Jacksonian Democracy
and the Working Class

Stanford Studies in History, Economics,
and Political Science, XIX

Jacksonian Democracy and the Working Class

A STUDY OF THE NEW YORK WORKINGMEN'S MOVEMENT 1829-1837

Walter Hugins

STANFORD UNIVERSITY PRESS

Stanford, California, 1960

Preface

FOUR DECADES ago two books were published, one written by a political historian, the other by an economist. Though unlike in subject matter and focus, both dealt in part with the Workingmen's movement in Jacksonian New York. In the *Decline of Aristocracy in the Politics of New York* Dixon Ryan Fox viewed the activities of this group as a culminating episode in the gradual democratization of political life in the Empire State. John R. Commons and his associates in their *History of Labour in the United States* discussed the Workingmen's parties as early examples of the labor movement in politics. The story of the Workingmen is now generally familiar, as other historians writing of the Jacksonian era have built upon the findings of Fox and Commons. Some intellectual spokesmen of the movement have received further study, but little effort has been made to explore more deeply this significant episode in the attempt to determine with more exactness its composition and objectives.

This I have endeavored to do here. No important historical sources unknown to my predecessors have been discovered; our knowledge of the movement still comes largely from the contemporary press. But an intensive investigation of the available record reveals the Workingmen in all dimensions—the trees as well as the forest. As a political entity this movement was often more than the sum of its parts. Yet it was at the same time essentially the expression of the interests and aspirations of the individuals who participated in it. Our knowledge and understanding of these men, their economic roles and political objectives, contributes to our comprehension of the social climate of Jacksonian America.

My exploration of this subject has benefited from the guidance and encouragement of friends and counselors. Richard Hofstadter has shown a generous interest and offered discerning criticism at all stages of my work. I am especially indebted to Richard B. Morris for several careful and perceptive readings of the manuscript and for his penetrating comments and suggestions. I wish also to express my gratitude to John A. Krout, Joseph Dorfman, Henry F. Graff, and Marvin Meyers for helpful criticism of this study in whole or in part. I owe a special obligation to my wife, Jo Ann Thacker Hugins, for her critical encouragement of my efforts. My debt is large, but I alone am responsible for any errors of fact or interpretation.

I am obligated to the Trustees of Columbia University for the Erb Fellowship in American History, which gave me a year of uninterrupted time for research. The assistance of the Bancroft Fund in obtaining microfilm copies of vital newspaper files in distant repositories is gratefully acknowledged. I wish to thank the staffs of the New-York Historical Society, the New York Public Library, and the Columbia University library for aid in the use of manuscripts and newspapers.

A portion of this work first appeared in a slightly different version in an article, "Ely Moore: The Case History of a Jacksonian Labor Leader," in the March 1950 issue of the *Political Science Quarterly*, and is used here with the kind permission of the publisher.

WALTER HUGINS

Contents

Tables

*Jacksonian Democracy
and the Working Class*

Introduction

WHATEVER THE DISADVANTAGES of the "presidential synthesis" as a method of organizing the raw data of American history,[1] both the drama and the significance of the past appear on occasion to have been inextricably bound up with the personality and the program of the Chief Executive. More than folklore is responsible for the conception of Jacksonian Democracy as largely inspired by Andrew Jackson—that "the American people looked through his eyes, and thought with his brain."[2] It is undeniable that he was in many ways a genuine man of the people, sharing in large part their prejudices and idiosyncrasies, but Jackson was more the product than the prime mover of that social, economic, and political upsurge that we know as Jacksonian Democracy.

To discover the essence of this movement, we must search beyond the public career and pronouncements of "Old Hickory." Like other forceful political leaders in our history, he was both supported and opposed by a wide variety of factions (in the Madisonian sense) throughout the country. While Jacksonian Democracy had a different meaning to a New York merchant, a Tennessee backwoodsman, and a Virginia planter, a central thread, characterized by the "rise of the common man," runs through this period. Because the John Doe of the 1830's is less vocal in a historical sense than his political leaders, he cannot easily be isolated and examined. Nevertheless, in order to investigate and analyze this ferment, we must shift our attention almost wholly away from the national capital and focus upon the activities, interests, and aspirations of the ordinary citizen.

The effort to epitomize the Jacksonian period in these terms has given rise to varying interpretations. Frederick Jackson Turner, for example, found the wellspring of Jacksonian Democracy on the frontier,[3] while Arthur M. Schlesinger, Jr., asserted in contradiction that the movement drew its strength "in the main from the seaboard, not from the forest."[4] Similar to the controversy concerning its source is a difference of opinion regarding the nature of this liberating impulse. Schlesinger saw the Jacksonian era as a "phase of that enduring struggle between the business community and the rest of society," in which the radical wage-earning class of the eastern cities took a leading part.[5] Others have disagreed, maintaining with Joseph Dorfman that the movement was "antiaristocratic rather than anticapitalistic," composed largely of "capitalists, enterprisers, and ambitious workingmen" who "sought to eliminate or hedge law-created privileges."[6] According to this view, therefore, "the democratic upsurge was closely linked to the ambitions of the small capitalist," and the principal contribution of the Jacksonians was "the democratization of business."[7] The debate on the character of the protagonists notwithstanding, there has been essential agreement in recent years that this contest was somehow related to the rise of urban capitalism. The difference is one of emphasis, ranging from a dichotomy between business and labor at one extreme to a competitive struggle between two segments of the business community at the other. One view tends toward a two-class interpretation of Jacksonian America, while the other implies its virtual classlessness. Yet neither is based upon a systematic examination of the stratification of urban society, nor upon an analysis of the working class—the "labouring classes" or "producing classes" in the terminology of the period—and its relationship to the main currents of Jacksonian Democracy.

The cities of the Northeast with their increasingly complex socioeconomic organization obviously provide the most fruitful field for the study of this popular ferment, demonstrated particularly by the entry of "mechanics and workingmen" into politics and the concurrent emergence of militant journeymen's organizations. John R. Commons and his associates were the first to make a detailed investigation of the development and relationship of these political and economic activities. To them, they formed a single movement, representing "the first painful efforts of wage-earners to extricate themselves both from the existing political parties and from the guild-like organizations which their employers controlled."[8] In focusing upon a search for the origins of modern trade unionism, this pioneering study was little concerned with the larger meaning of Jacksonian Democracy, nor in determining its relationship to the labor movement of the period. Renewed interest in the Age of Jackson has led to a reassessment, in terms largely ignored by the Commons school, of labor's political role in the major urban centers.[9] Yet these more recent studies, though placing the movement in broader perspective, have generally followed Commons in interpreting the political activities of "workingmen" as a complementary manifestation, with wage earners' combinations, of a bona fide labor movement, demonstrating (in Commons' words) "the repeating cycle of politics and trade unionism."[10] This underlying assumption is often apparent despite the admission that many leaders of these Workingmen's parties were not journeyman mechanics; moreover, the discovery that they oftentimes opposed the local Democratic candidates is cited as proof that "labor" did not support Jackson with any unanimity or consistency.

The developments in New York City from 1829 to 1837, nearly coterminous with Jackson's administration, were particularly significant manifestations of this democratic ferment. The Workingmen's Party in that city was surprisingly successful in the 1829 election and, even though soon divided by factionalism, survived for two years. Following a brief hiatus, during which journeymen's associations multiplied and a formidable city central trades' union was organized, the Workingmen reentered politics and formed an alliance with the Democracy to aid in Jackson's struggle with the "Monster" Bank. But this contest against monopoly, translated to the local scene, led to the Locofoco secession, in which the Workingmen in a new guise renewed their demand for "equal rights" and reform of the state banking system. Reunion with Tammany came in 1837, after two years of independent political action; although the Workingmen were absorbed into the Democratic Party, the impress of the movement remained evident throughout the succeeding decade.

In Commons' view, the Workingmen's Party of New York, in

comparison with the earlier movement in Philadelphia, was "more radical in its demands, more distinct in its cleavage of classes."[11] Other scholars have pointed to the "indisputable evidence of its ties and sympathies with bona fide workingmen."[12] This modern emphasis on the radicalism and proletarian nature of the movement is in part a reflection of a contemporary view, expressed by its political opponents: not only were its objectives "injurious to the cause of law, order, and morality," but the new party represented a revolt by "the restless, the turbulent, and the needy," directed against "those who have a valuable stake in the community."[13] In attacking existing social institutions and offering seemingly drastic solutions for the ills of society, the Workingmen undeniably belong on the left of the Jacksonian political spectrum. But neither the socioeconomic roots of this radical movement nor its vision of the "new society" falls easily into a clear pattern of proletarian protest.

It is the purpose of this study to determine the class basis of this movement in an effort to elucidate the aspirations of a significant element in the Jacksonian coalition. The investigation consists of a threefold analysis, approaching the Workingmen through the aspects of the party, the personnel, and the program. The chronicle of the Workingmen's and Locofoco parties is generally familiar, though it has often been told in terms of separate and unrelated political organizations. But a close examination of the so-called "labor press"—principally George Henry Evans' *Working Man's Advocate* and its successors— and other newspapers of the period demonstrates an evident continuity, the years from 1829 to 1837 dividing into three periods. The Workingmen's Party in 1829–30 rose, split into factions, and declined. Between 1831 and 1834 it gradually disappeared, only to emerge as an influential segment of the Democracy during Jackson's Bank War. Finally, from 1835 to 1837 it moved again, as Antimonopoly Democrats and then Locofocos, toward political independence. All these dissenters from Democratic orthodoxy have, therefore, been denominated Workingmen in this study, and their organization termed the Workingmen's movement. In an endeavor to clarify its connection with the Workingmen, the parallel evolution of journeymen's associations and unions from 1831 to 1837 has also been reassessed, in part through an investigation of its leadership.

The Workingmen themselves, aside from a few of the more prominent leaders, have never been investigated as a group of individuals. A search of the newspaper accounts of party meetings, on both a city-wide and ward level, has revealed a total of 850 names of men active in the Workingmen's movement. Data contributing to a life history of some of them are available in biographical encyclopedias, from which significant conclusions can be drawn regarding the socioeconomic basis of the movement. This has been supplemented by an occupational tabulation of the entire group of 850 men, 700 of whom have been identified from city directories and other sources. This analysis of life histories and occupations has then been related to the program proposed by the Workingmen in an effort to discover both the roots and the concrete objectives of their radicalism. A statistical analysis of the source of its electoral support, in comparison with the vote for the major parties, sheds further light on the class basis of the movement and its contribution to the evolution of the Democratic Party in New York. This many-faceted examination of the New York Workingmen's movement demonstrates the complex composition of the Jacksonian working class, the unprivileged "producers of wealth." In sharing the interests and objectives of the rising middle class, the Workingmen drew their support from a broad stratum of society ranging from wage earners to the professions. The study of this minority movement assists in defining the political developments in New York City from 1829 to 1837, and thus contributes to a deeper comprehension of the political, economic, and social aspirations of Jacksonian Democracy.

The Party

The Rise of the Workingmen

THE ELECTION of Andrew Jackson in 1828 has been viewed as a result of "the rising of the masses"; certainly the scenes at his inauguration seemed, in the eyes of the old order, to demonstrate that King Mob had been enthroned.[1] In New York, the most populous city in the Republic, citizens for the first time voted directly for Presidential electors, and Jackson's triumph was overwhelming. Yet this was not wholly attributable to "the common man," for the Jackson ticket received widespread support in all but the formerly Federalist lower wards.[2] Although both were doubtless symptoms of the same ferment, the rise of the Workingmen's Party during the first year of Jackson's administration was totally unrelated to the political changes in Washington. Neither was it a conscious imitation of the similar political organization which had been active the previous year in Philadelphia.[3] The New York movement, although its origins are somewhat obscure, was largely the result of local factors, economic and social as well as political.

The initial impetus was economic, a protest against unemployment and a defense of the ten-hour day, but social and political grievances soon came to the fore. Increasingly conscious of their subordinate status in society, "mechanics and workingmen" listened avidly to the lectures of Frances Wright and Robert Dale Owen at the newly opened Hall of Science, and pored over their editorials and articles in the *Free Enquirer,* recently transferred to New York from the defunct New Harmony community.[4] Not all shared their anticlericalism, but their attacks on banks and other "aristocratical tendencies," and their emphasis on mass education as a solution to social ills, found receptive ears. To this social unrest was joined a deep-seated animosity to caucus politics, as exemplified particularly by the entrenched Tammany machine. Not only were the recently enfranchised restive under its control, but many former adherents of the discredited Adams-Clay party were in search of a new political alignment as their only hope for the future. In many instances disenchantment with apparent obstacles in the way of the popular will was reinforced by specific complaints against the ruling party; significant among these were the lack of a mechanics' lien law and the failure to reform the auction system.* All these elements played a part in the rise, and ultimate decline, of the Workingmen's Party.

During the winter of 1828–29 New York City suffered from business stagnation. Unemployment, combined with unusually severe weather, produced widespread destitution, as evidenced by numerous meetings held in February and March to encourage the leading citizens of the metropolis to practice "benevolence" as a palliative for pauperism.[5] When spring came, some employers attempted to revive the eleven-hour day, even though ten hours had long been established as the norm in most trades. On April 23, 1829, a meeting of "mechanics and others" was called to resist this demand, and the Workingmen's Party was born.[6] This meeting was sparsely attended, so after some discussion it was adjourned until April 28, when a second and much larger meeting was held. At this time a resolution was passed announcing that all concerned would refuse to work for any employer asking more than "ten hours, well and faithfully employed." A Committee of Fifty was then appointed to collect a relief fund, but little use was made of the money as the employers quickly retreated from their stand. The Committee was also instructed to prepare a report for later presentation on "the causes of the present condition of the poor."[7] According to George Henry Evans, one of the leaders and first historian of the movement, "great care was taken to have no 'Boss' on the committee . . . [so] a large majority . . . were journeymen."[8]

While the Committee was drafting its report, Robert Dale Owen and Fanny Wright were agitating the education question in the columns of the *Free Enquirer*. On September 10, at their suggestion, the Association for the Protection of Industry and for the

* An anti-auction ticket was nominated in 1828 in opposition to the Democratic Congressional candidates. For further discussion of this issue see Chapter 8, below; for the lien law see Chapter 7.

Promotion of National Education was organized with the objective of "carrying through the State Legislatures a system of Equal Republican Education." The second meeting of the Association two weeks later heard the report of a committee condemning the existing educational system as a major cause of economic distress among mechanics. Too many apprentices, it was asserted, were competing for the available jobs, and many of them had been bound out only because their parents could not afford to educate them. The committee further recommended that ward committees and a general committee be organized, and that candidates be nominated for the coming election.[9]

This was the prelude for the meeting on October 19 of "Mechanics and other Working Men" to hear the long-awaited report of the Committee of Fifty. Demonstrating the unity of purpose of the two groups, Robert Dale Owen was invited to be one of the secretaries of the meeting.[10] The Committee had fallen under the sway of Thomas Skidmore, one of its members who was a machinist but certainly no journeyman. Until recently an active supporter of the Adams party, he had just written a book, *The Rights of Man to Property!* and the report which he read was obviously a digest of this tract.[11] Denouncing "the hereditary transmission of wealth" as the "prime source of all our calamities," he outlined an elaborate scheme to provide for its "equal transmission to every individual of each succeeding generation on arriving at the age of maturity." Combined with this plan was Owen's educational system, providing equal food, clothing, and instruction for all children at public expense. The report as approved by the assemblage named "banking institutions" as a further cause of economic misery, calling upon the community to "destroy banks altogether," and attacked the auction monopoly and tax exemption of churches and church property. After advocating a mechanics' lien law on buildings, the report concluded by declaring that the immediate remedy was to "elect working men to the Legislature" and inviting "all those of our fellow-citizens who live on their own labor, AND NONE OTHER," to meet four days later to nominate a slate of candidates.[12]

Little time remained for deliberation, since the election was less than two weeks away; but at the same time the Workingmen wished to avoid the onus of caucus nominations, so often charged against the major parties. So the October 23 meeting adopted a complicated procedure, by which nominations from the floor were processed by the Committee of Fifty and then three days later voted upon in open meeting as the names were drawn from a hat.* A full legislative ticket, eleven State Assembly candidates and two for the State Senate, was chosen, but it was decided to make no nominations for the Common Council of the city, instead supporting those nominees of other parties who "lean most to the protection of the interests of the poor and industrious classes." The Workingmen's Assembly ticket listed the occupations of the candidates: two carpenters, two machinists, a painter, a whitesmith, a brassfounder, a printer, a cooper, a grocer, and a physician. The Senatorial candidates were Edward J. Webb, an architect, and Silas Wood of Long Island, an Adams party candidate for Congress the preceding year.[13]

Other former National Republicans than Skidmore and Wood had found refuge in the new party, a fact that did not go unnoticed by the Tammany braves. Of those on the Assembly ticket, Alden Potter (a machinist) and Frederick Friend (a brassfounder) had both been active Adams men and "Friends of the American System." Moreover, Dr. Cornelius Blatchley was until recently secretary of the New York Antimasonic General Committee. "This ticket is not what it pretends to be," warned the Tammany organ. "From the names placed on it, and the individuals known to have taken an active part in it, we are perfectly satisfied it is the old enemy in a new disguise. It is Clay at the bottom, and tariff to the very destruction of the trade and commerce of this city. . . . The true mechanics' ticket will be nominated at Tammany Hall."[14] A few days later an effort was made to obtain official National Republican endorsement, when a Workingmen's meeting called by Owen's Association adjourned to a gathering of that party. Accounts differ

---

* The Committee selected the names of twenty-two persons who were willing to be candidates for the Assembly, and they were drawn one by one from the hat until eleven men received majority approval; the same procedure was used for the nomination of the two candidates for the State Senate.

as to what occurred, although the Workingmen claimed that they had "carried everything before them," taking over the meeting and reapproving the resolutions and nominations previously made. The National Republicans admitted that there had been "a delectable degree of confusion," but insisted that the regular slate of candidates was nominated before "the 'Agrarian' party . . . took possession." According to the Tammany version, however, "the Adams party was captured bag and baggage . . . by a detachment of the 'Working Men,' alias the Fanny Wright men."[15]

The Democrats, meanwhile, were having troubles of their own. Not only were they fearful of losing votes to the Workingmen on the lien law issue, but some of their Assembly candidates were attacked for supporting Van Buren's Safety Fund Act, adopted to prevent banking abuses but denounced by city bankers as discriminatory. Bolters from Tammany, derisively called the "Pewter Mug" faction, drew up an opposition ticket, substituting three names for those of the erring brethren. The election showed the result of all these political currents. Although eight of the Tammany Assembly nominees were successful, two of the "Pewter Mug" candidates and one Workingman—Ebenezer Ford, a carpenter—were elected.* Defections from Tammany were more than matched by the losses of their opposition, implying that some of the Adams men had been captured by the new party. The National Republican strength amounted to only 12 percent of the total vote, decreasing about 7,300 votes from the 1828 total, while the Workingmen polled over 6,000 votes for their entire ticket.[16]

The Democrats, comforting themselves with the belief that the Workingmen were basically "Jackson men" misled by "broken down politicians," immediately took steps to woo them back to their rightful allegiance, promising that "a lien law will be adopted to secure the permanency of their influence in every subsequent election in this city."[17] Some supporters of the Workingmen undoubtedly returned to the Tammany fold on the strength of this pledge, but

---

* Six other Workingmen's Assembly candidates ran less than 50 votes behind Ford, and Silas Wood carried the city but lost Long Island, and the election, to the Democratic Senatorial candidate.

many were not receptive to these blandishments, their relative success at the polls having given them renewed confidence for the future. They had gained new allies, including the *Evening Journal,* which urged the mechanics to continue their struggle to "gain a proper standing in the community, and a representation in the councils of the state." This could best be done, it was pointed out, by learning from past mistakes in passing "violent resolutions" and nominating unqualified candidates when there were many in their ranks with "great ability and talent." A prospectus was also issued for a new paper, the *Daily Sentinel,* to be "devoted chiefly to the interests of the Artists, Mechanics, and other Working Men."[18]

Of greater significance for the party's future was the influx of quondam National Republicans, reading their fortune in the election returns. While many were no doubt attracted by one or more planks in the Workingmen's platform, and by the possibility of seeing them enacted, others plainly were governed by the desire to develop and use the party as an effective counterpoise to Tammany. Chief among the latter was Noah Cook, a commission merchant who had been a delegate to the 1828 National Republican state convention. Clarkson Crolius, Jr., also a leader in this group, had been for several years associated with his father in both the manufacture of stoneware and the vigorous support of the Adams-Clay party.[19] Throughout the winter and early spring of 1830 these men and others with similar backgrounds took an increasingly active role in party deliberations, their first objective being the elimination of Skidmore, his partisans on the Committee of Fifty, and his visionary panacea.

They were aided in this endeavor, not only by the *Evening Journal,* but by the proponents of Owen's educational plan. To George Henry Evans, whose *Working Man's Advocate* had become the spokesman of this group, the primary issue was party organization: decentralization of power through the establishment of ward associations in place of Skidmore's plan of an all-powerful permanent General Committee. The contest was joined at a general meeting of the party on December 29, 1829. The steamroller was well oiled, for Skidmore was shouted down whenever he rose to speak, and the Evans plan, calling for a General Executive Committee of five delegates from each ward, was adopted. The new party platform, moreover, "succeeded in wiping away the stigma of Agrarianism," as the *Evening Journal* triumphantly announced, although continuing to endorse "universal education" without referring specifically to Owen's scheme of state guardianship.[20]

The Executive Committee which convened in January demonstrated the growing influence of the Cook faction. Henry G. Guyon, a master carpenter and former National Republican, was elected chairman, and Aaron L. Balch, a teacher who was another recent convert to "workeyism," recording secretary. After a sharp contest Simon Clannon, a painter and one of the original Workingmen, defeated Crolius for the office of corresponding secretary. In addition all persons not members of the Committee were barred from the room, and it was rumored that a doorkeeper would be appointed. Foreshadowing the future split in the party, Evans attacked this action as an "anti-republican" device to "exclude free citizens from a knowledge of what their servants are doing," and sharply condemned the gagging of Skidmore at the general meeting.[21]

Meanwhile, the "Agrarian" leader, although read out of the party, refused to remain quiet. Castigating the Executive Committee with the declaration that at least nineteen of the seventy delegates were "rich men, living on the labor of others," Skidmore started publication of a newspaper, the *Friend of Equal Rights,* to circulate the views of his faction.[22] Evans, in reply, termed it "preposterous" to denounce as rich men "all who happened to have saved a few hundred dollars," but cautioned the Workingmen against embracing uncritically all who offered friendship. "Designing individuals may," he warned, "have the power to make the cause of the working men subservient to the advancement of their own speculating and ambitious views." Let us then, he added,

> scrutinize the political history of those who now array themselves in our ranks, but *did not number with the 6000* who went hand and heart last election, before their own strength was ascertained. . . . Those who waited *to count the 6000 votes,* before they made up their minds as to whether they were friends to the mechanics or not . . . *are too busy among us now.* . . . They

may have their own axes to grind, and may choose to have us turn the grindstone.

Arguing further that the Workingmen's Party should insist for the most part of "plain, practical mechanics," he predicted that two or three "aristocratic" members would probably be expelled from the Executive Committee in the near future.[23]

While the germs of discord were multiplying in the metropolis, the Workingmen's movement had spread upstate to Albany, Troy, and Utica. These groups, especially the party at the state capital, soon developed close ties with Cook's faction, whom Evans accused of "intriguing at Albany" to "induce the working men . . . to abandon their principles." According to Jabez Hammond, a close and astute observer of the political maneuverings in the state during this period, "the intelligent men who joined it were many of them zealous Clay men." While professing their independence of existing parties, "masons and other men who could not or would not join the anti-masonic party, but who were opposed to the Albany Regency and the Jackson party, seeing no prospect of resuscitating the national republican party, flocked to the standard of the working men."[24] After the Albany and Troy Workingmen had been notably successful in their first electoral campaign, a victory celebration was held in New York. Cook threw down the gage of battle when, after describing the purging of the Skidmore faction, he warned of the danger to the movement of further "fanaticism" and argued that "too much zeal" was undesirable. While continuing to endorse a "republican system of education," he emphasized that the second leading principle of the party should be "the protecting and fostering of our own industry." It is not surprising that Evans now began to "suspect the *purity* of the motives" of "those who contend for *too* little."[25]

The conflict mounted behind the façade of unity, as journalistic skirmishes were carried on in the columns of the *Evening Journal,* of which Noah Cook had recently become co-editor, against the *Working Man's Advocate* leagued with the *Daily Sentinel.*[26] But open contention did not break out in party conclaves until spring, when the report of the subcommittee on education was presented to the General Executive Committee. Largely an attack on Robert Dale Owen and the alleged "infidelity" of his educational plan, the report took issue with his proposal to separate children completely from their families during their education, favoring "a plan that shall leave to the father and to the affectionate mother the enjoyment of the society of their offspring." A minority report was presented but not read, as the Cook faction carried the day by twenty-five votes against twenty-one. Counterattacking almost immediately with a "History of the Unmasking," the opposition journals listed the infamous "Twenty-five," alleging that "a large proportion (we believe a decided majority) . . . opposed us at the last election."[27] Accusations of subservience to a major party were hurled by both factions. Although, according to Owen's supporters, "an anxious regard for religion and good order" was the ostensible cause of the controversy, "those who took the lead against us cared about as much for religion as the Great Mogul. . . . We are fully convinced that their plan . . . has for its sole object *the election of Henry Clay as our next President.*" The Cook faction countered with the charge that the *Sentinel* was "but a mere tool of the Tammany faction, sent into our ranks to betray us," and took steps to consolidate its position.[28]

During succeeding weeks ward meetings were called by both groups to eliminate "traitors" on the Executive Committee, so that two rival parties were soon claiming to be the legitimate representatives of "honest workingmen." The rivalry was acute in most wards, resulting in several pitched battles and an occasional "forcible ejectment" as each faction continually invaded meetings called by the other. The *Sentinel* party, accusing the opposition of using various "caucus manoeuvres," claimed superiority of numbers, although the issue was often in doubt.[29] The first real test of strength between the two groups came in July, when a special election was held in the Fifth Ward to fill a vacancy on the Common Council. The Cook faction selected General Anthony Lamb, a National Republican Assembly candidate in 1829, whose nomination was seconded two days later by a meeting of "Republican electors," many of whom were prominent Clayites. William Leavens, a cabinetmaker and owner of a mahogany yard who had been an Adams supporter in 1828, was the choice of the *Sentinel* party. Victory went to Lamb, with the Tammany candidate running second by 100 votes and Leavens trailing with only 445 of the nearly 1,800 votes cast. Although convinced that many Workingmen had been deluded into voting for the opposition candidate, the supporters of Leavens found consolation in the fact that he had polled more votes in the ward than the party ticket had received in November.[30]

In the months remaining before the 1830 autumn election, the Workingmen were increasingly subject to solicitations from the major parties. The Owenites were torn between the desire to maintain their independence and the importunities of Tammany, while the Cook faction was moving in the other direction. When the *Courier and Enquirer* declared that the votes for Leavens, as well as those for their own candidate, were "pure, unadulterated Jackson votes," Evans replied that it was "futile" to assert that the Workingmen favor either Jackson or Clay, for neither "has ever evinced any particular anxiety or interest in the measures of reform that the Working Men are advocating." Although he admitted feeling "a lurking kindness for their party still, because Jefferson first founded it," the editor warned that "they cannot catch us, and had better not waste their time in the attempt."[31] At the same time the *Sentinel* faction was showing signs of retreating from its uncompromising stand in favor of Owen's educational plan, the Executive Committee declaring itself opposed to any scheme which would send children to schools without the consent of their parents. The *Evening Journal* interpreted this statement as an overture toward consolidation of the two factions, but Evans was cool toward the suggested amalgamation. Accusing the opposition of attempting to "sit between two stools," he further explained:

> We will unite with no party, *as a party*—and with individuals of all parties, *if* we believe them to be sincerely the friends of the people. . . . We indentured our labor and our money for something more than political influence and party triumph. . . . Our object is, not to put down Tammany, or any other faction,

as such; but simply to unite, if we can, the honest from all parties. . . . We will not league with one enemy to crush another.[32]

Meanwhile, the Cook faction was moving toward coalition with other anti-Democratic forces in the state. They ratified the earlier suggestion of the Albany Workingmen that General Erastus Root, a rebellious Democratic politician, be nominated for Governor, and answered the call for a state convention of the party in late summer. As expected, New York City sent two rival delegations, but the credentials committee seated only those whose certificates of appointment were signed by Henry Guyon, chairman of the Cook Executive Committee. Root received the nomination, with Nathaniel Pitcher, another disgruntled Democrat, being chosen for Lieutenant Governor, and the platform adopted was almost wholly a virulent attack on Van Buren's Albany Regency for its past record. Only momentarily taken aback a month later when both men declined the nominations, the Cook party soon followed the National Republican remnant in endorsing the Antimasonic nominations of Francis Granger and Samuel Stevens, the latter a New York "mechanic," clearly chosen to appeal to the Workingmen.[33]

This action virtually eliminated the possibility of reconciliation between the two wings of the party, to the dismay of the *Evening Journal* and the Albany Workingmen. Since their overtures had been rebuffed, largely at the instigation of the New York *Reformer,* a new paper edited by Noah Cook, the *Sentinel* faction proceeded to select its own candidates for Governor and Lieutenant Governor. Earlier, Evans had urged the party to

> take a man from the plough or the workshop, even though his name has never been heard beyond the lines of his county, if his character stands fair among those who have the best opportunity of knowing him—if he is believed thoroughly to understand, and honestly to approve our principles. We may not, perhaps, be so sure of success . . . as we should in rallying round a man who had been long known as the leader of a political party. . . . In one case, our measures would be entirely forgotten amid the scrambles for office; in the other, they would be gradually and firmly gaining ground.[34]

This advice was essentially followed with the nomination for Governor of Ezekiel Williams, a leather manufacturer in Auburn, with Isaac S. Smith, a Buffalo merchant, as his running mate. An involved nominating procedure was again used to choose the other candidates on the Workingmen's ticket. Only one, Ebenezer Ford, was a holdover from the previous year, while three "original workingmen" were nominated by the Skidmore party, which hopefully revived during the fall. The election was a victory for Tammany, but the newly organized anti-Democratic Coalition, showing an increase of more than five thousand votes over the National Republican strength of 1829, was a serious challenger. The Workingmen on the other hand received only 2,200 votes, a decrease of nearly four thousand from their impressive total the year before.[35]

Many of those who had originally supported the Workingmen's ticket were now evidently enlisted under the banners of the opposition parties. Despite the despondency of some in the movement, Owen declared that "the result neither surprises nor disappoints me." Many hundreds, he believed, "if not thousands," were deceived by the Coalition ticket, and even more had voted for "the modified aristocracy and semi-liberality of Tammany" as the lesser of two evils. Evans agreed that "the *Ins* have kept their places by the votes of the Working Men," which was regrettable because the Democrats would henceforth take their support for granted. Nevertheless, "Tammany, with all its imperfections, is a hundred times preferable to the piebald and motley squad who attempted to unhorse the 'Regency.' "[36]

Thus, the Workingmen's Party, which had arisen out of economic and social grievances and opposition to Tammany management, found itself drifting reluctantly into the Democratic orbit. Its initial success had not only wrung concessions from the enemy—causing some desertions at the hour of triumph—but induced National Republican adventurers to infiltrate its ranks in an effort to capture and utilize the enthusiasm generated by the new party. Personal animosities intensified doctrinal differences until party objectives were nearly subordinated to factional striving for advantage. But, although this movement of "the producing classes" was sundered by ambition and dogmatism, the basic aspirations of the Workingmen remained. Optimistic even in the face of disaster, "A Mechanic" wrote Evans after the election, urging his fellows never to despair of "the progressive improvement of the human mind," which would in time bring the triumph of their cause.[87]

The Workingmen Become Jacksonians

THE NEW YORK Workingmen's movement in the period from 1831 through 1834 passed through a second stage in its history, as the followers of George Henry Evans moved gradually toward union with the Democracy under the standard raised by Andrew Jackson. As his titanic struggle with Nicholas Biddle took the center of the stage, the "measures of the Working Men" were increasingly identified with the program of the administration in Washington. But in local politics the inveterate suspicion of both Tammany and the Albany Regency continued. Clinging tenaciously to a semblance of party organization, the Workingmen finally succumbed in 1832, circumstances and sentiment combining to render untenable the position of an independent third force. As the Bank War reached its climax early in 1834, they reentered politics in the Democratic cause. The social unrest which had given rise to the movement was still present, but it was now channeled into an effort to overthrow monopoly in its various guises, banks and paper money becoming the special scapegoat. With Jackson supplanting Jefferson as their lodestar, the Workingmen formed an uneasy alliance with Tammany, leaguing to crush the minions of the "Monster" Bank while endeavoring to enlist the old enemy in a war against the "privileged aristocracy" at home.

Following the disastrous defeat of 1830, the Workingmen's Party remained active for nearly two years, though with ever decreasing strength. Evans, from his editorial rostrum in the *Working Man's Advocate,* conducted a vigorous but largely ineffective campaign to rally and augment his forces. "Was it generally understood," he asked, "that because the working men were unsuccessful last year they should not make another effort? . . . It *may* be that working men contending for their dearest rights are discouraged by *one* defeat . . . but we do not *believe* that such is the case."[1]

Attempting to overcome the general apathy, the editor met with the faithful nucleus of the party late in 1830 to draft plans for the coming year, establishing a Workingmen's Political Association with a written constitution and subsidiary ward associations. In an effort to prevent infiltration by "pretended friends" and politicians, the associations were organized as private clubs with members admitted only by ballot. Evans had high hopes as the plan was quickly put into operation in several wards, pointing to the example of England, Ireland, and France where "associations have been found most efficient engines in the cause of the people . . . who are struggling for their rights."[2]

This new scheme failed, however, to arouse the interest of more than a handful of his erstwhile colleagues, many of whom had quietly found sanctuary in the major parties. Only a handful of ward associations had been formed at the time of the so-called Charter election of city officials in April, so Evans recommended that the Workingmen support many candidates of the opposition parties.* "It can make little difference to those who contend solely for principles," he declared in justification, "whether the nominations of candidates to support those principles originate with ourselves or with others," for "a large proportion of the individuals composing the different political parties joined such parties with good motives, and have been misled—not corrupted—by the party leaders. . . . The mass will either revolutionize the party to which they are attached, or retire from its ranks and array themselves under the banner of principle which the working men have unfurled."[3] Nevertheless, this group remained uncompromising in its antagonism to all proposals for amalgamation or alliance, condemning alike "the two great parties who are led by *office holders* on the one hand, and *office seekers* on the other." Some correspondents in the *Working Man's Advocate,* while warning against "the overheated zeal of misguided enthusiasts . . . and the reckless and cold blooded cal-

---

* Nominations by duly constituted ward associations were made only in the Fifth and Eighth wards, while a "Working Men's ticket" was presented in the Tenth and Fourteenth wards. The election returned an anti-Tammany majority to the Common Council, including a candidate endorsed by the Workingmen in the Eighth Ward.

culations of interested and ambitious demagogues," urged the Workingmen to unite "without reference to what you have been, or what party flag you have marshaled under." An effort was made at a fall meeting of the Association to loosen the membership requirements in the hope of improving their chances in the election. But, to Evans' obvious satisfaction, it was finally agreed that principle would not be sacrificed to political expediency.[4]

Yet an effort was made to form a united front in opposition to "the *ruling* party." Without receding from "the principles of the working men," Evans endeavored to obtain National Republican and Antimasonic endorsement of the nominations, predicting that "no candidate can succeed against those nominated at Tammany Hall, *unless they are on the working men's ticket.* . . . We believe that a sufficient change of public sentiment has been effected to make it almost certain that any candidate who can receive the support of *all,* or nearly all, the opposition to the office holding party, will be elected."[5] Although a few of the Workingmen's candidates were also found on other tickets, no coalition was made; as a result, Tammany won easily, the Workingmen's Party with only eight hundred votes reaching the nadir of its strength.* Evans attributed the debacle chiefly to "want of Union and want of organization," but also blamed "the cursed general ticket system" for giving the Democracy an unfair advantage. Echoing the sentiments expressed by "A True Republican," he called for unity and perseverance and urged his readers not to disband the associations, converting them instead into "schools of moral and political instruction, or *Lyceums,*" and inviting all "working men" to attend.[6]

With the dawn of the Presidential election year a few weeks later, the Workingmen in their meetings and discussions began to turn their attention to national politics. It had long been assumed that Andrew Jackson would be a candidate for reelection, though Evans had refused to express joy at the prospect. Regarding the President as "too violent a party man" and primarily a "caucus candidate," he had declared as early as 1830 that "the times demand

---

* Interest was slight in this election, for the total vote showed a 25 percent decline from the previous year.

another Jefferson who will take the side of the people." The choice of the Workingmen had long been Richard M. Johnson of Kentucky, principally because of his fight in Congress against imprisonment for debt and his reports in opposition to the Sunday mail agitation. But, in view of "the present state of party spirit, fostered . . . by executive patronage," Evans reluctantly abandoned the hope that he might receive the Presidential nomination and endorsed him for the Vice-Presidency.[7] Following a rally early in 1832 of "the friends of Col. Richard M. Johnson," the Workingmen's Executive Committee met to discuss the Presidential ticket. There was little argument over supporting Johnson; but as some feared an endorsement of Jackson might cause disunion, it was finally concluded that "though many of the working men might not approve of all the conduct and measures of Andrew Jackson, yet . . . there are few who do not *prefer* him [over Clay] for his support of some of the most important measures which the working men advocate."[8] This sentiment was ratified by a general meeting, and Evans placed the names of Jackson and Johnson on the masthead of his newspaper. "The working men will not be *Jackson* men, nor *Johnson* men," he wrote in elucidation of the resolution, but "our exertions in promoting their election will be exerted as far as they can be consistently with our support of the great *measures* contended for by those who have now nominated them. . . . We have no doubt that the election of the candidates nominated would tend incalculably more to produce the desired effect, than the election of the persons who are now named as their competitors."[9]

The Baltimore Convention of the Democratic Party a few months later deflated the Johnson boom by nominating Martin Van Buren for Vice-President on the first ballot. Evans had earlier expressed his antipathy toward the Little Magician, asserting that "no man knowing the sentiments of this state . . . would think of hanging him to the neck of Andrew Jackson." Now, citing his opposition to universal suffrage in the constitutional convention of 1821, he declared: "Every *real* republican would . . . cut off his right hand sooner than vote for Martin Van Buren."[10] Yet it soon became apparent that continued support of Johnson was quixotic, and the

Executive Committee called a meeting "in regard to the expediency
of substituting the name of Martin Van Buren." Unhappy with
this move, Evans announced: "We feel no obligation to acquiesce
in the nomination"; although agreeing to remove Johnson's name
from the masthead, he categorically refused to put Van Buren's
in its place.[11]

In the meantime Jackson's veto of the bill to recharter the Bank
of the United States had removed the Workingmen's doubts as to
the desirability of his reelection. The message, according to the
Sentinel, stated "principles which approach nearer to the doctrines
of the illustrious Jefferson than any state paper issued from the city
of Washington for twenty years," and it was suggested that "the
old democratic party of mechanics" be reorganized to support the
President. When Tammany came out unequivocally in support of
Jackson's stand, Evans recommended that the Workingmen, in
order to avoid being "seduced by partizans," nominate their own
candidate for Governor. Arguing that this would enable them "to
express their opinions on the 'regular nomination' system now in
use by both the Tammany and the Bank parties," he predicted that
"as soon as the *outs* and *ins* get nearly balanced, to secure our support they will adopt our candidate." At the same time, however,
he warned that "too much should not be risked" which might endanger the struggle against the "Mammoth Monopoly."[12] During
the ensuing campaign the National Republicans, hopeful of capitalizing on the Workingmen's antipathy to "rag money," stressed
the role of the Bank in maintaining a "sound currency" despite the
operations of local banks, and emphasized that "upon none do the
evils of depreciated paper more sorely press, than on the industrious,
enterprizing, and working classes of society." Several Workingmen, notably Ralph Wells, a broker who had been a member of
the original Executive Committee and later a supporter of the
Sentinel faction, gravitated to the support of Clay and the Bank,
but the majority followed Evans into the Tammany fold to help
elect the Democratic ticket, which received almost three-fifths of
the total vote in the city.[13]

With Jackson's triumph in 1832, therefore, the Workingmen

as an organized political group had disappeared, dissolved into the ranks of the contending parties. Tammany now seemed in the ascendant in the city, a result which some found incomprehensible. One editor, citing the anti-Jackson "current of opinion as found in the business circles, in the newspapers . . . and among the readers of newspapers," deplored the existence of "another current deeper and stronger than we had supposed, among the whole people," concluding: "We have lifted up a voice without effect."[14] Nevertheless, the ensuing year saw defections from the Democracy as a result of the President's determination to order removal of the government deposits from the Bank. While politics excited little general interest in 1833, with the opposition still disorganized after its defeat, Tammany's margin of victory in the fall election was uncomfortably small;* this could be ascribed, however, to the small turnout of voters, reflecting political apathy in a period of general prosperity.[15] Further evidence of the upward swing of the business cycle was the marked increase during the year in the organization and agitation of trade societies, culminating in the formation of the General Trades' Union of the City of New York.†

Although a few Workingmen took an active part in this non-political organization, most of them as 1834 dawned were more concerned with the reviving political struggle. Prosperity had been succeeded by recession, as Jackson's removal order was answered by Biddle's severe curtailment of credit. Political cleavage between the friends and enemies of the President became more bitter, the opposition gaining strength from the imminence of large-scale bankruptcy and unemployment. Workingmen were to be found on both sides of the controversy, depending upon whom they blamed for the prevalent economic distress, although the majority appeared to agree with Evans that the Democracy was preferable to the "Bank vermin."[16] Several of them, for example, took a prominent part in turning a City Hall Park meeting of the Bankites into a fiasco.

---

* The total vote was approximately 15,000, about half that cast in 1832, and the Tammany Assembly ticket won by only 1,200 votes, compared with the nearly 6,000-vote margin the previous year.

† A detailed account of this movement is given in Chapter 4, below.

With other Jackson supporters, they invaded this assemblage of "Mechanics, Merchants, Manufacturers, and other Citizens . . . who disapprove of the recent removal of the Public Deposites," over which the aristocratic Philip Hone was presiding. Edward J. Webb, an "original" Workingman, was elevated to the chair, and John Windt, a long-time associate of Evans and Owen, was named secretary. Following a violent struggle for the rostrum, during which the dignified Hone was "handed to the outside of the Park," a series of anti-Bank resolutions was passed, and the meeting closed with a mighty "Hurra for Jackson." That evening Windt was discharged, nominally because of the "depression of business," as was an employee of the *Courier and Enquirer*, by this time an anti-Tammany paper; James Watson Webb, the editor, advised all employers to follow his example by dismissing workers who supported Jackson.[17]

This occurrence set the pattern, with editorials and meetings increasing in frequency and heat as the annual spring election approached. Additional excitement was generated by the fact that this was the first time in the city's history that the choice of Mayor was given directly to the people. Moreover, the anti-Jackson forces, newly christened Whigs, had united and nominated for that office Gulian C. Verplanck, a former Democrat who had left the party in protest against the veto; his rival was Cornelius W. Lawrence, a retired merchant and Congressman. The campaign was centered, therefore, on national politics, with no reference to local issues, banking and monopoly becoming the leading questions of the day. The Whigs exhorted merchants to "organize as a political body" to defeat the "spirit of *agrarianism*" which intended to "destroy the honestly acquired wealth of the industrious and enterprising." Employers were now urged, not to discharge Democratic employees, but to "take pains to make them understand the reasons why we are all suffering . . . and then require them to vote for members of the city government who are their friends—not their enemies." Anti-Jackson meetings were held by clerks, cartmen, sailors, printers, carpenters, and blacksmiths (including some former Workingmen), all of whom passed ringing resolutions supporting Verplanck and denouncing the President's policies for causing the "contraction of commerce, and consequent unemployment and dislocation of the currency."[18]

Democratic "Mechanics and Working Men" were also active in the campaign, though Evans suspected at first that Tammany was dominated by "miscreants who merely oppose the present Bank that they may profit by the erection of another." Moreover, he had long shared the perturbation of those, alarmed by the increase in applications for bank charters, who noted that many Tammany leaders were officers of banks which would benefit from the demise of the "Monster." Regarding the policy of placing the federal deposits in state banks as going "out of the *fire* into the *frying pan*," Evans expressed the hope that "the determination of the people to put an end to the most powerful . . . of the *Rag Money Mills*, is an indication of their determination to put an end to the whole system." He was particularly alarmed by Democratic Governor Marcy's proposed six million dollar loan "to prop a ruinous and rotten Banking system" against the onslaughts of Biddle's Bank, remarking: "Suppose the Banks are at war! What need the people care should they suffer the fate of the Kilkenny cats?" Not only would the loan put the state into debt, Evans believed, but it would "enable the Banks of this State to undo much of the good that the 'removal of the deposites' has done by driving Rag Money out of circulation." Despite these objections, he finally urged his readers to support the Democratic nominees in order to check "the dangerous power of the United States Bank." The Workingmen responded at a large and enthusiastic gathering at Tammany Hall a week before the election, at which Ely Moore, president of the General Trades' Union, gave the principal address.[19]

The three-day election showed the results of the bitter campaign. Virtually all stores and shops were closed throughout the contest, and bands of men, both Whigs and Democrats, surrounded the polls or roamed the city. Violence flared, especially in the Sixth Ward where mobs, said to be mainly Irish, armed with knives, clubs, and stones, attacked Whig committee rooms, tearing down banners and destroying ballots. After the "Bankites" had broken

into the arsenal in search of weapons, the combatants were finally
disarmed by federal troops from Governor's Island. When the
smoke of battle had cleared, it was found that, despite a heavy rain
on the first day, nearly thirty-five thousand ballots had been cast
in the election, more than in the last Presidential contest. Lawrence
was elected Mayor by the slim majority of fewer than two hundred
votes, but the Whigs captured the Common Council and, with the
city patronage at their disposal, envisioned a more complete victory
in November.[20]

The Democrats were equally determined to win the fall elections,
but a rift appeared in their ranks as opposition became more pro-
nounced to the state banking system and to the Democratic politicians identified with it. Evans, speaking for the Workingmen,
continued to warn that Marcy's State Loan was "a dead weight
on the democratic cause," identifying "the prosperity of the . . .
State . . . with the destinies of a paper money aristocracy." Urging Tammany to "examine the ground on which they now stand,"
he emphasized that

> they must consider that the question "Bank or no Bank?" on
> which the late Election turned . . . will, at the fall Election,
> be understood in a general sense, or . . . BANK OR NO BANKS?
> We consider that the United States Bank question is now defi-
> nitely settled, as far as the people of this city and state are
> concerned. . . . But a man may be *opposed* to a United States
> Bank . . . merely because it interferes with the exclusive
> privileges given to a favored few by means of State Banks;
> and there is too much reason to fear that a considerable portion
> of those who have just aided to make Mr. Lawrence Mayor of
> this city are of this class.

The election can be won, he concluded, only by nominating candidates "who will oppose the granting of new Bank Charters and the
renewal of old ones, and advocate the restoration of the Constitutional Currency" by gradually eliminating paper money. "If a
bank charter granted by Congress is unconstitutional," wrote Edward J. Webb in summarizing the Workingmen's view of the inherent contradiction in the Tammany position, "*Banks* chartered by

our Legislature at Albany are equally so. . . . The degree alters not the constitutionality."[21]

The Workingmen, during the spring and summer, began to implement these principles by taking steps to organize for the coming campaign and, in Evans' words, "to follow up the victory over the now prostrate United States Bank, by a war of extermination against the smaller engines of fraud and corruption." Announcing as their objective the election of men who would "oppose the granting of ALL PRIVILEGES, and especially *the privilege of making paper money*," they established a temporary General Committee, consisting of two delegates from each ward, and adopted a Plan of Organization. It was further agreed that no candidate would be supported unless he had pledged himself against all chartered monopolies and in favor of gradually prohibiting the circulation of small notes. Although banks and paper money were the major source of dissatisfaction, other grievances were revealed by their resolutions attacking the auction system, imprisonment for debt, the militia system, unequal taxation, and the "aristocratic" system of civil law.[22]

They received unexpected support in this agitation from the *Evening Post*, an official Tammany organ; under the editorial direction of the "chaunting cherubs," William Cullen Bryant and William Leggett, this paper published a series of attacks upon "the rotten Banking system." Rejoicing that "the *Post* has now risen above party and taken a stand among the true advocates of the people's cause," the Workingmen regarded this as an indication that the Democratic organization had been converted to "correct principles."[23] But the *Times*, spokesman of the pro-bank wing of the party, quickly disabused them of this notion, charging that "the [United States] *Bank men were at the bottom of the whole affair*," attempting to alienate the mechanics from "their Democratic friends." The officers of the Workingmen's meeting replied to this imputation, declaring: "The working men belong to no *party*, nor are they to be cajoled by any party. . . . With us 'Democratic Republicanism' is something more than a *name*, and all we wish is to make it a *reality*."[24] Furthermore, Evans argued in defense of his insistence on the pledge, not only would this "republican measure . . . give new vigor to thousands of democrats who though disgusted, have never left the party," it would also "be the certain means of recovering hundreds of votes that have been given to the Wigs [sic], not on account of friendship to their principles, but merely to break down a dominant party that professed republicanism, but whose candidates when elected, practised nearly everything that was hateful in aristocracy."[25]

With election time approaching, the party began to close ranks, as it became apparent that concessions would be made to guarantee the support of the antimonopolists. "The *bone* and *muscle* . . . the *hard hands* and *honest hearts*" of the Democracy met at Tammany Hall, overflowing into the adjacent City Hall Park, to hear exhortations and approve resolutions endorsing the principle of "equal rights." This was followed by ward meetings to choose delegates to the Tammany nominating committee. Evans importuned the Workingmen to "be on the spot" to prevent "the voice of the many" from being stifled by "the dictation of a few," recommending that delegates be selected by ballot instead of the usual method of *viva voce* approval of a prepared list. Leggett seconded this appeal in the *Post*, but the *Times* maintained a discreet silence. Nearly half the wards followed this advice, with even more resolving in favor of the pledge for all party candidates.[26]

Governor Marcy, running for reelection, was also moving to conciliate this faction. He had previously ingratiated himself with those mechanics who had long and loudly denounced the so-called State Prison Monopoly, the contract-labor system by which convicts were taught a trade and hired out to contractors.* Although refusing to consider its abolition, he had appointed a commission—one of whom was Ely Moore, the trade-union leader—to conduct an investigation. The Workingmen welcomed this step, although Evans insisted that this issue was secondary to "that ten times greater monopoly and hundred times greater curse the RAG MONEY MONOPOLY."[27] Now, the Governor delighted them with a forth-

* See also the discussion in Chapter 8, below.

right reply to their request for his views on the broader issue. Advocating the prohibition of small notes and opposing an "unwise increase of banking institutions with exclusive privileges," he avowed:

> Legislation goes beyond its proper sphere of action when it undertakes to regulate the business pursuits of our citizens, unless it is required to do so in the exercise of its guardian power of affording protection against certain and obvious evils. This guardian power should, however, be exercised with the utmost caution, and with a special regard to the equal rights of all classes of citizens.[28]

If Marcy's statement appeared to attest that the Albany Regency had capitulated to the Workingmen, further evidence of their victory was offered when the Democrats met to hear the report of the nominating committee. Although Evans' insistence that "a *majority* of the candidates should be men who subsist by useful labor" was unavailing, he and Leggett professed themselves generally satisfied with the ticket presented. The nominations of Ely Moore for Congress and Job Haskell, a "coalman," for the Assembly were especially hailed, but the most heartening news was the fact that all candidates had signed a pledge against "the extension of monopolies and other exclusive privileges." These concessions, combined with a return of prosperity to the business community, many of whom had been alienated by Biddle's policies, brought victory to the Democratic cause. The entire Tammany ticket was elected by a majority of over two thousand votes, seeming to promise Democratic ascendancy for years to come.[29] Thus the Workingmen, after five years of agitation, had finally asserted their influence by inducing Tammany, on the surface at least, to nominate only antibank men. Fearful of the rising power of the Whigs, the Democracy at the risk of alienating its more conservative supporters catered to the antimonopoly faction by adopting the pledge and nominating some of its candidates. Though forced by circumstances to disband as a political party, the Workingmen had reached the climax of their power and prestige. The party of Jefferson and Jackson had seemingly embraced the principles of the party of "Mechanics and Working Men."

The Workingmen as Locofocos

THE SURFACE harmony in the Democracy scarcely survived the 1834 election. Now that victory had been won, pledges were soon ignored and the Workingmen chastised as nonconformists. Their principles repudiated and their counsel unheeded, the anti-monopolists in the ensuing three years gradually abandoned the hope of reform from within and reentered the lists against Tammany. Inflationary pressures fed their political discontent, the party in power bearing the odium for the "evils" of banks and other monopolies, and the Locofocos emerged as a reincarnation of the Workingmen's Party. Overtures were made, on the one hand, to journeymen whose economic weapons were being blunted by the courts and, on the other, to the hitherto despised Whigs. But this political bargain, like the earlier alliance with the Democracy, brought disillusionment, and, as panic succeeded prosperity in 1837, the Locofocos were reunited with a "purified" Tammany. Van Buren, the onetime object of obloquy, received their allegiance as the rightful heir of Jefferson and Jackson, for the principles of the Workingmen had become Democratic doctrine.

The uneasy truce of 1834 between the two wings of the party was first broken in the editorial columns. Attacks by Evans and Leggett on "chartered monopolies" prompted the *Times* to assert that "the *Man* is leading the *Post*, and the *Post* is driving the party." Democrats, declared the spokesman of the conservatives, were "merely opposed to monopolies properly so called, and *not* to whatever the *Post*, may deem to be monopolies."[1] "The *Times*," Evans wrote in rebuttal, "has thrown off the mask. The election being over, it thinks it can, as it could not before, *afford* to show its face. . . . 'The party will not receive new *principles* at the hands of the *Man* and the *Post*, nor adopt implicitly the wild changes devised by the spirit of ultraism,' says the *Times*. . . . The Democracy will not receive '*new* principles' at our hands, for we advocate none."[2]

Conflicting editorial opinions are seldom enough to sunder a political party, but the behavior of the recently elected Assemblymen soon gave the antimonopolists a concrete issue. Ignoring the pledge they had signed, most of them proceeded to vote favorably on a number of incorporation bills. By the end of the session, with nearly one hundred charters approved, only three names (including Job Haskell's) had been recorded consistently in the negative. The Democratic Workingmen's General Committee, still active, met to censure this "perfidious violation of a solemn engagement." Evans, adverting to his earlier suspicion that "they gave the pledge, not because they were in favor of its requirements, but because they could not go to Albany without it," maintained that "the political hypocrites were . . . *compelled by their fears* [of defeat] to make radical democratic professions . . . to ensure success."[3]

The debate continued throughout the spring and summer, exacerbated further by the report on prison labor, in which the commissioners concluded that complaints against the system had been based upon "erroneous impressions." The invective grew more heated, the *Times* characterizing the *Man* as "the dirty little paper which acts as tender and toadeater to the *Evening Post*"; Evans replied in kind, denouncing the " 'Organ of the party,' i.e. a mere party hack."[4] In October the antimonopolists, in the hope of making "political capital" for their cause, took the lead in arranging a public dinner to honor Richard M. Johnson, slated to be Van Buren's running mate in the next Presidential election. By the ancient and honorable device of a series of toasts, the principles of Equal Rights were restated and the defenders of monopoly denounced for their "heresies." The dissidents from party orthodoxy took heart especially from the endorsement of the pledge by Churchill C. Cambreleng, a New York Congressman and a close personal friend of Van Buren. But when the Democratic nominating committee was chosen, the "monopoly democrats" won the day, and it became obvious that the pledge would be dropped and no concessions made in the selection of candidates. The professional politicians and the conservative businessmen had determined to reassert their control over the party.[5]

With the crucial test of strength between the two factions approaching, the Equal Rights Democrats found themselves without the leadership of both Evans and Leggett. The former had discontinued the *Man* during the summer, being induced to move to Rahway, New Jersey, "by the prospect of cheaper and more eligible accommodations for business and residence than could be obtained in the city." Though continuing to publish the weekly *Working Man's Advocate* at that place throughout the remainder of the year, Evans was in poor health most of the time and essentially out of touch with the political activities of his former colleagues. Leggett's uncompromising editorials, meanwhile, had almost bankrupted the *Post*, for the all-important government patronage had been withdrawn. But it was his defense of the abolitionists which was regarded as the major heresy, and he was excommunicated by the principal organ of the Democracy, the Washington *Globe*. In addition to his financial difficulties Leggett became ill and on the eve of the election seemed near death, not fully recovering for nearly a year.[6] The result, according to Fitzwilliam Byrdsall, chronicler of the Locofoco movement, was that

> the *Evening Post* was bereft of the mighty spirit which gave it power over men's minds, and it seemed as if the sun was standing still in the political world. So deep and intense was the interest felt by the friends of Equal Rights in behalf of the champion of their cause, that it threw an aspect of solemnity over their councils, which perhaps induced more caution in their preparations, and the more necessity for reliance on themselves in the approaching contest.[7]

This group, consisting of old Workingmen and Democrats converted by Leggett's editorials, had been meeting privately to discuss strategy, believing that secrecy was necessary because of the political maxim that "nothing could justify a disorganizer." Evans, from his sanctuary across the Hudson, suggested that their "only course" was to select substitutes for all unsatisfactory Tammany candidates, "to offer these substitutes in the general meeting if there be time, and to support them whether they shall be adopted by the general meeting or not."[8] This advice was essentially followed. Although some advocated a complete repudiation of the Tammany ticket, it was finally agreed to oppose strenuously only five of the twelve Assembly candidates; Byrdsall, one of the extremists, later epitomized this decision: "To go the whole length either way, was not agreeable to the majority of the prominent men, who were not distinguished for great decision of character—but to go nearly half way, was to hit the medium point which medium men strive to arrive at."[9]

The general meeting on October 29, 1835, was a scene of pandemonium; both factions having foreseen the struggle, the regulars were prepared to use steamroller tactics and the dissidents to resist them. When the doors were opened, the party rank and file found the Tammany leaders, who had come up the back stairs, already on the platform. While the "regular nominations" and resolutions were being read and declared approved, a struggle surged around the chair between the Tammany supporters of Chairman Isaac Varian and the partisans of Joel Curtis, an old Workingman nominated from the floor. After the chair was overturned and Varian thrown from it, the meeting was declared adjourned. The departing party leaders turned off the gas, but the insurgents were prepared for this. As seen by James Gordon Bennett, an interested observer from the other side of the political fence, "Every man pulled out his tallow candle and lucifer [or locofoco] match, and in a second two hundred fat tallow torches blazed over the hall. They deserve credit for this contrivance, for heretofore, turning the gas cock, turned out all opposition. It was one of the most decent and pleasing rows we ever saw." The Antimonopoly ticket was then voted on and declared to be "almost unanimously carried," after which a series of resolutions was approved opposing monopolies, especially banks, and calling for an end to paper money.[10]

Rejoicing at the split, the Whig press dubbed the dissidents "Locofocos," a label they proudly adopted. The *Times,* understandably, reported the meeting with vituperation against "disorganizers" and "noisy discontented politicians," but concluded: "We are glad that they are going to run a ticket . . . as by that means only can we effectually weed our ranks. We shall get rid now of the interlopers who have tried so long to force honest republicans into supporting their new-fangled doctrines, and a good riddance it will be." Tammany enforced party discipline against the "irregular" ticket and, to counteract Leggett's influence, exerted pressure upon the Democratic Young Men's General Committee to repudiate the *Evening Post*.[11] "Party attachments were appealed to," Byrdsall revealed,

> the ligatures of self-interest were drawn tight, and fears of extrusion from the party were awakened. Many of the anti-monopolists began to lose a portion of their enthusiasm for principle, when brought in conflict with party attachments. Others flattered themselves that they were in the advance of their fellow-citizens, and that they had better remain quiet in the Monopoly Democracy until it became as far advanced and enlightened as themselves. In short, the fate of Mr. Leggett was a warning to all Reformers not to set themselves against "the party."[12]

In spite of these defections the Locofoco ticket polled nearly four thousand votes in the unsuccessful contest with Tammany. The turnout was disappointingly small, about half the vote of the previous year, which Evans ascribed to "a feeling of disgust" by the electorate. But, he wrote consolingly, considering their "utter want of organization" and virtual lack of a public press, "the result of the election is no cause of discouragement. . . . In another year the Anti-monopoly Democrats should win." The *Evening Post,* also, was optimistic, pointing out that "the Disorganizers Hold the Balance of Power," for "not an election can be carried but by their aid." The Locofocos were urged to "act as a distinct body," and were told that "the time must soon come when our co-operation will be coveted with far more ardor than it is now repudiated, and when it shall fall to us to dictate the terms of the compromise."[13]

Considerable discussion ensued, however, before an independent party was organized, the dissidents vowing at first that they did "not intend to institute a new party, but to form a union with those of their fellow-citizens whose political principles are truly Democratic." Leggett was known to oppose a new political alignment, and his prestige was sufficiently high to deter an immediate move for separation, despite the growing sentiment in favor of a complete break with Tammany. It was finally agreed to postpone the final decision until the election of delegates to the Democratic General Committees in December; when the result indicated that Tammany was still in control, the Equal Rights Party came into being.[14] Several of the original antimonopolists refused to join the secession movement, so the February organizational convention was attended, as Byrdsall noted, by "few of the prominent names conspicuous in the original anti-monopoly movement." The Declaration of Principles adopted by the convention emphasized: "We utterly disclaim any intention or design of instituting any new party, but declare ourselves the original Democratic party, our whole object being political reformation by reviving the landmarks and principles of Democracy." Invoking the doctrines of "the revered Jefferson," they flew the banner of "equal rights" and the pledge, declaring their hostility to all monopolies, paper money, and "the dangerous and unconstitutional creation of *vested rights* by legislation." A plan of organization similar to that of the Workingmen's Party was adopted, Dr. Moses Jaques being elected treasurer and Byrdsall recording secretary, the only permanent officers designated for the new party.[15]

The Locofocos attempted to consolidate their position in the succeeding months, challenging Tammany at the polls and recruiting adherents from organized labor. In the spring election, candidates for the Common Council were presented in eleven of the sixteen wards; following Leggett's declination, the mayoralty nomination was given to Alexander Ming, Jr., the son of Skidmore's former associate and until 1835 a faithful Tammany supporter. Though none of the Locofoco candidates was successful, the votes taken from the Tammany ticket resulted in an equal division between Whigs and Democrats on the Council; the Tammany incumbent, Mayor Lawrence, was reelected as Ming polled 2,700 votes, a decrease from the strength shown in November.[16] In the meantime, the Trades' Union, reflecting the grievances of journeymen in an inflationary period, was becoming increasingly militant under the presidency of John Commerford, once active in the Workingmen's Party and now a Locofoco. Strikes by its affiliated societies led, in the case of the Journeyman Tailors, to violence, followed by conviction on charges of conspiracy and riot. A mass meeting in the

Park to protest against the trial cheered an address by Ming and approved a resolution calling for a state convention to organize "a separate and distinct party." The Locofocos then voted to join the "mechanics and working men" at Utica in mid-September, since "the objects and measures must necessarily be founded on the same principles, and in favor of the same reforms in government, as are urged by the anti-monopoly democracy."[17]

In the interim the party held a protracted county convention from May to the end of July to discuss plans for the coming campaign, the session being prolonged primarily by debate on the endorsement of a Presidential candidate. Evans, hitherto implacable in his opposition to Van Buren because of his earlier stand on universal suffrage, had modified his opinion and placed his name on the masthead of the *Working Man's Advocate*. "We should have more readily acquiesced in the nomination of Mr. Van Buren," he explained, "had he never been wrong on a fundamental doctrine of republicanism; but having been satisfied that he is now right, on the subject . . . and on all the important questions which have lately occupied the public mind . . . we have, after due deliberation, determined to render our feeble aid towards the election of Mr. Van Buren to the Presidential chair."[18] Although this view was shared by a number of the Locofocos, the opposition was equally determined, the long-standing distrust of the politician warring with the desire for a continuation of Jacksonian policies in Washington. A committee was appointed to correspond with Van Buren and Johnson, the Democratic nominee for Vice-President; the Whigs were ignored because, it was agreed, "either the consistency, or the ability, or the democratic faith of the other candidates, is a matter of great doubt in the minds of the people." While Johnson's reply was deemed to be in full accord with the Declaration of Principles, Van Buren's letter failed to mitigate the controversy. In reply to the detailed questions of the committee, he tersely referred them to "a public course of no inconsiderable duration in the state and federal government, and to a succession of public declarations heretofore made by me." Byrdsall and others termed this letter "evasive, unsatisfactory, and unworthy of a great statesman," and a resolution to support both Van Buren and Johnson was tabled. Finally reaching a compromise, the party agreed to endorse no Presidential ticket, leaving each member free to make his own choice in the election.[19]

The county convention had no difficulty reaching agreement on a gubernatorial candidate, tendering the nomination to Colonel Samuel Young, a Democratic State Senator who had opposed the "banking mania." Though ratifying the Locofoco principles, Young declined because of his opposition to a third party, so the Utica convention in the fall was faced with the necessity of finding a substitute. Isaac S. Smith of Buffalo, the Workingmen's candidate for Lieutenant Governor in 1830, was selected, Moses Jaques receiving second place on the ticket. The ninety-three delegates from all sections of the state, after resolving unanimously to "institute a political party separate and distinct from all existing parties or factions," adopted the Locofoco Declaration of Principles and endorsed the pledge. An Address to the People was issued, denouncing "all monopolies and all partial and unequal legislation," attacking the "aristocratic" practices of the legal system as demonstrated by the labor conspiracy cases, and calling for a state constitutional convention to eliminate these evils. Resolving to "divest ourselves of all party feeling, party prejudices, and attachments to party leaders," the convention declared: "The leaders of the two great political parties under which the people have arrayed themselves are selfish and unprincipled; the objects of both are power, honors, and emolument; they are the enemies of the equal rights of the citizen; be therefore no longer deceived; let us withdraw ourselves from both. . . ."[20]

When the local election campaign opened a month later, however, the Locofocos, despite their manifesto, nominated prominent Whigs for three legislative and Congressional offices. Although doubts were expressed regarding the propriety of this step, it was justified as the most effective means of defeating Tammany and thus converting the Democracy to "correct principles." Edward Curtis and James Monroe (the nephew of the ex-President) were proposed for Congress, largely on the recommendation of Dr. Alexander Vaché—"a man," in Byrdsall's words, "in whom the party had the

fullest confidence," although a "most ingenious casuist." In spite of
the assertion that Curtis had expressed his opposition to some party
tenets, Vaché convinced the assemblage that both men "were as
radical and thorough as any present" and "would strenuously maintain the principles of the party." The Congressional ticket also included Dr. Stephen Hasbrouck, an "original" antimonopolist, and
Ely Moore, who had been renominated by Tammany.[21] The Locofocos bitterly opposed Morgan L. Smith, the Democratic candidate
for State Senator, because of his close association with the Tammany Old Guard and his position as a bank director. "What though
he is!" the *Times* indignantly replied. "Is the director of a bank a
felon, an outlaw! . . . We fancy that few . . . seriously hold that
a place in a board of directors is incompatible with integrity or
reputation, or that it disqualifies a man for any other social or
political station." The Equal Rights Party nominated a Whig,
Frederick A. Tallmadge, for that office, "not because they preferred
him personally . . . but because they could use him to defeat a
candidate of the Monopoly principle." The ticket was completed
with the selection of thirteen Assembly candidates, two of whom,
Robert Townsend, Jr., and Clinton Roosevelt, were endorsed by the
Whigs along with Curtis, Monroe, and Tallmadge.[22]

The Democrats, attempting to capitalize on the strange alliance,
expressed doubt that "conscientious whigs" could support men
pledged to Locofoco principles; the *Times* pointed out in regard to
Curtis that "the whigs expect him to go for a protective tariff, a
national bank, etc.—the Loco Focos deem him pledged to oppose
all banks, restrictions upon trade, etc. Which is to be deceived and
disappointed?" To disarm the doubters in the antimonopolist camp,
Curtis appeared before a meeting of "working-men and others
friendly to Equal Rights," informing them that his father had been
a blacksmith and avowing that "some might call him a Whig, but
he called himself an Equal Rights Democrat." He likewise assured
the Whigs that he had given only qualified assent to the Locofoco
principles, having been nominated primarily because of their hostility to Tammany, "the common enemy" of both parties.[23]

The Locofoco strategy succeeded, the election dealing a crippling blow to the power of Tammany. Curtis and Moore were elected to Congress, Tallmadge to the State Senate, and Townsend and Roosevelt to the Assembly; the other Congressmen elected were Ogden Hoffman, a Whig, and Cambreleng, supported unofficially by many Locofocos, while only six of the thirteen Tammany Assembly candidates were successful. The new party did not fare so well with its independent nominations, the gubernatorial ticket receiving only fourteen hundred votes in the city and thirty-five hundred throughout the state. The *Democrat,* the Locofoco organ, ignored reality by hailing the triumph of party principles, declaring with reference to the successful candidates that "the infatuated Whigs lay claim to them as Whigs . . . one of the many egregious errors of that absurd party."[24] Although Curtis and Tallmadge quickly forgot their pledge to the Equal Rights Party, Byrdsall, among others, was not disconcerted. The principal objective, he believed, had been attained with the discomfiture of Tammany, for the Locofocos "knew that all the arguments and clear reasonings in the world would effect no reform in the policy of the Republican party, so long as it was annually elected into power. To defeat it therefore . . . was the only way to reform it, by compelling it to fall back upon its original principles which it never fails to do as its last resort."[25]

As 1836 ended, it became evident that prosperity was preparing to leave with Jackson. The inflationary spiral, fed by extensive speculation in land and securities and the flood of paper from state banks, reached its culmination as Martin Van Buren entered the White House. Prices of necessities and rents rose to new heights just before the crash, especially in the cities, and early in February the Locofocos called a meeting in the Park to demand action to end the widespread distress. Addressing the large crowd huddled together against the cold and wind, Alexander Ming, Jr., put the blame upon "our monstrous banking system," for "as the currency expands, the loaf contracts." Volunteer orators then began to harangue the crowd, charging that flour was being hoarded to keep the price up, and soon a mob was moving toward several flour stores. Before the riot was brought under control, wheat and flour were thrown into the streets and several heads were broken. The Locofocos, as well as trades' unions and foreigners, were held responsible by the press, Ming being discharged from his position at the Custom House, but of the fifty-three rioters arrested none was a member of the party. Conditions worsened throughout the spring, and Panic arrived on May 10 when suspension of specie payments by the New York banks brought business failures and consequent unemployment. "There are vastly too many with nothing to do, and precious little to eat," Horace Greeley reported, estimating that at least fifty thousand people in the city were suffering for lack of "the common wants of life."[26]

The economic distress added to Tammany's woes, the Whigs continuing to benefit while the Locofocos increased their electoral support. This was demonstrated in the Charter election, Jaques' four thousand votes for Mayor guaranteeing the success of the Whig candidate.[27] Furthermore, President Van Buren's conversion to hard-money views, revealed by his continuance of Jackson's Specie Circular and his advocacy of an Independent Treasury, caused a rift to appear in the New York Democracy. Supporters of state banks and paper money, including the majority of the Tammany General Committee, attacked the President's message as a Locofoco-inspired document and, as Conservative Democrats, moved gradually toward an open alliance with the Whigs.[28] The Equal Rights Party, of course, wholeheartedly approved Van Buren's course, and welcomed the endorsement of the President by the Democratic Young Men's General Committee and a mass meeting in Tammany Hall. This chain of events led to discussions regarding Locofoco reunion with the apparently "purified" Democracy, but action was deferred while a ticket was chosen for the coming election. In the meantime a committee had been conferring with Tammany representatives to discuss "the propriety of requesting their candidates to subscribe to the Declaration" of Principles. As a result of these meetings, it was reported that "the branch of the party at Tammany Hall had given evidence of their disposition to unite with us in sustaining the administration," and had nominated "a ticket composed of men politically and morally satisfactory," all of whom had pledged their support of the principles of equal rights. The committee concluded:

"Principle and patriotism demand that we should meet them in a like spirit of conciliation. . . . In union there is strength: to produce union a mutual concession of personal feeling must be made—which concession sustains our principles, will elect our ticket, defeat our enemies, and strengthen the confidence of the people in the administration of the General Government."[29]

The majority of the Locofocos were willing to claim victory and return to Tammany, especially after five of their Assembly candidates were placed on the Democratic ticket. But a group of "ultras" led by Byrdsall and Windt refused to surrender to these overtures, despite accusations by the party majority that they had been bribed by the Whigs. Issuing an Address to the Citizens, the Locofoco "Rump" asserted its fidelity to the President but maintained that "no permanent good can be expected from the Democratic party in this city, unless a radical Democratic change takes place in its organization"; moreover, they added, "no reformation can be expected among 'the leaders,' while they can command lucrative official patronage."[30] The crushing Democratic defeat in the election led Byrdsall to grumble that since "no advantage resulted from the reunion . . . there would have been nothing lost by acting in good faith." Horace Greeley, from the Whig side, exulted: "The Loco-Foco party, as such, has exploded"; but he warned his triumphant colleagues not to read too much into the results. Victory should be attributed, he declared, neither to the adherence of the Conservatives nor to a desire for another National Bank, the votes of the majority implying "dissatisfaction with what is, far more clearly than they designate what in their opinion should be."[31]

Most of the Rump Locofocos, their ticket receiving fewer than four hundred votes, gradually rejoined their fellows in Tammany Hall, now the bastion of "correct principles." The former meeting place of the Equal Rights Party, the Military and Civic Hotel at Broome Street and the Bowery, was now deserted,

> for there was only one Loco-Foco, Robert Hogbin, who made it his haunt as usual. . . . [He] went there regularly, month after month, on the evenings appointed by the constitution for the meetings of the faithful; and he would bide there, solitary and

alone, until ten o'clock. . . . The old Military and Civic Hotel fell into decay, and at length was pulled down. Poor Hogbin saw it lying prostrate in its last ruins, and he turned away and wept.[32]

Byrdsall's sentimentality was unnecessary, for there were far more enduring monuments to the Locofoco movement than a decrepit frame building. For the next decade Locofoco principles were generally in the ascendant in the New York Democracy. The state constitution of 1846 embodied many of the demands of the Workingmen and their successors. The changed atmosphere at Tammany Hall provided an opportunity for many of the radicals to rise in the party hierarchy, some even becoming Sachems. Their contribution was perhaps best exemplified by the Democratic beatification of William Leggett. When he died in 1839, all his fulminations were forgotten as the party paid him tribute. The 1835 resolution excommunicating him from the Democracy was expunged from the record, and his bust was placed in Tammany Hall. William Leggett was now not merely a Locofoco martyr; he was a Tammany saint.[33]

The Men

The Labor Movement

PARALLELING the progress of the political Workingmen was the development of an organized labor movement. Because defense of the ten-hour system served as the impetus for organization of the Workingmen's Party, and because the Locofocos led the opposition to the doctrine of labor conspiracy, many writers have seen a close relationship between the political and industrial movements of the period. John R. Commons and his associates, in their pioneering studies of American labor history, have interpreted the rise of trade unionism, reaching its height between 1833 and 1836, as a continuation of the earlier political movement for "citizenship." According to this view, "wage-earners" after joining with their employers in the Workingmen's Party rejected politics to organize "wage-conscious" journeymen's societies, but then returned to politics with the Locofocos as the boom economy was succeeded by Panic.[1] Others have accepted this interpretation, overlooking the distinction (recognized by Commons) between "wage-earners" and "mechanics and workingmen," and presenting both movements as class conscious or "proletarian."[2]

While there was interaction between the political and trade-union movements, they were essentially independent, supplementary rather than complementary manifestations of social unrest. The basis of the confusion is the meaning of "mechanics and workingmen." This problem is essentially one of semantics, as an investigation of the terminology of the period reveals.[3] "Mechanic" was the more definite term, being used generally to describe anyone working at one of the mechanical "arts"—that is, crafts or trades. These were characterized by an apprenticeship system in which the "mystery" of the craft was learned by working in the master's shop and then practiced by journeymen who eventually would in their turn become master mechanics. Although the old system was beginning to break down during this period, the term did not yet imply any distinction between employer and employed.

Political usage, of course, often enlarged this rigid definition, both Democrats and Whigs on occasion going to such lengths that, as Dorfman concludes, only politicians of the opposition party were excluded.[4] Gideon Lee, the Tammany Mayor in 1833, was a banker and a leading merchant capitalist in the leather industry, but was termed a mechanic because he had begun his career as a tanner.[5] Silas M. Stilwell, a Whig candidate for the Assembly the following year, was called a mechanic in the party press because he owned a shoe store; the Democrats charged, however, that he was a "small lawyer . . . without brains sufficient to gain a livelihood by his profession," who had become a "retailer of the slop manufactures of the Bay State" and, even more heinous, a dealer in prison-made shoes.[6] Despite this abuse in terminology, "mechanic" had a more circumscribed meaning than "workingman," which was considerably more elastic and hence more difficult to define. The term apparently included small merchants and retail tradesmen, cartmen, and even some clerical and subprofessional occupations. As an example, a notice of a Workingmen's Party meeting early in 1830 was addressed to "Mechanics and Working Men, including Grocers, Traders, Firemen, and Cartmen—in a word, all that support society by useful employment."[7]

The Workingmen themselves were concerned about the problem, as evidenced by the discussion in their party organs. The *Evening Journal* early in 1830 defined "Working Men, or Producing Classes" as "all who are industriously engaged in any necessary occupation, whether he be a farmer, a mechanic, a tailor, a hatter, a shoemaker, etc., a carman, a day-laborer, a necessary grocer or merchant." The writer continued by emphasizing that some men, like "forestallers" and fruit pedlars, "who labor hard . . . no more belong to the Producing Classes, than the overgrown rich monopolist, or the auctioneer," because "their labor produces nothing; . . . their living . . . is extorted from the labor, the hard earnings of real producing citizens."[8] Similarly, Evans in the *Working Man's Advocate* attempted to distinguish between "useful" and "useless" occupations, indicating that the former should not be limited to the mechanical trades. While excluding lawyers, bankers, and brokers, even though "some of those occupations are already among us," he listed "general shipping merchants, or their clerks, retail dry good dealers, grocers, druggists, etc.," as useful. Conceding even that porterhouse keepers, while not useful in the accepted sense, should not receive a blanket condemnation, he agreed with a correspondent, "formerly a Mechanic," who urged the Workingmen: "Do not spurn every man who does not labor with his own hands, or who wears a ruffled shirt; many of whom have labored . . . as you do now, and are as friendly to your cause, as you are yourselves." Later, in writing his "History of the Origin and Progress of the Working Men's Party in New York," Evans defined the term as "including not merely the manual laborer, but every man who earns his bread by *useful* exertion, whether mental or physical."[9]

The Jacksonian period was a crucial time for the mechanical trades. Economic developments such as widening markets, improved transportation, and a more sophisticated use of credit were creating dynamic changes in the social structure.[10] Both horizontal and vertical cleavages were becoming more evident in commercial and industrial society. Increasing rivalry between the dominant mercantile community and the rising mechanic-manufacturer was succeeded by rivalry within the trades between master and journeyman, exacerbated by the emergence of the merchant-capitalist as employer in place of the master craftsman.[11] These men, with easy access to credit, began to invade the mechanical trades and to establish small-scale factories. The master craftsman with a handful of journeymen and apprentices continued to rely upon the quality of his products, but he found it difficult to compete when he was undersold by quantity production in a market increasingly oriented toward price.

A correspondent in the *Evening Journal* denounced the invasion of "monopolists and capitalists usurping the rights of mechanics . . . abridging their privileges by opposing them in their business with the advantages of a large capital." Describing the situation in more detail, he declared that "men who are no mechanics . . . are engaged in mechanical concerns . . . at the expense of the interest of the legitimate mechanics; . . . and in many cases, preventing the industrious, enterprising, but, perhaps indigent mechanic, from following his trade to advantage, or from following it at all." This, he continued, deprives the mechanic of the opportunity to benefit fully from the knowledge he had acquired from an arduous apprenticeship. "The ideas of an apprentice are constantly buoyed up by the prospect, not only of being franchised from his indentures, but . . . by a desire to become a proprietor himself; which is . . . necessary alike to master and apprentice, for it increases and strengthens the appetite to become an adept, and gives a zest to all his efforts."[12]

Furthermore, the master mechanic because of the credit situation either found it difficult to enlarge and improve his business in order to maintain his position, or lost everything in the inflationary spiral induced by paper money and speculation. A writer in the *Working Man's Advocate* complained bitterly: "As those who labor produce all the wealth of a community, why is it that they must fight so hard to participate, even in a small degree, in that wealth? . . . The citizen is tempted to launch into extravagant schemes, which may yield a fortune or may produce beggary. This . . . renders all business a sort of lottery."[13]

Combined with and aggravating the economic situation was the social rivalry between merchants and mechanics. On the eve of the 1829 election the *Evening Journal* declared that "although the Mechanics are the most useful and powerful body of men in the community, and . . . as respectable as any other class, they are . . . considered in many points inferior. . . . Is it a stain upon the character to gain an honest livelihood by useful industry? . . . There are more real gentlemen among this than any other class."[14] This rivalry became more acute in 1834, when the Bank War and economic recession intensified political and social conflicts. "A Working Man" advised his fellows to "permit no violence from any person, whether he wear a fine coat and shirt or not." Evans, describing a Whig meeting, reported that "these silk stocking tape and buckram gentry really appeared a degraded race, compared with the assemblage of the hardy sons of useful labor at Tammany Hall," adding somewhat apologetically that "they *force* us to these comparisons, by their unwarrantable attempts to set themselves above the useful classes."[15]

Economic and political conditions were also causing a gulf between master and journeyman. During the 1832 and 1834 elections, for example, many instances were cited of journeymen being discharged, or threatened with loss of their jobs, because of political differences with their employers.[16] Even more significant were the differences arising from economic and technological changes. Journeymen saw a threat to their status because the traditional apprenticeship system was breaking down. Since the old hand process was being supplanted by machinery in many trades, and the master was forced to be more concerned with marketing than craftsmanship, the need for trained craftsmen had diminished. Apprentices were now taught only the rudiments of the craft, becoming a source of cheap labor to supplant the more highly paid journeymen. As Paul Douglas has emphasized, this process degraded not only the status of the journeyman but the craft itself by producing "a constantly increasing number of half-trained men who were thrown out of employment by a fresh batch about to go through the mill from which they had just emerged."[17]

Many master craftsmen endeavored to maintain the old relationship. The journeymen recognized this and at first directed their denunciations toward the merchant-capitalists, seeing no conflict of interest with masters as such. "It is well known," declared the *National Trades' Union,* a weekly journal which began publication in the summer of 1834, "that innovations upon the rights of Journeymen have seldom originated with employers who have themselves served a regular apprenticeship, and worked as Journeymen. Almost always do they come from speculators, who steal into a business as adventurers."[18]

A writer in the *Man* went further. "The interest of all who obtain their living by honest labor," he insisted, "is substantially the same." To illustrate his contention, he added:

> . . . since the bos [*sic*] is often brought back to journeywork by hard luck, and the journeyman may expect in his turn to become an employer, while both of them are invariably imposed

upon and treated as if belonging to an inferior grade of society by those who live without labor, it surely seems quite desirable that . . . both journeyman and employer should come together. There are in truth but two parties in our country that can be said to have distinct interests. . . . Mechanics, farmers, artisans, and all who labor, whether as bos or journeyman, have a common interest in sustaining each other—the rich men, the professional men, and all who now live . . . without useful labor, depending on the sweat of their neighbor's brow for support, have also a common interest. And their interest is promoted by working us hard, and working us cheap.[19]

Fostering this mutual interest were a number of mechanics' fraternal or benevolent societies, many of which had been founded during the early years of the nineteenth century. Two of the oldest and most respectable were the Mutual Benefit Society of Cordwainers and the New-York Typographical Society, founded in 1808 and 1809 and both subsequently chartered by the State legislature.[20] Most other trades organized similar societies, open to masters and journeymen alike, as was demonstrated late in 1830 when the mechanics of New York celebrated the recent revolution in France with a colorful procession. The newspaper accounts listed some thirty trades as participating, about half of which were represented by benefit societies—including the Bakers, the Tailors, the Gas Workmen, the News Carriers, and the Pilots.[21] Other organizations, like the General Society of Mechanics and Tradesmen and the Mechanics' Institute, were not restricted to a specific trade, providing reading rooms and lectures for all young mechanics. Another group, typified by the Association for Moral Improvement of Young Mechanics, showed more concern for their religious habits than their mental or occupational development.[22] These various societies not only demonstrated the mutual interest of all mechanics but, as Paul Douglas concludes, gave evidence, along with the contemporary flowering of the Sunday school and day school movements, of the decline of the apprenticeship system; the general education formerly provided in the home and shop of the master now had to be sought elsewhere.[23]

While most of these societies continued to flourish throughout the 'thirties, journeymen increasingly found a need to form separate associations through which to channel their grievances against their employers. The experience of the printers was typical. The New-York Typographical Society was founded two decades earlier as both a protective and benevolent society of journeymen, but after an early period of militancy it had become merely a mutual benefit association. Forbidden by its charter to "interfere in respect to the price of labor," its members included both master mechanics and journeymen. Many of the latter finally became convinced that a protective organization must be established in order to maintain an adequate scale of wages. This sentiment culminated in 1831 with the formation of the Typographical Association of New York by a group of journeymen, most of whom continued their membership in the Society.[24]

The previous decade had been marked by sporadic "turnouts," notably the 1829 movement to defend the ten-hour day, but the resultant printers' strike opened the floodgates, and within a few years an irreparable breach had been made in the doctrine of mutual interest. In the same year both the masons and the sawyers turned out briefly, one for wages and the other for hours. Early in April 1833 a small group of twenty-four journeymen instituted the New York Society of Journeyman House Carpenters, which in two months numbered more than one hundred fifty members. Their constitution enumerated their objectives, indicating both protective and benevolent features:

> To establish equitable prices and obtain just and reasonable wages to promote mechanical Knowledge to raise a fund for the relief of such of its Members as shall suffer by accidents while engaged in their mechanical occupations for the decent interment of its deceased Members to provide for such of its Members as shall have lost their tools by fire and finally by adjusting disputes and endeavouring to cherish and maintain a good understanding between employers and those who are employed—to advance the general interest of all who are concerned in the business of House Carpenters. . . .

The document provided further that an applicant for membership must be "a regular Journeyman House Carpenter of the age of

twenty one years of good moral character and not working for less
than the then established wages or prices," and authorized strikes
if approved by two-thirds of the membership. Dues of twelve and
one-half cents per month were assessed, and benefit payments were
authorized amounting to twenty dollars for funeral expenses and a
maximum of three dollars per week for a disabling injury; but any
member receiving such relief payments could be expelled from the
Society if it were found that he was "engaged in his employment
or in spending his time in brothels or gambling."[25]

Within a month after organization of the Society, a strike was
called to maintain the daily wage of twelve shillings, or one dollar
fifty cents, against an attempted reduction by the Master Builders.
The support of other trades enabled the carpenters to win their
demands after a month's turnout, which led to discussion of making
the alliance permanent. The Typographical Association, "on account
of the many facilities which Printers possess for disseminating information," took the lead by issuing a circular calling for a convention of trades and presenting a tentative plan of organization.[26] Nine
journeymen's societies sent delegates to the first meeting, three
others sending letters approving the plan. At subsequent meetings
the General Trades' Union of New York was organized and a constitution was adopted. It provided that each society would be represented by three delegates chosen annually, and levied a capitation
tax of six and one-quarter cents monthly, "to maintain the present
scale of prices to all members who are fairly remunerated; to raise
up all such as are oppressed; to alleviate the distresses of those suffering from the want of employment; and to sustain the honor and
interest of the 'Union.'" It was agreed, however, that "no Trade
or Art shall strike for higher wages . . . without the sanction of
the Convention." The remainder of the year saw the rapid growth
of the Union, until twenty-one societies in New York, Brooklyn,
and Newark were represented, some four thousand members affiliated with it parading up Broadway and the Bowery in December
to demonstrate their unity.[27]

The organization of the New York Trades' Union was followed
by similar organizations in other cities, and in the spring of 1834 a

call was issued for a convention of delegates from these unions to meet in New York during the summer. This step, it was declared, was desirable in order to "consult on such measures as shall be most conducive to advance the moral and intellectual dignity of the laboring classes, sustain their pecuniary interest, succor the oppressed, and by all just means maintain the honor and respectability of the mechanical profession." Thirty delegates, two-thirds of them from the New York metropolitan area,* assembled in the heat of late August—and in the midst of a cholera epidemic—to organize the National Trades' Union, characterized by Commons as "merely a national medium of agitation without administrative or disciplinary control over local unions."[28] Also during that summer a new weekly newspaper appeared, fittingly named the *National Trades' Union,* dedicated to "advocate the cause and defend the rights of the producing classes."†

The next few years saw a crescendo of labor activity, with about ten new trade societies being organized. The increased volume of agitation was reflected by an eightfold increase in dues for the Union to twelve and one-half cents per week. Nearly a score of strikes were called in 1835 and 1836, most of which were a direct result of inflationary pressures, either demands for higher wages or defenses against proposed reductions. The Ladies' Cordwainers (or shoemakers), who had first turned out in 1833 at about the same time as the Carpenters, struck again in 1834 and 1835. The Journeyman Tailors struck in 1833 and 1836, and the Carpenters again in 1836; other trades taking similar action ranged from Cabinet Makers and Masons to Horse Shoers and Weavers.[29]

In justification of their demands the *National Trades' Union* stated early in 1835 that "the expenses of living, and supporting a family in this city, are annually increasing at the rate of 10 or 12 per cent," emphasizing that "if the mechanics do not demand a pro-

---

* The delegates were divided as follows: New York—15, Brooklyn—1, Newark—3, Poughkeepsie—1, Boston—3, and Philadelphia—7.

† The first issue, from which the above quotation is taken, appeared July 5, 1834. This newspaper was in no way an official organ of the Trades' Union, receiving no financial support from that body, but it was sanctioned as an unofficial spokesman of the organization.

portional . . . advance of wages, they will, in fact, be annually reduced in the same ratio." The paper declared further:

> Rents are enormously high; and in many cases . . . owners of houses demand, for the ensuing year, an advance of 25 or 30, and even as high as 40 per cent on the rent of the current year. The grocer must add the amount of the advanced rent to the price of his articles—every other dealer must do the same; and the mechanic must pay more than he did last year for every thing which he or his family eat, drink, or wear. . . . And must the journeyman look quietly on, and see his expenses annually increased against his consent, while his wages remain the same? Must he alone bear the sole burden imposed upon society by the landlords? . . . Has he not as good a right to demand an advanced price for his labor, as the purse-proud landlord has to turn his family into the street, because his scanty wages do not enable him to pay the enormous rent demanded of him?

A year later the same journal stated that "the cost of maintaining a family is 60 percent higher than it was five years ago; yet wages are not on the average 30 percent higher than five years ago."[30]

Wages were not the only issue facing the journeyman. The first strike under the jurisdiction of the General Trades' Union was that of the Journeyman Loaf Bread Bakers in June 1834; while basically a wage dispute, their demands also included the limitation of apprentices to one per employer, an indenture period of at least five years, and no Sunday work. The Union, after appointing a committee to investigate the justice of the Bakers' complaints, authorized the strike and called for a boycott of all "unfair" establishments. During the same year the printers expressed concern at the proposal of Duff Green, a Washington publisher, to establish an institute to instruct boys in the printing business, thus circumventing the traditional apprenticeship system.[31] After the influential *Niles' Register* had denounced as "in utter repugnance to the public welfare" the attempt of the Bakers to regulate apprenticeship, the *National Trades' Union* defended the attitude of the journeymen's societies, declaring:

> . . . the consequence of our measures will be, to exclude from employ all incompetent workmen! Clumsy, idle or intemperate

hands will find no employ; boys will be under the necessity of
serving their time out, instead of leaving their masters after a
year or two's service—of learning their trade, before they get
employment as journeymen; *rats* and two-thirds men will be
discountenanced: and journeymen induced to be steady and industrious in their situations, and temperate in their habits. Thus
. . . we shall actually be the means of improving our own condition as journeymen, of promoting and securing the interests
of the employers, and of advancing the welfare and happiness of
the whole community![32]

As the strength of organized labor grew, the right of "combination" itself became the main issue. Some newspapers, like the
dignified *Journal of Commerce,* had from the first taken a dark view
of journeymen's societies, holding that "all combinations to compel
others to give a higher price . . . are not only inexpedient, but at
war with the order of things which the Creator has established for
the general good, and therefore wicked." Others saluted the organization of the Trades' Union, but soon became apprehensive that
"this confederacy . . . will ultimately prove a very dangerous body
to the country." As the editor of the *Evening Star,* a Whig paper,
asserted: "However innocent and justifiable may have been the
original motives . . . to protect the laborer against a mercenary
and unjust spirit on the part of the employer, these associations when
they become formidable by their numbers . . . control employers
. . . [and] prescribe rules and regulations for the government of
society at large, according to their own views and interests." Editor
Hezekiah Niles in 1834 had seen little harm in "turn-outs," for he
believed that "high prices for honest labor . . . injure no one";
but within a year he was denouncing the Union for attempting to
"dictate the rate of wages to employers," warning that "the step
from combining to threatening is so short, that the one almost always
leads to the other."[33]

In answering these attacks and denying that strikes and trades'
unions were synonymous, the *National Trades' Union* asserted on
the contrary that "*strikes* are scarcely considered, by the projectors
of Trades' unions, as essential to their purposes." Criticism of
journeymen's combinations, the paper maintained, was based prin-

cipally upon the fact that, as in the case of the carpenters and bakers, "their members, when not adequately compensated, may leave their work, and not at once perish with hunger; that, by these associations, they are secured from the tender mercies of those, who would grind them to the earth!"[34] Late in 1834 the Journeyman Hatters experienced the effect of the animosity toward combinations, after acceding to two downward revisions of their "list of prices." Employers then began discharging all members of the society, an action which was formally denounced by the General Trades' Union as "proscription, and a direct infringement of personal rights." A strike was called and, business fortuitously increasing, most of the discharged hatters were back at work in a month.[35]

Within the ensuing year master mechanics in a number of trades had begun to form a united front against the journeymen's societies by organizing employers' protective associations. One of the strongest was the Master Tailors "combination" which early in 1836, after the journeymen had struck in protest against a wage reduction, resolved not to employ members of the Union Trade Society of Journeyman Tailors. This organization, the masters declared, is "subversive of the rights of individuals, detrimental to the public good, injurious to business, restrictive of our freedom of action, and unjust, and oppressive towards industrious journeymen, who are not members of the said society."[36] Frequent clashes between strikers and "rats" led to police action and eventually to the arrest and trial of twenty-five journeymen on charges of riot and conspiracy to restrain trade. The judge in his charge to the jury relied upon the opinion of New York Chief Justice Savage in a similar case, and a blanket verdict was returned against the defendants, who were fined a total of $1,400. The Union and its friends understandably attacked the decision; the Locofocos held a vociferous Park meeting in protest, and even the Whig editor Horace Greeley deplored the verdict. "To convict men of . . . combining to obstruct trade and commerce," he declared, "where they have only associated themselves to demand a certain compensation for their labor . . . is not exactly the way we would wish to see justice administered."[37]

In another year the organized labor movement in New York had disappeared. But it was not the legal weapon of conspiracy which destroyed the Trades' Union and its affiliated societies. It was instead the Panic of 1837, which brought a general collapse in all business and resulted in widespread unemployment. Greeley reported in June 1837 that "one-half of the artists, mechanics, clerks, women and laborers of every class in our city are wholly out of employment, and could not earn their daily bread for their labor in any capacity." As winter approached the situation worsened, Greeley declaring in October that "there is not now employment at any price for three-fourths of those who seek it," adding discouragingly, "it is hardly better in any of the Atlantic cities."[38] Under these conditions the specter of joblessness was of greater moment than wages or hours, and so this brief period of labor militancy came to an end, not reviving until the return of prosperity in the mid-'forties and 'fifties.

While the relationship of this labor movement to the Workingmen's parties is complex and difficult to evaluate, it can be approached through a biographical study of some of the men associated with both. The most prominent labor leader in New York during this period was ELY MOORE. Although never formally affiliated with the Workingmen, he was allied with them in 1834, when he was elected as "labor's first Congressman," and two years later was the only Tammany candidate nominated on the Locofoco ticket. Furthermore, as first president of both the General Trades' Union and the National Trades' Union, he was regarded as an official spokesman of organized labor.[39]

Moore was born in 1798 on a farm near the village of Belvidere, New Jersey, and as a boy was apprenticed to a printer in the nearby town of Newton. He arrived in New York in the early 1820's, where he married a daughter of Gilbert Coutant, a well-to-do grocer and lumber merchant who was also active in Tammany politics.[40] He then, it appears, abandoned the printing trade for the more promising spheres of land speculation and politics, assisted in both activities by Coutant. In 1827 he purchased a large tract in upper Manhattan which he later sold in parcels at a profit.[41] Three years

later his political career began with an appointment as assistant
county register, serving under Coutant who had been elected register on the Tammany ticket.[42] While holding this position Moore
made his debut as a political orator early in 1832, joining a group of
Democratic insurgents in advocating the nomination of Richard M.
Johnson for Vice-President. By October, however, he had returned
to the Tammany fold, demonstrating his party fidelity by speaking at a meeting called to endorse the regular slate of candidates,
including Martin Van Buren, the choice of the party.[43] Throughout
the following year he took a leading part in the agitation against the
New-York & Harlem Railroad and its supporters on the Common
Council, and was a leader of a faction in the Fifteenth Ward which
successfully opposed the reelection of an alderman who was a stock-
holder in the company;* Moore was joined in this campaign by
the *Evening Post* and a number of prominent Democratic politicians.[44]

Although he was a guest speaker at the anniversary celebration
of the Typographical Association in 1832, Moore's association with
the labor movement actually began in 1833. After the issuance of
the circular calling for a convention of trades which resulted in the
establishment of the General Trades' Union, the Typographical
Association named Moore a delegate to this preliminary convention,
and he was subsequently elected first president of the Union. These
circumstances seem to validate later charges that he "was smuggled
into the Trades' Union as one of the Delegates from a trade at
which he had entirely ceased to work many years before," and that
"numerous meetings were held, and several societies had agreed to
organize themselves into a General Society, before Ely Moore made
his appearance among them."[45]

During the ensuing two years his principal activity as a labor
leader, including his service as president of the National Trades'
Union in 1834–35, seems to have consisted of passively presiding
over Union meetings or delivering stirring addresses at labor cele-
brations. As far as can be determined, he neither led nor partici-

* See the detailed account of this episode in Chapter 8, below.

pated in a strike, nor made a speech to a group of strikers. Nor was he instrumental in organizing a single trade society, although he defended with vehemence, both in New York and Washington, the right of journeymen to combine in order to protect themselves against their employers. At the same time he enunciated a spirit of moderation in his speeches to the journeymen, declaring that the Union, instead of encouraging strikes, should try to "allay the jealousies and abate the asperities which now unhappily exist between employers and employed." Furthermore, he cautioned them that "their claims must be founded in justice, and all their measures be so taken as not to invade the rights, or sacrifice the welfare of employers."[46]

In 1834, as the Bank War reached a climax, Moore became more active in political affairs, becoming a member of the Democratic Workingmen's General Committee.[47] At the same time he associated himself with another popular issue, opposition to the contract-labor system in the state prisons, which as the "State Prison Monopoly" had long been an object of attack by "honest mechanics," both masters and journeymen. Meetings of the aggrieved mechanics were held and a memorial was submitted to the legislature calling for abolition of the system. Moore, who had taken no part in the earlier agitation, now went to Albany to lobby for a bill providing for the appointment of three commissioners to investigate prison conditions.* His appointment to the commission after its passage met with opposition from some of his erstwhile supporters who maintained that the bill had been weakened through Moore's connivance with a Democratic machine hesitant to change a system in which it had a vested interest. This issue later formed the basis of strong denunciations of their president by several Trades' Union members, especially after the commissioners' report concluded that the amount of competition from convict labor had been exaggerated. Although his resignation was called for, the storm finally subsided, but the end of his term as president in August 1835 marked the termination of his official relationship with the trades' union movement.[48]

* This issue is discussed further in Chapter 8, below.

Moore in the meantime had received the Tammany nomination for Congress and, after pledging himself to oppose recharter of the Bank of the United States and other "exclusive privileges," obtained the endorsement of Evans and the Workingmen; although trailing the rest of the ticket by almost five hundred votes, he was elected for the first of two terms in the House of Representatives.[49] His Congressional career was undistinguished, marked primarily by several speeches defending labor combinations against the charge that they promote "agrarianism . . . sedition and revolution." As a member of the Committee on Naval Affairs, he attempted to raise seamen's pay and advocated increasing the salary of warrant officers, but neither measure was approved. In 1836 he presented a memorial from the National Trades' Union, calling for a ten-hour day on all public works, but his support of this proposal was far from enthusiastic and it was similarly dismissed by the House. In most respects he was a model Congressional freshman, seldom participating in debates and almost never crossing party lines when the vote was taken.[50] In spite of this record, he was the only Democratic candidate for Congress in 1836 who was also nominated by the Locofocos, and as a result he was reelected while Tammany went down to defeat.[51]

Before the campaign of 1838 Moore had spoken in Congress in favor of President Van Buren's Independent Treasury plan,* which he declared was favored by "ninety-nine out of every hundred workingmen."[52] Since the campaign in New York was fought almost wholly on this issue, he became the special target of the Whig press. The rumor that he would be the Tammany candidate for Governor was broadcast to alarm conservatives, while the prison-labor controversy was disinterred to arouse the mechanics against him. A letter from "Five Thousand Workingmen" demanded: "Away with the trumpet tones . . . of idle demagogues who call themselves workingmen, but never lifted a hammer or made a shoe string." The election was a blow to the Democracy as the Whigs swept New York and Moore's bid for reelection was spurned.[53] He was not forced to leave politics, however, for President Van Buren ap-

---

* See the discussion of this plan in Chapter 9, below.

pointed him Surveyor in the Custom House, and he remained active in New York political life for the next decade, although failing repeatedly in his pursuit of elective office. In 1845 President Polk appointed him United States Marshal in New York, after which he returned to his birthplace where he purchased a weekly newspaper and participated in New Jersey politics. When Pierce became President in 1853, Moore was appointed special agent to the Indian tribes in Kansas, later serving until his death in 1860 as register of the territorial land office.[54]

Moore's career exemplifies, not the success story of a worker's rise to a position of leadership through trade-union activity, but that of an ambitious politician who, by capitalizing upon a brief early history as a journeyman printer, endeavored to advance his own and his party's political fortunes. Despite his prominent role in the labor movement, he consistently viewed political action as the chief road to the salvation of labor, an attitude revealed as clearly by his numerous speeches and writings as by his overt activities. While defending the right, and even the necessity, for workers to combine as a protection against employers, he continually impressed upon his hearers that such organizations were only a temporary expedient, worthless without "the acquisition of knowledge and correct habits of thinking." Without "severe mental discipline," he emphasized, journeymen "may complain in vain—in vain organize—in vain form Unions and associations," but knowledge would enable them to "elevate men whose interests . . . feelings and sympathies are identified with . . . [their] own."[55]

But he neither expected nor demanded that such men should advocate ameliorative legislation in behalf of labor, for he was consistent in his exposition of the twin Democratic doctrines of strict construction and laissez faire. In spite of his demand for the elimination of all special charters and "exclusive privileges," he gave no open support to political parties like the Locofocos which were dedicated to that end, preferring instead to battle for his program within the Democratic organization. Throughout his life he was an avowed exponent of party discipline, summarizing his practical political philosophy in the assertion that "the key to party success," and hence the eventual defeat of the "aristocracy," is to "forego our own private feelings and predilections and to support the candidate of whom a majority of our party friends shall have made the choice."[56]

Moore, therefore, was no more a bona fide Workingman than he was a journeyman, although he formed brief connections with both movements. Furthermore, his career epitomized the interaction of the two realms of political and industrial action found in varying degrees in the lives of other trade-union leaders. ROBERT BEATTY, for example, had been prominently associated with the Bookbinders Association since 1830, and was a delegate of that society to the preliminary convention which organized the General Trades' Union. He remained active in the Union throughout its history, serving as a member of the finance committee. No record has been found of his participation in the Workingmen's Party before 1834 when he became affiliated with Evans' Democratic Workingmen's organization, acting as vice-president of several meetings and serving on the General Committee. Joining the Locofocos in 1836, he was their candidate for assessor in April and vice-president of the famous Park meeting the following year which culminated in the "flour riot."[57]

Another leader of the Trades' Union was JOHN H. BOWIE, a member of the Journeyman Curriers and Leather Dressers Society. Serving as secretary of the preliminary convention and corresponding secretary thereafter, he was also a delegate to the first meeting of the National Trades' Union. He expressed great interest in the prison-labor question, and led the attack on Moore in the Union for his endorsement of the commissioners' report, introducing the resolution demanding his resignation. He first affiliated himself with the Workingmen early in 1834, officiating at some of their meetings and serving as chairman of the General Committee. After participating in Democratic ward politics in 1835, he joined the Locofocos the following year; an active Democrat again in 1840, he formally joined the Tammany Society, and in 1846 was elected a Sachem. In the meantime his business career had also prospered, for the city directory of that year listed "John H. Bowie & Co., hosemakers."[58]

The most notorious of these politically oriented labor leaders was LEVI D. SLAMM, whose connection with the Union began with his election in April 1835 as a delegate of the Journeyman Locksmiths. Although he may have served an apprenticeship at that trade, the *Directory* listed him as a grocer from 1833 to 1837, giving rise to the suspicion that he was in reality no more of a mechanic than Ely Moore. He continued in the Union into 1836, serving for a time as secretary, but shifted his principal attention to politics and the Locofoco Party.[59] Receiving their nomination for the Assembly in both 1836 and 1837, he became known as such a forceful and colorful speaker at party meetings that James Gordon Bennett in the *Herald* began referring to the Locofocos as "Slamm Bang & Co." Byrdsall regarded him as the "executioner" of the party for failing as Recording Secretary to call meetings after the 1837 election, and concluded that "Mr. Slamm is deficient in logical as well as philosophical powers of mind; he has more perception than thought. . . . He is an active political partizan, the man of the present, the surface of which engages his whole attention. . . . Whatever or whoever is the popular rage of the day, has charms for him, and if he can, he will use the same to promote the present success of himself or party." Subsequently becoming active in Tammany politics, Slamm joined the Society in 1842, and edited two lively but scurrilous papers, the *New Era* and the *Plebeian*. Meanwhile, his reputation as a political opportunist, allegedly for sale to the highest bidder, worsened in the 'forties. He flirted for a time with the Calhoun faction which attempted unsuccessfully to "beg borrow or steal enough to render him independent" of Tammany. But Van Buren's partisans retained his allegiance with cash instead of promises, after which a Calhoun supporter described him as "the personification of contemptible meanness and base treachery," and he was henceforth branded with the stigma of political unreliability.[60]

Not all labor leaders were affiliated with the Democrats. Some could be found active with the Whig opposition. This was especially true in 1834. Before the spring election for city officials, the first under a new charter providing for popular election of the Mayor, the Whigs sponsored a number of meetings of anti-Jackson "mechanics" including jewelers, cabinetmakers, printers, and cartmen.

With the approach of the November election their efforts increased, and the General Trades' Union found itself split between the opposing political forces. While Moore, their president, was nominated on the Tammany ticket, other officers took an active part in the Whig Party. David Scott, a tailor who was vice-president, and James Anderson, a printer and corresponding secretary, were both prominent among the Whig mechanics, and ISAAC ODELL, a delegate of the Journeyman Carpenters who had served as chairman of the preliminary convention of the Union, was the Whig candidate for county coroner.[61] Odell and his fellow delegate from the Carpenters, ROBERT TOWNSEND, JR., had long been prominent in anti-Tammany politics. The former had been an early leader of the Workingmen's Party, presiding over several of the 1829 meetings. As the schism developed in the party in 1830, Odell allied himself with the Cook faction, being elected to their Executive Committee and representing them at the state convention. He joined the Whigs early in 1834, moving on to the Locofocos two years later; in 1838 he was back in the Whig Party as an officer of a city-wide pre-election rally.[62]

Townsend's case was even more noteworthy. His origins are obscure,* although it is known that he became a member of the

---

* According to Byrdsall, *History*, pp. 70–71, Townsend's speech to the 1836 Locofoco state convention contained a biographical sketch in which he claimed that he was the illegitimate son of a "gentleman of high respectability" who had at one time served in the State Senate. As a result, he declared, he and his mother had been "exposed to reproach and suffering" while his father "lost not his caste in society"; he added that after a long apprenticeship he had known only "hard toil." Some of the implications of this statement can be questioned on the basis of the research of the late Morton Pennypacker, author of *General Washington's Spies* (Brooklyn, 1939). As reported in the *New York Times,* July 7, 1948, and reaffirmed in a letter to the present author dated March 26, 1953, Townsend was the son of Robert Townsend, the New York merchant and coffee-house owner, who as Samuel Culper, Jr., served as one of Washington's spies during the American Revolution. Pennypacker believed that he was secretly married to Townsend's mother, who was incarcerated on the British prison ship *Jersey* following the execution of Major André. There she died after giving birth to a son who was taken from the ship and brought up by two prominent Brooklyn women, his father secretly contributing to his financial support. As further evidence of this connection, Pennypacker indicated that young Townsend led the crusade for the erection of a monument to those who died on the prison ships, his efforts succeeding in April 1808. A more sensationally written version of this story appeared in *American Weekly* for September 19, 1948.

Tammany Society as early as 1807 and had been listed as a carpenter in the *Directory* since at least 1825. Joining the Workingmen's movement after the 1829 election, he, too, soon became a leader of the Cook faction and was chosen president of the 1830 state convention dominated by this group and its upstate supporters. In 1832 he was vice-president of the Antimasonic state convention, moving on two years later to the Whig Party, the latest solvent of anti-Tammany sentiment.[63]

He had in the meantime assumed an important role in organizing the General Trades' Union, attending the preliminary convention as a delegate from the Journeyman House Carpenters and subsequently being elected treasurer. Both he and Odell, like Ely Moore, could be charged with being "smuggled" into the Union, for neither took part in the carpenters' strike, their affiliation with the Carpenters' Society coming nearly three months after the turnout and only a few weeks previous to the organization of the G.T.U.[64] During the summer of 1834 Townsend was a delegate to the first convention of the National Trades' Union, where his resolution on "the social, civil, and political condition of the laboring classes" caused a spirited debate; fears were expressed that the organization might be shattered on the rock of politics, and over Townsend's protests the word "political" was deleted in favor of "intellectual" before the resolution was passed. At about this time, as the fall political campaign was getting underway, he resigned as a delegate to the Union, bringing his career as a labor leader to an end after slightly more than a year; Odell also resigned shortly after the November election but was reappointed by the Carpenters the following year.[65]

Townsend's relationship with the Locofocos began late in 1836, when he was chosen president of the state convention which founded the Equal Rights Party. He declined their nomination as Lieutenant Governor in favor of Moses Jaques, but in November was nominated for the Assembly by both the Locofocos and the Whigs. He was elected and served one term in the legislature with Clinton Roosevelt, also a bipartisan candidate; the Democratic Governor Marcy later observed that he preferred Roosevelt to Townsend "because I prefer a combination of folly and craziness to downright knavery." In

1837 Townsend presided at the Park meeting which called the second
Locofoco state convention, was again chosen president of that con-
clave, and was again nominated for the Assembly. Although receiving the support of a "purified" Tammany as well as the dissident
Rump Locofocos, he was defeated for reelection in the Whig land-
slide. Two years later he was appointed city sealer, serving until
1843 when he became a city weigher of merchandise.[66]

Other labor leaders were less guilty of political expediency than
Moore and Townsend, but few of them remained aloof from the political controversies of the day. JOHN COMMERFORD, who succeeded
Moore as president of the Union, was politically active most of his
life but seemed to have no personal political ambitions. A chairmaker,
he spent his early life in Brooklyn where in 1830 he was one of the
leaders of a Workingmen's group which supported the nominations
of the *Sentinel* faction for State offices. Moving to New York the
following year, he took no active part in the Workingmen's movement until 1834, when he was a leader in the agitation against prison
labor and was appointed to the Executive Committee. Later that
year after the Journeyman Chairmakers had organized a society,
Commerford was chosen a delegate to the National Trades' Union
convention, at which he was elected corresponding secretary and
introduced a resolution attacking the prison labor system. A few
months later he was elected to represent the Chairmakers in the
General Trades' Union and at the same time headed the short-lived
United Working Men's Association whose objectives, though obscure, were probably concerned with the prison question.[67]

During 1835 he became increasingly active in both labor and
political affairs. Continuing to agitate against the competition of
convict labor, he made a number of speeches at political meetings
and soon joined the antimonopolists under the standard which
Leggett had raised. Associated with the Locofocos virtually from
the beginning, he was a vigorous advocate of separation from the
Democratic organization. Byrdsall characterized him as "a mechanic, of considerable talent as a political speaker, but more as a
writer," adding that "his independence of mind is not agreeable to
expedient politicians, nor those who have influence in the disposal

of office. . . . As an opponent, he is open, and as a friend he has the very rare merit of being a better and kinder friend in adversity than in prosperity." He was a delegate to the 1836 county and state conventions of the party, but presumably dropped out of the movement after the fall elections.[68]

He had in the meantime been chosen orator for the second anniversary celebration of the General Trades' Union, as well as president to succeed Ely Moore, and took a prominent part in the second convention of the National Trades' Union. Under his leadership the New York Union became more energetic in supporting the demands of its member societies and in stimulating the organization of new journeymen's associations. Union dues were increased and a new daily paper, the *Union*, was issued, supported by stock subscriptions from the journeymen's societies. Moreover, Commerford traveled to Poughkeepsie, Newark, and Philadelphia as the representative of the Union, extolling the virtues of combination and urging a united front against the depredations of employers in all Eastern cities.[69]

With the onset of the Panic and the collapse of the labor movement, Commerford's name disappears from the public press until 1841, when he headed a committee on prison labor at a mechanics' convention in Albany. The following year he became involved in the Calhoun movement as president of a Free Trade Association founded by Byrdsall, who as late as 1847 still considered him a supporter of the Carolinian.[70] When Evans returned in 1844 from New Jersey to organize the National Reform Association as a vehicle to agitate for a homestead law, Commerford became one of his principal lieutenants and was nominated for Congress by this group. For him, this was no new panacea, his 1835 address to the Trades' Union having contained the warning that

supply and demand must have its influence on the prices of labor as well as other exchangeable property.; therefore, it ought to be one of our main objects to assist in opening avenues for drawing off any surplus labor. . . . The Public Lands will furnish us with this means. . . . We should look upon this vast domain . . . as an available magazine, for supplying the wants of the

people instead of having it made a commodity, on which the
stock-jobber and speculator can prowl with impunity.

In supporting this program in the 'forties, moreover, Commerford
disagreed with the Nativists, then coming to the fore, by maintaining
that European immigrants should be invited here once the land
became available for settlement.[71]

In 1850 Commerford was a delegate, along with Evans and
Horace Greeley, to the New York City Industrial Congress; by
this time he was no longer a journeyman, having been listed in the
Directory since 1842 as proprietor of a chairmaking shop. In politics
he remained a Democrat until 1859, when he was placed on the
Republican Assembly ticket, and the following year he was one of
their candidates for Congress. His changed allegiance was due
primarily to Republican support of free homesteads, but he viewed
the Homestead Act of 1862 as only a partial victory, continuing to
agitate for land reform. In 1874 when the officers of the Land
Reform Association paid a visit to Evans' New Jersey grave, Commerford was the only one of them whose career spanned the years
since the beginning of the Workingmen's movement, nearly a half-
century before.[72]

Another prominent Workingman, JOHN WINDT, was only briefly
a labor leader and never was affiliated with the General Trades'
Union. Of German and Irish descent, he was born in New York
City in the first decade of the nineteenth century. Becoming a journeyman printer and an agnostic, he printed and edited a number of
Frances Wright's essays and lectures, but was not active in the
Workingmen's Party. He was a member of the Typographical
Society in 1830, but when the journeyman printers turned out for
a wage increase the following year, he was a leader in organizing
the Typographical Association and was one of its officers in 1833
when the General Trades' Union was founded. He played no
further part in the labor movement, although a journeyman as late
as 1834 when he was discharged by Hoe and Company, the typefounders, for political activity; by 1835 he had established his own
printshop.[73]

Meanwhile, during 1834 Windt had become extremely active in the Workingmen's movement, officiating at a number of meetings during the spring electoral campaign and being chosen secretary of the Workingmen's General Committee. When the Democrats espoused the cause of the Workingmen, he transferred his allegiance to that party. But, as Byrdsall said, he was an "ultra anti-monopolist" and became a leader of the early Locofocos, being one of those nominated in 1835 for the Assembly in opposition to the Tammany slate. He was increasingly active during the succeeding two years, publishing the *Democrat* as the party organ, attending party conventions, and receiving their nominations for Third Ward Alderman and Assemblyman. In 1837, after gaining notoriety at the time of the flour riot, he became a leader of the Rumps, receiving with Byrdsall the bitterest denunciations of the majority which wished to rejoin Tammany.[74] Like other Locofocos, he flirted with the Calhoun movement in the 'forties. He then joined Evans in the land reform movement, publishing the new *Working Man's Advocate* and running for Congress on the Reform Association ticket, his printshop serving as the unofficial headquarters of the group. A "good printer" during the remaining years of his life, he died in the 1870's in his sixty-fifth year. According to one of his associates in the land reform movement, Windt "so appreciated the rights of the laboring man, and the hardships of the hire and wages system, that he always punctually and fully paid his journeymen. He was so moderate in charging his customers, that he amassed no more than a bare competence. He was ever ready to print posters and open halls for any meetings upon reformatory measures."[75]

The association existing between organized labor and the Workingmen's movement, exemplified by these biographical accounts, falls into no simple pattern. In their relationship with both movements Moore, Townsend, and Slamm seemingly were actuated primarily by political opportunism, while Commerford and Windt were more sincerely concerned with broader and more legitimate objectives. Each in his own way was typical of the Jacksonian labor movement.[76] An accurate statistical study of the movement as a whole is impossible because of the paucity of data available. But a sample of the membership indicates a definite lack of correspondence between trade unionism and politics, in contrast to the activities of some of their spokesmen. A tabulation of 458 names, compiled from newspapers and other sources, includes the officers of most journeymen's societies and delegates to the Trades' Union; nearly half of these were members of the Journeyman House Carpenter's Society. In comparing these names with a list of 850 participants in the Workingmen's movement from 1829 to 1837, only forty-one, or about 9 percent of the total, were active in both movements. This group as a whole was almost equally divided numerically among the three periods of the political movement, although sixteen of these men, including all eight of the previously discussed labor leaders except Levi Slamm, were active in more than one period.[77]

This does not imply that the laboring man was apolitical, but rather that he was more often practical than visionary in his political allegiance, supporting one of the major parties in preference to the more doctrinaire Workingmen and Locofocos. Moreover, most leaders of the labor movement consciously endeavored to prevent the Union and its affiliated societies from embroilment in partisan politics, citing the fate that had befallen the Workingmen's parties in New York and Philadelphia.[78] The labor press, the *National Trades' Union* in particular, continually reiterated that organized labor had no political objectives or partisan affiliations. This newspaper, pointing out in 1834 that "candidates from the Union will probably be on both tickets at the coming election," denied on behalf of the General Trades' Union that "political movements are contemplated—or, that we are seeking the personal advancement of some of our members." Trades' Unions, it was emphasized,

> are not intended to interfere in *party* politics; nor will they attempt to favor either of the two great political parties now agitating the body politic. . . . We do not suppose there are any among us . . . who desire an entire renunciation of every thing having a political bearing; for it is generally conceded, that many of the subjects upon which we are to act, are political in their

nature; many of the evils under which the workingmen are suffering, are of political origin, and can only be reached in that way. . . .

The measures proposed by the Unions, are such as their members coming from both parties, can unite to carry into effect.[79]

At a time when the bank question was convulsing the electorate and producing deep political animosities, organized labor avoided taking an official stand, for it was realized that such a move would shatter the Union. The principal political issue discussed by laboring men was prison labor, for all journeymen regardless of political affiliation could agree that it should be abolished or modified. Even though the Democrats had established the system, it could be denounced in the chambers of Tammany Hall without fear of excommunication, and the Whigs quickly realized that it was a convenient rallying point to obtain the support of the mechanics. Moreover, the competition of convict labor was an issue upon which most employers could unite with their journeymen, for only a few "speculators" and "unscrupulous" contractors marketed prison-made products in the city. The importance of this issue can be seen in the foregoing biographical sketches of the most prominent labor leaders, as well as in the Prospectus of the *National Trades' Union*, which declared: "The subject of the STATE PRISON MONOPOLY, in particular, will receive . . . the examination which its importance to the whole community, and particularly the mechanic branches demands." But the inconsistency of labor's attitude toward politics was revealed by this issue, as emphasized by an anonymous correspondent of that paper.

I do not see how the Trades' Unions can ever procure the adoption of several of their measures without using political means to do it. I do not mean that they shall attach themselves to any of the political parties now in existence. . . . But that they must elect men to serve them . . . who are in favor of their measures, before they can expect to procure the accomplishment of such measures, is as evident to me, as my existence. How can the State Prison Monopoly be done away with, until men are sent to the Legislature who are convinced of its impolicy and

injustice? . . . If ever these evils are remedied, it must be done
through the instrumentality of politics.[80]

The importance of this issue was exemplified in the career of Ely
Moore. Since his stand on the question in 1834 undoubtedly secured
him the support of a large segment of organized labor, their disillusioned reaction the following year was particularly bitter and
violent.

The labor movement as a whole took no sides in the intramural
warfare which led to the Locofoco schism, although many individual
journeymen doubtless severed their allegiance to Tammany at that
time. It was not until the labor conspiracy cases a year or so later
that an actual alliance was formed between the Locofocos and the
Union, largely at the instigation of the former. Even here, it is
difficult to say how many journeymen actively supported the Equal
Rights Party; if the election returns are any real indication, the
number could not have been large.[81]

The tenuous relationship between the Workingmen's movement
and organized labor can be demonstrated by the attitude of Evans
and Leggett, neither of whom was an uncritical supporter of the
labor movement. Evans maintained that reform of the currency and
the public lands, rather than "combination," would provide a solution of the ills besetting the laboring man. But he admitted that
journeymen's associations were "temporary . . . remedies for the
inadequate compensation of useful labor," while at the same time
asserting:

> We do not believe in the entire efficacy of *strikes* to raise the
> wages of labor to the proper standard. . . . We would much
> rather see matters amicably arranged between employers and
> employed . . . [for] we believe that it is the interest of both
> . . . to *unite* to counteract the causes which tend to depress
> labor, and think those organizations ill judged which exclude
> either employers or employed. . . . We shall exert ourselves
> to bring about . . . *a union of the useful classes, employers and
> employed,* to obtain the full value of their labor.[82]

Leggett defended the right of labor to organize, stating that "our
notions of free trade . . . dispose us to leave men entirely at liberty

to effect a proper object either by concerted or individual action." To him, the "Principle of Combination" was a legitimate means by which "mechanics and labourers may safely rally" to prevent such evils as payment in depreciated currency. Nevertheless, the abolition of monopolies was the keystone of his political philosophy, and he always emphasized to "the labouring classes" that "their only safeguard against oppression is a system of legislation which leaves to all the free exercise of their talents and industry, within the limits of the GENERAL LAW, and which, on no pretence of public good, bestows on any particular class of industry, or any particular body of men, rights or privileges not equally enjoyed by the great aggregate of the body politic." Furthermore, he was extremely violent in his condemnation of the Trades' Union after the flour riot, maintaining that "the chief actors . . . were, beyond question, members of some of the numerous associations of artisans and labourers affiliated under the general name of the Trades' Union."[83]

As the above statements reveal, the interests and objectives of the Workingmen generally transcended the narrow vision of the labor movement. Evans and his fellow Workingmen often expressed great concern on the subject of female and child labor and took steps to alleviate their situation. On the contrary, the Trades' Union, as an instrument of the elite of the wage-earning class, seldom recognized the plight of the unskilled in their struggle to prevent the worsening of their own position. While the *Working Man's Advocate* and the *Man,* for instance, were publicizing the unfortunate economic condition of the seamstresses and the female shoe-binders, the *National Trades' Union* was agitating on behalf of journeyman tailors and shoemakers.[84] The factory system which was coming to dominate New England industry was hardly known in New York, although "slop shops" were increasing in the clothing and shoe trades, degrading the status of the craftsman. The fear of this threat to their status, as much as wage consciousness, doubtless accounts for the exceptional militancy of the skilled tailors and cordwainers; the latter especially felt the effects of New England competition, and in 1836 held a national convention in an effort to standardize wages and working conditions.[85] With a few exceptions,

industry in New York still offered a high degree of occupational
mobility, so that the journeyman, even though wage-conscious in
an inflationary period, did not consider himself a member of a
permanent proletariat, nor did his objective of an entrepreneurial
position seem chimerical. Upon occasion the attainment of this objective was unexpected, as in the case of some striking journeyman
tailors who set up their own shop with apparent success in competition with their former employers.[86]

Journeymen, having gradually been freed, politically and socially,
from the strait jacket of a stratified society, were not yet reconciled
to surrendering this freedom to the demands of an increasingly
industrialized economy, based on the multiplication of credit and
the division of labor. In their resistance to this pressure they followed different avenues. To some, the immediate threat to their
job and standard of living seemed most important, so "combination"
and the strike became the main recourse; others, in the expectation
of both immediate relief and long-term benefit, joined in a political
movement dedicated to the democratization of society. Although
sometimes in agreement on specific issues, the two movements were
far from identical in either personnel or objectives. Moreover, if
the Trades' Union was not basically class-conscious in its orientation, there is even less evidence for interpreting the Workingmen
in those terms. In seeking and unquestionably receiving support
from unskilled laborers and employers as well as journeymen,
neither the Workingmen's Party nor the Locofocos can be explained
as the political expression of the organized labor movement. The
New York Workingmen represented a cross-section of society,
including yet transcending the demands and aspirations of the
journeyman mechanic.

The Workingmen:
A Biographical Catalogue

THE FOREGOING historical narrative of the Workingmen's movement provides little enlightenment on the fundamental question of its socioeconomic position. Neither the relative place of this group in the class hierarchy of the period nor the more dynamic factor of ascent or descent within the stratification of society has been demonstrated by this account. Were the Locofocos—and the Workingmen's parties which preceded them—a "nascent proletarian party"?[1] Was this movement in any sense anticapitalist, a "conscious class alignment between capital and labor"?[2] Were the Workingmen, in short, representatives of a self-conscious working class, organized politically for radical economic and social ends? Even an analysis of the contemporary labor movement, as in the preceding chapter, is not particularly helpful in answering these questions, both because of the nature of that movement and because of its tenuous relationship with the Workingmen's parties. Only an investigation of the Workingmen themselves, not only their program and political pronouncements but their life histories, can shed further light upon the nature and objectives of the movement.

The ideal approach to this problem is the career-line study.[3] By this method, statistically sound generalizations could be made comparing the Workingmen with another group, such as Tammany supporters. The panels so established would be analyzed on the basis of significant information including the occupation or socioeconomic status of the previous generation, recency of the family in the United States and in New York City, rural or urban background, education, religious denomination (or lack of it), and detailed occupational history. Although this type of study would provide an answer to our basic problem, unfortunately the information required for such a statistical analysis is not available for the majority of the Workingmen, nor for most of the Tammany braves. Nevertheless, some conclusions can be reached from a biographical study of those Workingmen who attained sufficient prominence to be listed in biographical encyclopedias. Furthermore, these facts can be supplemented by data on others in contemporary sources, from which biographical deductions can be made. While the biographical profiles of these men cannot, because of their prominence in the movement, be considered necessarily typical of the Workingmen as a whole, any pattern that can be found should at least be regarded as indicative.

Of the early leaders of the movement, THOMAS SKIDMORE's life was probably the shortest, for he died in 1832 of "cholera morbus" at the age of forty-two, less than three years after attaining political notoriety in the Workingmen's Party.[4] According to a brief memoir written by a contemporary, he was born in 1790 in the village of Newtown, Fairfield County, Connecticut, the oldest of ten children; his father's background is unknown. Young Skidmore was such an avid scholar that at the age of thirteen he was appointed teacher in the district school, leaving five years later because his father was appropriating all his earnings. He then spent a year teaching in an academy in nearby Weston, living with an uncle whom he offended by writing political articles. During the next five or six years he taught in academies and other schools in Princeton and Bordentown, New Jersey, Richmond, Virginia, and Edenton and New Bern, North Carolina; no reason is given for his brief tenure in each of these localities.[5]

In 1815 Skidmore moved to Wilmington, Delaware, and changed his career to chemical and mechanical research, attempting to develop improvements in the manufacture of gunpowder, wire drawing, and paper making. He was successful in the latter, but another received the credit. After brief residences in Philadelphia and New Brunswick, New Jersey, where he was married in 1821, he came to New York, where he apparently led a precarious existence as a machinist.[6] He worked on various projects, including a new reflecting telescope about which he wrote in 1822 to Governor DeWitt

Clinton in the fruitless hope of obtaining financial support.[7] He became an active supporter of John Quincy Adams and the National Republicans in the 1828 political campaign, attending the city nominating convention and serving on the correspondence committee of the Friends of the American System.[8]

As a member and the guiding spirit of the Committee of Fifty in 1829, he helped to formulate the original creed of the Workingmen's Party, expanded in his book *The Rights of Man to Property!* which appeared late that same year. Nominated for the Assembly, he received only twenty-three fewer votes than the successful Ebenezer Ford. After being forced out of the party following the election, a move dictated apparently as much by his personality as by the opposition to his "agrarian scheme," he delivered a series of lectures and edited a short-lived newspaper, *The Friend of Equal Rights*.[9] Although he seems to have disappeared from the political scene after the 1830 election, he carried on a controversy with Robert Dale Owen on education and birth control, publishing in reply to some of Owen's theories *Moral Physiology Exposed and Refuted*; this work combined an acceptance of Ricardo's "iron law of wages" with a denial of the validity of Malthus' reliance on "moral restraint."[10] At his death Skidmore had returned to mechanical pursuits, attempting to cast metallic shells for terrestrial globes by "producing transverse rotary motions in a hollow sphere."[11]

The obituary notice in the *Working Man's Advocate,* which had generally opposed his program for the party, deplored the "wildness of his schemes," but praised "his open candor, his independence of spirit . . . and talented mind." The writer of his memoir emphasized the "confusion in his ideas," which were maintained "in a most uncompromising disposition, in an independent and uncourteous manner," permitting not the slightest deviation. Suspecting the motives of all who opposed him, regardless of the basis of their disagreement, he died with the firm belief that "some, who publicly espouse the cause of the producers of wealth, were its secret enemies . . . and . . . felt chagrin on the failure to form a permanent, increasing party around him."[12]

Considerably less is known about NOAH COOK, the principal

instrument of Skidmore's political destruction. Listed as a commission merchant in the *Directory,* his activities are known to have included serving as the local agent of an Erie Canal boat line and selling such varied items as cordwood, country real estate with mill and water privileges, and patent rights for a cast-iron grist mill bushing and a filtering machine for purifying cider.[13] Like Skidmore, he had been an active Adams supporter in 1828, having been a delegate to the National Republican state convention.[14] Early in 1830, after joining the Workingmen, he became an associate editor of the New York *Evening Journal* and later edited a paper of his own, the *New York Reformer.*[15] By the time of the 1834 spring election, he had attained a prominent position with the new Whig Party, serving as secretary of the victory celebration.[16] Cook's connection with the Workingmen's movement was brief, opportunistic, and divisive in its effect, but he was representative of an important faction and hence cannot be lightly dismissed.

Another leader whose relationship with the movement was brief, but even more influential, was ROBERT DALE OWEN, the eldest son of the British reformer, Robert Owen. Born in Glasgow, Scotland, and educated both by private tutors and in the New Lanark school associated with his father's cotton mills, Owen spent four years at the famous Fellenberg school in Hofwyl, Switzerland, probably the most significant influence in his life. Returning to New Lanark, he then took charge of the school for a time and managed the factory in his father's absence. In 1825 at the age of twenty-four he accompanied the elder Owen to his cooperative colony at New Harmony, Indiana, where he taught school and edited the *New Harmony Gazette.* When the colony failed two years later, he joined Frances Wright in her Nashoba, Tennessee, colony, later accompanying her to Europe and back to New Harmony to assist in the work of the "Free Enquirers."[17]

Early in 1829 Miss Wright came to New York to deliver a series of lectures, and Owen decided to follow and publish the *Free Enquirer,* successor to the *Gazette,* in that city. Shortly after his arrival in June, the Free Enquirers opened the Hall of Science in Broome Street, in the same building in which the paper was published. Owen immediately began a series of articles on the Hofwyl school, agitating for "a National System of Education."[18] When the Workingmen met in October to hear the report of the Committee of Fifty, Owen with some of his friends "attended that meeting as a stranger, ignorant what were the objects of those who called it, what the measures to be proposed, or who the individuals who were to propose these measures." As he later explained, "I acted as secretary, when requested to do so, simply because I am willing at all times to aid those whom I believe deprived of any just rights; and was requested to do so, probably, because I was believed to be friendly to the people's interests; and totally without reference to my speculative opinions."[19]

Owen took no active part in the movement after the 1829 election, other than giving it his editorial support. By 1831 the Hall of Science, the fortress of "infidelity," had been sold to a Methodist congregation, Owen spending much of his time traveling. In April 1832 he married the daughter of Samuel Robinson, a shoe manufacturer formerly active in the Workingmen's Party.[20] After traveling in Europe for a year, the Owens settled in New Harmony, where he embarked on a successful political career. He was elected to the Indiana legislature, served two terms in Congress as a Democrat, and was minister to Naples under Presidents Pierce and Buchanan. He continued to work for improvements in the educational system and was a leading advocate of emancipation during the early years of the Civil War, maintaining until his death in 1877 an active interest in both philanthropy and reform.[21]

In the same rationalist tradition as Owen was GEORGE HENRY EVANS, another immigrant from the British Isles, and probably the most influential leader and spokesman of the Workingmen during the first five or six years of the movement. He was born in 1805 in the village of Bromyard, Herefordshire, into a middle-class family. His father had held a commission in the British Army during the Napoleonic Wars, serving in 1801 in Egypt, but his peacetime occupation has not been identified. Evans' mother was of a slightly higher class, the landed gentry, for her family owned a manor house with eight or ten servants and many dogs and horses, farming and sheep-raising being their principal source of income. She died in 1812 and Frederick, the younger son, was sent to live with her family, George remaining with his father and receiving a "scholastic" education. In 1820 when the elder Evans decided to emigrate to the United States to join his two brothers in Binghamton, New York, his sons accompanied him. After a short stay in Binghamton they moved on to Ithaca, New York, where George became a printer and apparently edited a newspaper while Frederick was apprenticed to a hatter.[22]

Evans probably came to New York in 1828 or 1829, for he was not listed in Longworth's *Directory* prior to that, and it is known that he printed the New York edition of the *Free Enquirer* from March to July 1829. During this period he also published a series of tracts entitled "Messengers of Truth," designed to "disseminate useful knowledge and promote free enquiry," and was an active member of the Society of Free Enquirers.[23] By late September he had taken a leading part in Owen's Association for the Protection of Industry and Promotion of Education, and on October 31 the first issue of the *Working Man's Advocate* appeared with Evans listed as printer and publisher. As a leader of the Workingmen's movement, Evans, in contrast to Skidmore, "possessed great evenness of temper, . . . was mild and courteous in his intercourse with others; . . . he was patient in argument, and never allowed himself to arise to a passion."[24]

For all but five of the next twenty years Evans published a New York newspaper devoted to social reform, deriving some of his income during most of this period from a job-printing business. In June 1830 the weekly *Working Man's Advocate* merged with the *Daily Sentinel,* Evans serving as one of the seven publishers of the combined papers until October 1831, when he took sole charge of both papers. The daily paper was discontinued in June 1833 "because of insufficient patronage," but in less than nine months he issued a new daily, the *Man,* which became the organ of the early antimonopolists. This journal was discontinued in August 1835, when Evans moved to Rahway, New Jersey, because of disgust with the turmoil and expense of urban living, and in the expectation of obtaining additional subscribers to the weekly paper. A combination of bad health and economic difficulties, due partly to his inability to collect from his New York debtors, led him after six months to abandon journalism for agriculture, and he subsisted on a small farm near Granville, New Jersey, for the following five years. In January 1841 the first issue of a new monthly paper, the *Radical, in Continuation of the Working Man's Advocate,* appeared, to be continued sporadically over the next two years; although published in Granville, it was distributed in New York by several of his former colleagues.[25]

Evans' disillusionment with the Workingmen's movement was revealed in a history of the party appearing serially in this journal. This feeling, combined with his experience as a New Jersey farmer, led him to adopt a new program, "Abolition of the Land Monopoly," and to proclaim editorially: "let us . . . emancipate the white laborer, *by restoring his natural right to the soil.*" In February 1844 he left his farm and returned to the city. Meeting with a handful of friends at the printshop of John Windt, a former Free Enquirer and Workingman, Evans proposed a plan for the agitation of land reform. Within a month he once again began the publication of a paper, known successively as *People's Rights, Working Man's Advocate* and *Young America.* He also organized the National Reform Association by collecting a dedicated group of supporters, some of them former Workingmen and Locofocos, and others veterans of the Hudson Valley anti-rent wars.[26]

For Evans now, the land monopoly was the greatest evil besetting the workingman, the only solution being to open the land to actual settlers and to limit the holdings of any one person. "Vote yourself a farm" became the cry of these latter-day Workingmen. Opposing Nativism, they urged that all Europeans who so desired should be invited to settle on the land, and advocated the annexation of Texas if it was reserved for settlers instead of speculators. In the fall a slate of candidates was nominated for Congress and the Assembly, pledged to "prevent all further traffic in the Public Lands" and "cause them to be laid out in Farms and Lots for the free and exclusive use of actual settlers." Tammany's defeat in the election

brought elation to the Reformers, Evans concluding that "we hold
the balance of power." He continued for five more years to agitate
hopefully for the adoption of his program, but finally admitted defeat
and retired, "worn out in health and means," to his New Jersey
farm. In 1856, just six years before the passage of the Homestead
Act, he died there, mourned by only a faithful few of those who
had first rallied to his cause a quarter-century before.[27]

Even more influential with the early Locofocos than Evans was
WILLIAM LEGGETT, associate editor with William Cullen Bryant
of the New York *Evening Post*. Although his background and
career were quite different from Evans', he came to many of the
same conclusions in regard to monopolies. Born in New York City
in 1801, four years before Evans, he was the son of Abraham
Leggett, a former major in the Revolutionary army. He was educated at Georgetown College, but did not graduate because of the
failure of his father's business in 1819. The family then moved to
Illinois, where young Leggett experienced the rigors of frontier
life. Three years later he received an appointment as a midshipman
in the United States Navy, but the combination of harsh discipline
and his hot temper caused trouble; in 1825 he was punished by a
court-martial for dueling and resigned his commission the following
year. In addition to a life-long hatred of authority, his naval experience resulted in a permanent impairment of his health from a
siege of yellow fever in the West Indies.[28]

Leggett then embarked upon a literary career. After publishing
some poems and short stories, he settled in New York in 1828 and
established a literary journal called *The Critic;* while a *succès
d'estime,* it was a financial failure, lasting only eight months. At
about this time William Coleman, senior editor of the *Evening Post*
since Alexander Hamilton's day, died, and Leggett became part
owner and Bryant's assistant on the editorial staff. Although insisting at first that politics was beyond his understanding and interest, he was within a year writing with vehemence and knowledge
on a number of political questions. In June 1834 Bryant sailed
for a lengthy tour of Europe, leaving his young assistant in charge
of the paper. The editorials in the *Post,* which for nearly a year

had been highly critical of conservative Democrats, now became more violent in preaching the doctrine of free trade and anti-monopoly. Leggett's course not only heartened the left-wing Democrats and led to the Locofoco schism, but alienated local advertisers and eventually cut off government patronage. During the winter of 1835–36 he became seriously ill, and Bryant was forced to return home to rescue the floundering paper.[29]

Leggett was too ill to work for almost a year, at a time when the new Equal Rights Party could most use his counsel. After returning briefly to the *Post,* he began in December 1836 the publication of the *Plaindealer,* edited in the same uncompromising fashion. He had been denounced as an "agrarian" for his banking views, but his conversion to the heretical doctrine of abolitionism, and his criticism of the Democrats for evading this issue, led to his virtual ostracism. The paper was discontinued in September 1837, nominally because of the failure of the publisher but in reality because of the unpopularity of the editor's views. The following year some of his friends attempted to nominate him for Congress, but he characteristically eliminated himself from consideration by stating that "abolition is, in my sense, a necessary and glorious part of democracy." After retiring to New Rochelle in bad health, he accepted an appointment from President Van Buren as chargé d'affaires in Guatemala, but died in May 1839 while preparing to leave. A monument erected by the Young Men's Committee of Tammy Hall marks the grave of this venerated yet misunderstood spokesman of Locofoco Democracy.[30]

These were the principal intellectual leaders of the Workingmen's movement. But others, considerably less influential in formulating and expressing the party program, were equally responsible for developing and nourishing the party organization. DANIEL GORHAM, an elderly merchant tailor, was most often listed as a party leader throughout the entire eight-year course of the movement; this "good-natured" grandfather, according to Byrdsall, "never sees the dark side of men or things, for he thinks no harm of others, and naturally concludes that others think no harm of him."[31] JOEL CURTIS was another perennial chairman, seemingly chosen by the Workingmen as their leader whenever a struggle over the chair was imminent—whether the opposition was the Cook faction as in 1830, or the Tammany regulars five years later. By occupation he was a tinsmith and sawfiler, proprietor of a hardware store, and successful manufacturer of cooking stoves.[32]

FITZWILLIAM BYRDSALL, the secretary and chronicler of the Locofoco Party, is a mysterious personality whose life remains obscure. The *Directory,* from 1825 to 1845, fails to list his name,[33] and no political affiliation with any party has been discovered prior to 1835. His association with the Locofocos from 1835 to 1837, known largely from the testimony of his own book, was one of unremitting hostility to the regular Democratic organization. He took the lead in favoring a separate party, continually distrusted Van Buren, and as a leader of the Rump faction refused to reunite with Tammany.[34] This attitude persisted, for Byrdsall next appears as an active participant in the early 1840's in the movement to nominate John Calhoun for President, originating in the main out of opposition to Van Buren. Helping to organize Free Trade Associations as a device to capture the Democratic Party, Byrdsall remained an ardent admirer of the South Carolina Senator for many years, corresponding regularly to pledge his support.[35] Between 1847 and 1853, and possibly later, he held a position in the New York Custom House, and in 1860 finally became an official member of the Tammany Society.[36]

The ALEXANDER MINGS, senior and junior, appear to have been more typical of the Workingmen. The elder Ming, since the early years of the century a printer and publisher of periodicals such as *Ming's New York Price Current* and the *Weekly Visitor, or Ladies' Miscellany,* had been one of Skidmore's earliest and most faithful supporters. A candidate for the Assembly in 1829, he remained with the "agrarian" minority, leading their electoral ticket in 1830 with 147 votes. By 1834, like most of the Workingmen, he had become an active Democrat, and in the following year was appointed inspector at the Custom House, where he remained for more than a decade.[37]

In contrast to his father, Alexander Ming, Jr., was a loyal Tammany supporter from 1828 to 1835. Originally a printer, he left this trade to operate a drygoods business and then a bookstore, before being appointed to a position in the Custom House in 1831. In 1835, although (as Byrdsall emphasized) "an office-holder with a large family," he became an active antimonopolist and took a leading part in the October 29 meeting, the Rubicon of the Locofoco Party. Although opposing complete separation from Tammany, Ming remained with the insurgents, receiving their nomination for Mayor in April 1836, for County Register in November, and for County Clerk in 1837. His greatest notoriety arose from his speech at the Park meeting which preceded the flour riot of February 1837, resulting in his dismissal from the Custom House; Ming, however, made a successful appeal to Washington, disclaiming any responsibility for the mob action, and was reinstated. Later that year he made his peace with Tammany, being one of the first Locofocos to accept the proffered alliance with the "purified" Wigwam, and by 1839 was on friendly terms with President Van Buren. Displaced at the Custom House by the 1841 political turnover, Ming operated a confectionery store in the Bowery for a time. He was active politically during this Whig interregnum, notably in 1842 during the Democratic agitation in support of "Governor" Dorr of Rhode Island; as a colonel in the militia, he offered the services of his military company to assist the Dorrites in maintaining themselves against the "legal" government of the state. Ming returned to his old job in the Custom House in 1845, when the Democrats returned to power in Washington, and in 1855 gave the Fourth of July oration at Tammany Hall.[38]

ROBERT HOGBIN was active in the Workingmen's movement from almost the beginning to the bitter end. Originally a grocer, he then worked as a turner and a tinsmith, manufacturing and selling anthracite stoves and other tin and sheet-iron ware. His political activity began in 1830, and a few months later he was elected to the Workingmen's Executive Committee. In 1833 he left New York for Tarrytown in Westchester County, where he remained two years and acted as local agent for Evans' paper. Returning in time to participate in the antimonopoly struggle of 1835, Hogbin remained loyal to the Locofocos through the succeeding two years and according to Byrdsall was the last of the Rumps to recognize the reunion with Tammany.[39]

FREDERICK S. COZZENS, variously a grocer, a chemist, and naturalist, was also active in the movement from 1830 to 1837. His father, Issacher, Sr., was a grocer who had been Tammany Wiskinkie or doorkeeper from 1810 to 1826, while his brother Issacher, Jr., a chemist and mineralogist, had served two terms as a Sachem in 1817–18 and 1825–26; Frederick became affiliated with the Society in 1807. His activity as a Workingman dated from June 1830, when he became a leader of the *Sentinel* faction, being subsequently appointed to the Executive Committee and proposed for a Congressional nomination. Serving again in 1834 on the Workingmen's General Committee, he continued active with the Locofocos, receiving their nomination in 1836 and 1837 for Fifth Ward Alderman.[40]

An important early leader and Evans supporter was SIMON CLANNON, a painter who was one of the 1829 Assembly candidates of the Workingmen's Party. Active after the election in organizing a Mechanics' and Workingmen's Political Debating Society, as well as being secretary of the House Painters' Society, he then was elected secretary of the Workingmen's Executive Committee in spite of opposition by Cook supporters. He continued to take an active part in the struggle within the Committee which led to the party split, his efforts in behalf of the *Sentinel* faction being recognized by his nomination (which he declined) for the Assembly in 1830. By 1832 he had apparently abandoned his original occupation, for the *Sentinel* carried his advertisement for "Liquors, Wines and Cordials." He embarrassed his "old friend" Evans during the campaign of 1834 by serving as secretary of a Whig meeting, although the editor assured his readers that Clannon "will vote the Democratic ticket" if the Tammany candidates were pledged to oppose "the *small fry* Banks as well as the *mammoth*."[41]

Another original member of the Workingmen's Executive Committee who supported the *Sentinel* faction but took refuge with the Whigs in 1834 was RALPH WELLS, the "Working Man" broker.

He joined the party shortly after the 1829 election, serving as secretary of the conference committee which preceded the expulsion of the "agrarians." First, Skidmore's adherents denounced him as a "rich man," and a few months later, after he had definitely aligned himself with the Evans faction, Cook's supporters denounced him for being "smuggled into the Executive Committee." Wells replied: "I shall be perfectly satisfied, to be considered a humble fellow labourer with those who have ascertained that true democracy consists in raising the oppressed to an equality with their oppressors." Later, as Evans said, Wells "seceded" from the Workingmen to join Tammany, supporting Van Buren over Johnson for the Vice-Presidency in 1832. By 1834, when the Bank War was at its height, Wells had become the principal orator for the newly christened Whig Party.[42]

Some Workingmen made good in the Democratic Party. NATHAN DARLING, elected to the Executive Committee early in 1830, remained loyal to Evans and the *Sentinel* faction in the struggle over the education issue. At this time he was a painter, but by 1834 he was not only an active Democrat but had been appointed inspector in the Custom House. Despite this preferment Darling did not completely surrender his independence during the stormy months of 1835, for he strongly supported Johnson over Van Buren for the Presidential nomination and, as a member of the Tammany Young Men's Committee, joined seven others in opposing the move to censure Leggett and the *Evening Post*. It must be noted, however, that he did not join the Locofoco bolters, yielding to the doctrine of party regularity.[43]

GEORGE W. MCPHERSON was another early antimonopolist who refused to maintain his principles to the point of party irregularity. A shoemaker, he apparently remained outside the Workingmen's movement until 1832, when by its support of Jackson it had virtually lost its identity. Two years later he became a member of the reconstituted Workingmen's General Committee, but was sufficiently orthodox to be elected to the Tammany Young Men's Committee in 1835. Like Darling, he supported the nomination of Johnson and defended Leggett's course in the *Evening Post*, his house serving as headquarters for informal caucuses of the "Friends of Equal Rights" during the fall of 1835. His party loyalty during the election was rewarded with an appointment as city weigher and then as Custom House inspector under Van Buren; he later worked as a grocer and then as an auctioneer after being supplanted in 1841 by a Whig appointee.[44]

Some appear to have entered the movement in part because of their antireligious views and their relationship with Owen and Evans. JOHN ALWAISE, for example, was secretary of Owen's Association, but took no active role in the party until late in 1829, being elected to the Executive Committee six months later. He reappeared as a leader when the Workingmen's movement revived in 1834, and was prominent in the Locofoco split the following year. His occupational history progressed from grocer in the mid-'twenties to cabinetmaker and then varnisher; finally, in 1839 his acceptance by Tammany was signified by his appointment as inspector and measurer at the United States Custom House.[45]

JOHN MORRISON was even more militant in the "infidelity" movement. After participating in 1829 in Universalist meetings, he joined the Free Enquirers and their successor, the Society of Moral Philanthropists, annually organizing a dinner in January to celebrate Tom Paine's birthday. Listed as a merchant in the *Directory,* he was the proprietor of a thread and needle store, declaring on one occasion that "although not at present an active Mechanic, I am a pretty hard *Working Man.*" A Fourth Ward leader of the Workingmen's Party from early 1830 through 1832, he continued to be close to Evans after this period, serving in 1841 as New York agent of the *Radical.*[46]

Another associate of Evans was JAMES A. PYNE, an English-born painter who in 1832 became proprietor of a store selling prints, picture frames, and "liberal books." After joining the Workingmen's Party in 1830, he remained active during the quiescent period which followed and took part in the Locofoco revolt. Upon Evans' removal to New Jersey, Pyne served as New York agent for the *Working Man's Advocate,* continuing in this capacity in 1841 with the *Radical.* In 1844, when Evans returned to the city to agitate for land reform, Pyne, now a baker, became one of his principal supporters.[47]

Other English immigrants were influential leaders of the movement. EDWARD J. WEBB, born in England about 1772, began working as a house carpenter at the age of eighteen. He had lived in New York since at least 1825, operating a building business. Early in 1830 he turned the business over to his son in order to devote his full attention to "Architecture, Mensuration, and the Valuation of Buildings," advertising "Plans, Elevations, and Working Drawings furnished at reasonable prices." Two years later he delivered a series of free lectures on architecture at the Mechanics' Institute, including "the science of bridge Architecture, and the best known methods of roofing."[48] He was remarkably articulate on other subjects, lecturing on the history of "Priestcraft" in connection with the Sunday mail question and speaking frequently at political meetings, and was an inveterate writer of letters to the editor.[49]

After receiving the Workingmen's nomination for the Senate in 1829, Webb was named chairman of the conference committee which took the first steps to reorganize the party. He remained active in the *Sentinel* faction during the succeeding year, although constantly urging harmony with the other Workingmen and decrying "party spirit," and appeared at party meetings during the years that followed. In 1834 he quickly became identified with the revived Workingmen, acting as one of their leaders at the famous Park meeting which ruffled the dignity of Philip Hone. He spoke frequently in support of the Antimonopoly Democrats and joined the Locofoco movement, in 1836 receiving their Assembly nomination and in 1837 their support for Fifteenth Ward Alderman.[50]

GILBERT VALE, another English immigrant, was described by Evans as "always . . . favorable to the measures of the Working Men," although with a "kind of vague apprehension that they would *ruin* themselves by some false step, or be ruined by 'their friends.'" It was not until 1834, however, that he became associated with them, his most important activity occurring two years later when he was a delegate to the Locofoco county convention. He was born in London, England, in 1788, and educated there for the ministry. Abandoning this vocation, he came to the United States in 1829, becoming a teacher of navigation, mathematics, and astronomy in New York. Now a "free thinker" and admirer of Tom Paine, whose biography he wrote in 1841, Vale in the words of Lewis Masquerier "attacked the errors of religions and governments as well as those of the physical sciences." During the 1830's he lectured, first at Owen's Hall of Science and then at Tammany Hall, on drawing, English grammar, logarithms, and a "Religious and Philosophical discussion of the Millenium"; his talks on astronomy, illustrated by a "planetarium" or "Transparent Orrery" which he had invented and patented, were especially popular. Late in 1831 he began the publication of the *Sunday Reporter,* a "moral, political, and scientific" journal which he continued for several years as the *Citizen of the World* and then the *Beacon;* he also edited a monthly periodical, the *Mechanics' Assistant in the Sciences and Arts.* In addition to his *Life of Paine,* Vale wrote a number of other books and pamphlets including *Fanaticism, its Source and Influence* and *Political Economy.* According to his friend and admirer Masquerier, "he had the irritable temperament so often attendant upon genius"—or as Evans tersely put it, "he is very apt . . . to go off at *half* cock." His daughter, Euphemia Vale Blake, became a well-known author, and his son, a printer. Vale died in his son's home in 1866.[51]

BARNABAS BATES was another English-born editor who was influential in the Workingmen's movement. Born in Edmonton, England, in 1785, he came to the United States as a child, his family settling in Rhode Island. Like Vale, he was educated for the ministry, apparently receiving a degree of Master of Arts, and in 1814 was chosen pastor of the Bristol, Rhode Island, Baptist Church. His increasing tendency toward Unitarianism caused a schism in the church, and he was deposed as pastor but, retaining control of the edifice, continued to preach. Appointed Collector of the port of Bristol during this period, he served his congregation without pay, even advancing some of his own funds to meet church expenses. Because of his outspoken support of the Freemasons and opposition to slavery and the slave trade, his renomination as Collector was rejected by the Senate and his property damaged by a combined antimasonic and proslavery mob. Late in 1824 he left for New York, where he opened a bookstore, gave occasional sermons, and began the publication of a weekly journal, the *Christian Inquirer,* devoted to "Free Inquiry, Religious Liberty, and Rational Christianity." Early in 1828 this paper was combined with the *Olive Branch,* a Universalist journal conducted by Abner Kneeland, and Bates became associated with the short-lived Pestalozzi Institute of Practical and Classical Education. Two years later he issued a prospectus for the *Every Day Mail,* dedicated to the "interests of Men of Business, viz. the Merchants, Mechanics, and Working Men," but denunciations in an opposition paper attached the odium of "infidelity" to this enterprise, and it failed through lack of financial support; Bates sued for libel, but collected only nominal damages.[52]

Although supporting their objectives, he was not formally associated with the Workingmen's Party until 1831 and 1832, playing an important part in switching its allegiance from Johnson to Van Buren for the Vice-Presidential nomination. Becoming increasingly active, he later became a leader of the antimonopoly movement, until the Locofocos determined to break with Tammany and form a separate political organization, a move he strongly opposed.[53] Byrdsall deplored his desertion of the movement, asserting:

> Had Barnabas Bates been present [when the resolution in favor of separation was passed], he might have prevented such a decision by some more proper and advisable course. . . . His absence was very properly felt, for no man labored more in the anti-monopoly movement that he did. . . . Doubtless he had proper reasons for his course now, as it is fair to believe that he is a man who always acts from a delicate, as well as profound sense of propriety.[54]

During this period he was Assistant Postmaster of New York, having been appointed to that position despite conservative protests in 1833, and serving there until 1837. Virtually deserting the political forum after his experience with the Locofocos, he became an earnest advocate of postal reform, traveling widely to study the postal service. From 1837 until his death in 1853 Bates devoted himself to the cause of cheap postage, writing and speaking extensively on the subject; his principal income during some of these years was derived from a position in the New York Custom House. His efforts to abolish the franking privilege and establish through postage stamps a flat rate of two cents per ounce led to the formation of Cheap Postage Associations in several cities. These activities eventually resulted in Congressional legislation which took the first steps toward the realization of Bates' democratic objective.[55]

DR. CORNELIUS C. BLATCHLEY, an 1829 Assembly candidate of the Workingmen who maintained his affiliation with them during the ensuing two years, was theologically even more conservative than Bates. Born in the village of Mendham, New Jersey, in 1773, he came from a large family of physicians, including his father and four brothers. His father, Dr. Ebenezer Blachly (as the name was usually spelled), was a descendant of an old New England family and one of the founders of the New Jersey Medical Society, while his mother was the daughter of Henry Wick, a prosperous Morris County, New Jersey, farmer. Cornelius studied and practiced medicine in New York City, sharing his office and home with two nephews, one a druggist and the other a physician. He had been active in the antimasonic movement and was apparently nominated by the Workingmen without his previous knowledge, but continued to work for a union of the two minor parties. Although labeled "a notorious follower of Fanny Wright" and an "infidel" by the opposition press, Blatchley held religious opinions considerably more orthodox than many of his compatriots. He constantly affirmed his belief in revealed Christianity, but he denounced "priest or churchcraft" and the "Christian party in politics" on the Sunday mail question, declaring: "We would not meddle with religion politically; but let that be between God and every man's own conscience."[56]

Some Workingmen gained fame or wealth in mercantile and mechanical pursuits. SAMUEL JUDD, a member of the Executive Committee early in 1830 and later a Democrat, was a well-to-do oil merchant with several stores in the city. Originally a pedlar selling from door to door, he eventually became a wealthy and accepted member of the commercial aristocracy, his daughters marrying prosperous merchants. JONATHAN GEDNEY, listed as a Workingman in December 1829, was a millwright and machinist, born in 1798 in Rye, New York. He moved to the city and in 1825 owned and operated a sawmill which was destroyed by fire four years later, ruining him and his partner. Gedney then turned to mechanical invention, his most successful devices being the wooden cogs in the cotton gin and a plow for digging potatoes. He later returned to Westchester County, where he died in 1886.[57]

GEORGE BRUCE and his nephew DAVID, associated together in the type-founding business, were affiliated only indirectly with the movement. David was nominated for the Assembly in 1830 by the *Sentinel* faction, while his uncle was the State Senatorial candidate of the Skidmore faction; in the following year George also received the Workingmen's nomination for the Assembly. George Bruce was born in 1781 in Edinburgh, Scotland, the son of a tanner, and was educated in the public schools. In 1795 he emigrated to the United States to join his elder brother David, who had settled in Philadelphia. George was apprenticed first to a bookbinder and then to a printer, where his brother was also employed. Fire and a yellow fever epidemic led the brothers to leave the city three years later, moving first to Albany and then to New York. He worked on newspapers until 1806, when the brothers began a book-printing business. Six years later David visited England, returning with the secret of stereotyping; they added several improvements and began casting their own type. In 1816 they sold the printing business to devote full time to their type foundry, which they operated in partnership for six years until David's health failed. George conducted the business alone and then with his nephew, David, Jr., inventing a successful type-casting machine. Living and working in New York until his death in 1866, George Bruce was for years president of the Mechanics' Institute and the New York Typefounders Association, and an officer in the General Society of Mechanics and Tradesmen.[58]

Another prominent type founder in the movement was JAMES CONNER, who presided at several 1834 meetings of the Democratic Workingmen. Born in Hyde Park, New York, in 1798, he learned the printing trade and worked as a stereotyper in Boston and New York. By 1830 he had established a type and stereotype foundry in the latter city, devising new styles and sizes of type, agate being the most famous. Although he participated in the memorable Johnson dinner in 1835, a landmark in the evolution of the Locofoco Party, he remained loyal to Tammany, which he had joined in 1829. In 1844 Conner was elected County Clerk, in which office he served for the next nine years, and was chosen Grand Sachem of the Tammany Society, a position he held at his death in 1861.[59]

JOHN FRAZEE, a marble cutter and sculptor, was a candidate of the Workingmen for two years, in 1830 for Congress and in 1831 for the Assembly, and was an admirer of Evans' "open and independent course." He was born in poverty in Rahway, New Jersey, on July 18, 1790, the son of a carpenter who had abandoned his family. He spent his early childhood working on his maternal grandparents' farm, obtaining virtually no schooling. At the age of seventeen he was apprenticed to a bricklayer and mason who was also a tavern keeper, receiving what little education he had in this home; three years later he went to work as a bricklayer with a New Brunswick masonry contractor, where he learned stonecutting in his spare time. During the War of 1812 Frazee began cutting tombstones, setting up a workshop first in Rahway and then in New Brunswick. He moved to New York in 1818, where he established a marble shop with his brother. Most of his work consisted of mantel pieces and monuments until 1824, when he completed a memorial bust in St. Paul's Church, the first carved in the United States by an American. In succeeding years he received many commissions for sculpture, including Daniel Webster and John Marshall, and helped found the National Academy of Design. In 1831 the partnership with his brother was dissolved, a new connection being made with another sculptor, Robert Launitz. Frazee's finest work was the new United States Custom House (later the Sub-Treasury) in Wall Street, where he was from 1834 to 1842 first construction superintendent and then architect, contributing especially to the design of the interior rotunda. Before his death in 1852, he also served there as a customs officer.[60]

The THREE COOPER BROTHERS from the rural Twelfth Ward were at various times affiliated with the Workingmen. The best known was Peter Cooper, the manufacturer and philanthropist. His connection with the movement was tenuous, consisting solely in his membership on the 1834 General Committee, but his younger brothers Thomas and Edward played important roles in the party. Their father, formerly a lieutenant in the Continental Army, was an unsuccessful businessman in New York City and the towns of the lower Hudson Valley, working variously as a hatter, a brewer, a storekeeper, and a brickmaker. Peter, the eldest son, born in New York in 1791, had only one year of formal education, assisting his father in his endeavors until his apprenticeship to a coachmaker. At the age of twenty-one he began working in a cloth-shearing machine factory, and within a short time was the owner of a similar machine from which he derived a good income. Selling this business after the War of 1812, he joined his brother-in-law in the grocery business in New York. In 1822 he bought a glue factory which became the foundation of his fortune, and six years later organized the Canton Iron Works in Baltimore, Maryland, where the famous "Tom Thumb" engine was built. Throughout this period he was sporadically interested in politics, being elected to the Common Council on the Tammany ticket.[61]

Thomas Cooper, Peter's junior by three years, was associated with him in the glue factory and later in the ironworks. He was a member of the original Workingmen's Executive Committee, aligning himself with the *Sentinel* faction in the education debate. A delegate to the 1830 state convention, he remained active in the movement in the early months of the following year.[62] The youngest brother, Edward, born in 1803, was a favorite of Peter's, who financed his medical education and assisted him in establishing a practice. His activity as a Workingman also began early in 1830, but continued into 1834 when he was appointed to the revived General Committee. After writing a number of philosophical works he began to show certain mental aberrations in 1837 and was committed to an asylum.[63] DANIEL F. TIEMANN, a close friend of the Coopers who married Peter's adopted daughter, was also a Twelfth

Ward Workingman in 1830. The owner of a paint business, he was elected Mayor of New York in 1857 on the Tammany ticket.[64]

Several sets of brothers, such as HENRY and JOHN RIELL, took a leading part in the Locofoco movement. Henry had been active during 1830 in the Workingmen's Party, representing the aristocratic First Ward on the Executive Committee. By 1834 he was an organization Democrat, being selected within a year as a member of the Tammany Young Men's General Committee. When the issue arose later that year of reading Leggett and the *Evening Post* out of the party and denouncing the Locofoco schismatics, Riell was one of a small minority on that committee refusing to be dominated by the "usages of the party." His brother John declared himself an Antimonopoly Democrat at about the same time, and both worked conscientiously for the success of Leggett's principles during the following year, and in 1837 for reunion with a Tammany which appeared sincere in offering concessions to the bolters. The Riells were tobacconists, like their father who had a well-established business, but in 1839 Henry was appointed gauger at the Custom House. He was removed during the Whig ascendancy in Washington, gaining his livelihood by first operating a picture shop and then an auction establishment; John, meanwhile, was working as a grocer. In 1845 when the Democrats returned to power, Henry Riell was made a weigher general.[65]

PHILIP and BENSON MILLEDOLER, the former a physician and the latter an attorney, were active in the antimonopoly movement of 1835, although neither was willing to make a complete break with Tammany. Their father was the Reverend Philip Milledoler, son of a Swiss immigrant, who after graduating from Columbia College became a popular pastor successively in the German Reformed, Presbyterian, and Dutch Reformed churches, serving in addition as president of Rutgers or Queen's College from 1825 to 1840. The younger Philip was Assembly candidate of the Workingmen in 1831, becoming increasingly active in the Democratic Party in 1834 and joining Tammany the following year. As chairman of the Democratic Young Men's General Committee, he gained a reputation as an antimonopolist, voting in support of Leggett and the *Evening Post;* the same was true of Benson, a member of the Old Men's Committee. In 1836 Philip was proposed as a Locofoco candidate for Congress but failed to receive the nomination. As characterized by Byrdsall, he was "sufficiently malcontent to have led on a revolution, but for his constitutional timidity."[66]

AUGUSTUS J. and GEORGE WASHINGTON MATSELL, the sons of a New York tailor, were active in the movement during the later period. George, born in New York City in 1811, was apprenticed at the age of fifteen to a dyer. By 1832 he had joined his brother, a bookseller and stationer, in operating the "Free Enquirer's Reading Room" and in publishing and selling "a large assortment of 'Liberal Books'"; these included works of Paine, Voltaire, Jefferson, the Owens, and Fanny Wright. Augustus' political activity was negligible, but George took an active part with the Locofocos, being nominated in 1836 for the Assembly and in 1837 for Sheriff. After joining the Tammany Society in 1838, he was appointed inspector at the Custom House; five years later he became police magistrate, while his brother received an appointment as clerk in the Hall of Records. George Matsell soon became noted as an efficient police justice, organizing the first municipal police force in the United States, and serving as its chief until 1857. In that year he became embroiled in a political controversy by supporting Mayor Fernando Wood against the state legislature. This led to a skirmish at the City Hall between Matsell's forces and the police created by the legislature, and Matsell's police were disbanded. He died in 1877 in New York.[67]

The careers of the THREE HECKER BROTHERS were quite different from the Matsells'. Their father, a skilled metalworker, emigrated from Germany in the early years of the nineteenth century and became foreman of the foundry and machine shop where Fulton's *Clermont* was built. He married the daughter of another German immigrant who operated a brass foundry; her brother, Frederick Friend (or Freund), was a follower of Thomas Skidmore and a Workingmen's Assembly candidate in 1829. Hecker opened his own brass foundry shortly after his marriage, but was generally unsuccessful in business. His eldest son John, born in

1812, became the principal support of the family, going to work as a boy in his uncle's bakery. George, six years his junior, later joined him there, while Isaac, the youngest, after attending public school for about six years worked for a Methodist weekly and then in a type foundry.

In 1834 John and George opened their own bakeshop, Isaac entering the firm the following year. At about this time the brothers became ardent Locofocos, John being listed by Byrdsall as a party leader. Setting up a hand press in the shop, they printed hard-money slogans on the paper money they received, their political activity increasing as the price of flour rose. Isaac, although at seventeen too young to participate officially, joined his brothers in passing out handbills and leading street-corner rallies. When the party majority reunited with Tammany in 1837, John remained with the Rump Locofocos, returning the following year to the Democratic fold. After being associated with the Calhoun movement in 1843, he was twice elected Alderman and in 1865 was nominated for Mayor on an independent ticket.

The Hecker brothers became successful bakers, expanding their business by 1844 to include five bakeshops and a flour mill. Furthermore, they patented several mechanical improvements and introduced farina and self-rising flour. Isaac, meanwhile, had begun studying metaphysics and theology in odd hours and became interested in Transcendentalism. After brief sojourns at Brook Farm and Bronson Alcott's Fruitlands community, he returned to the bakery and embarked upon a crusade to educate his brothers' employees by giving lectures and establishing a library. In 1844 he was converted to Catholicism, and after study and ordination in Germany returned to found the order of Paulist fathers, devoting the rest of his life to missionary work in the United States.[68]

One of the most prominent Locofoco leaders was DR. STEPHEN HASBROUCK. Although practicing medicine in New York at least as early as 1825, he originally lived in Fishkill, where he was married in 1815. He had been a Whig during the 1834 Charter election, but moved over to the Democrats in November. His party irregularity was evident again the following spring when he led a rebel Democratic faction in the Fourteenth Ward, so it seemed logical that he would join the Locofoco movement later that year. He was their Congressional nominee in 1836, received their support for Alderman the following April, and was nominated for the State Senate in 1837, but resigned his candidacy in an attempt to mediate between the two factions. His son Fenelon, who became a physician like his father, was also active in the Equal Rights Party, although only nineteen years old at the time.[69] Hasbrouck was active in Tammany in 1840, but by 1843 again revolted against party regularity, taking a prominent part in the Calhoun movement.[70]

DR. MOSES JAQUES, the patriarch of the Locofoco Party, was also a physician. He was born about 1770 in New Jersey, the son of a Revolutionary War officer, but came to New York early in the nineteenth century, joining Tammany in 1811. From 1825 to 1832 the *Directory* listed him as a merchant, partner in the druggist firm of Jaques and Marsh, after which he was listed as an M.D. He was one of the earliest and most militant Locofocos, urging the formation of a separate political organization almost from the beginning of the antimonopolist agitation. Serving continuously as party treasurer from January 1836 until he left the city for his farm in Rahway, New Jersey, in the spring of 1837, Jaques was also president of the first county convention of the new party, received their nomination for Lieutenant Governor in 1836, and was later the party candidate for the Assembly and the Mayoralty. Moreover, his influence in shaping and expressing the Locofoco platform was demonstrated by his drafting of the Declaration of Principles, adopted by the county convention, and his writing of the Address to the People which emanated from the state convention of the Equal Rights Party.[71] As Byrdsall characterized him, Jaques was

> mild yet immovably fixed in his views and principles, whatever were his convictions, they were the workings of his own mind; . . . consequently, such a man would be more of a thinker and a reasoner, than an impassioned speaker; yet he always spoke lucidly and with effect. His age, his qualifications, and his connection with the Revolution of 1776 combined to make him the

man to lead a body of democrats who thought and reasoned, and who had love of principle and of country at heart.[72]

Three of the intellectual spokesmen of the Locofocos had diverse backgrounds. THEODORE SEDGWICK, JR., a close friend of William Leggett, helped to edit the *Evening Post* during the latter's illness and after his death published a collection of his political editorials. Sedgwick's letters to the *Post,* signed "Veto," and his 1835 pamphlet *What Is a Monopoly?* were influential both in formulating and expressing the antimonopolist program, although he apparently took little active part in politics. The third to bear this name, Sedgwick was the grandson of the famous Massachusetts Federalist and the son of the equally well-known Jacksonian Democrat and writer on political economy. He was born in 1811 in Albany, New York; unlike his progenitors he graduated from Columbia rather than Yale, but followed the family tradition by studying law. After his admission to the bar in 1833, he traveled in Europe for over a year, being appointed attaché to the Paris embassy, but returned to establish his law practice, which he followed successfully until 1850. Upon his refusal of President Buchanan's offers of diplomatic posts, he was in 1858 appointed United States Attorney for the Southern District of New York, occupying this position until his death the following year.[73]

DR. JOHN W. VETHAKE, whose article "The Doctrine of Anti-Monopoly" was published in the *Evening Post* at the height of the political agitation of October 1835, was a more obscure figure. Better known was his brother, Henry Vethake, an academician and free-trade economist, who was born in 1792 of Prussian parentage in British Guiana and graduated from Columbia College; during the ensuing three decades he was a professor at Queen's (later Rutgers) College, the College of New Jersey (later Princeton), Dickinson, and New York University, finally being appointed professor and vice-provost at the University of Pennsylvania. John, too, taught for a time at Dickinson College and a medical school in Baltimore before entering politics in the early 1830's and editing the *Poughkeepsie Anti-Mason.* He apparently came to New York in 1833 to practice medicine, becoming active the following year in the Democratic Party. By the fall of 1835 he had taken a stand with the antimonopolists and was nominated for the Assembly by the insurgents. Opposing the formation of a separate party, he seemingly returned to the Tammany fold early in 1836, for he took no further part in the Locofoco deliberations. In 1840 he served briefly in the Custom House, practicing medicine until his reappointment in 1845 by President Polk.[74]

CLINTON ROOSEVELT was a more active intellectual leader. Born in 1804, his first listing in the *Directory* from 1828 to 1830 was "hardware" and "machinery"; he later appeared there as an attorney. In 1833 he first came to the attention of the Workingmen with his pamphlet, *The Mode of Protecting Domestic Industry, Consistently with the Desires Both of the South and the North, by Operating on the Currency,* in which he opposed both a high tariff and paper money. He became editor of the *Democrat,* the official Locofoco organ, early in 1836, and was nominated for the Assembly in October; also receiving Whig endorsement, he was elected and served for one year. Within a few years he had became a critic of the laissez-faire philosophy, continuing to write on a variety of subjects, but maintaining his interest in machinery as attested by his invention in 1869 of a new type of railroad car wheel. Byrdsall's character sketch seems remarkably apt in describing this man, who lived to the age of ninety-four: "an honest politician of considerable talent and some eccentricity. . . . His mind is fertile either to construct systems, mechanical machines, or literary matter."[75]

Among other candidates who obtained considerable support from the Workingmen were THOMAS HERTTELL and CHURCHILL C. CAMBRELENG, although only the former was actively affiliated with the movement at any time. Herttell, born in 1771, had been an attorney and a judge, but at the time of the Workingmen's political debut had given up his practice, serving as president of the Phenix Fire Insurance Company. Active in politics since 1803 when he joined the Tammany Society, he had been elected Third Ward Alderman in 1828, but declined the Assembly nomination the following year. From 1830 to 1836 Herttell and the Workingmen developed a mutual attraction, principally based on an affinity in their humanitarian objectives. The *Sentinel* faction of the Workingmen's Party nominated him for Congress in 1830 and for the Assembly in 1831; in the following year he was a successful Tammany candidate for the legislature, being reelected annually for the ensuing three years. Late in 1835 the antimonopolists endorsed his candidacy for the Assembly and he was seriously considered in 1836 for a Locofoco Congressional nomination. Herttell took a leading part in the movement to abolish imprisonment for debt and was active in the Franklin Temperance Society. As an advocate of "spiritual tolerance," he wrote a pamphlet attacking the religious test for witnesses, opposed the use of the Bible in schools, and strenuously denounced the appointment of legislative chaplains; his political opponents, as might be expected, continually described him as an "infidel," although the New York *Whig* emphasized that he was "radical" only in religion.[76]

Cambreleng, a close friend of Martin Van Buren and for a decade a Democratic leader in the House of Representatives, was consistently supported by the Workingmen, often to the detriment of their own candidates. Born in 1788 in Washington, North Carolina, and educated in nearby New Bern, he came to New York as a youth of sixteen. Little is known of his family, except that one brother, Stephen, became a New York attorney and another a naval officer. After working as a merchants' clerk, he advanced in commercial pursuits, being associated for a time with John Jacob Astor, and soon became an important merchant in his own right. He also served as director of a fire insurance company and during the 1830's as an officer of several railroad companies, being portrayed in the anti-Jackson press as an "accomplished stock-jobber" in railroad issues.[77]

Elected to Congress in 1820, he served nine terms with distinction, heading the House committees on Foreign Affairs, Commerce, and Ways and Means. There he soon gained a reputation as a staunch defender of free trade, despite which an influential segment of the New York mercantile community consistently opposed him. The antimonopolists were heartened in 1835 by his support, expressed at the fateful Johnson dinner, of the pledge system and the right of instruction, and he received unofficial Locofoco support the following year. Defeated for reelection in 1838, he was appointed minister to Russia in 1840, and later took a prominent part in the New York constitutional convention of 1846, the 1847 convention of the "Barnburners," and the Utica convention of 1848, the seed from which the Free Soil movement grew.[78] Van Buren, his political mentor, characterized Cambreleng as "clear headed, painstaking, indefatigable and conscientious, . . . ardent in politics but incapable of knowingly saying anything to advance his cause which he does not believe to be true." Byrdsall, who seldom agreed with the "Little Magician," portrayed Cambreleng as "a man in whom there is no dereliction of principle," and sincerely regretted his political defeat.[79]

From Skidmore the machinist to Cambreleng the merchant, the nearly fifty men discussed here seem to have no single common denominator. Perhaps this is due in part to the scanty evidence. Yet some inferences can be drawn from their careers. The origins of about half the men are known, being divided almost equally between urban United States (principally New York), rural (including small towns), and foreign (largely Great Britain). The proportion of foreign-born Workingmen in this group is especially noteworthy, lending some credence to the charge that the movement was dominated by foreigners,[80] although the migration from farm and village to the metropolis was doubtless of equal significance.

More important in placing the Workingmen in the status system of the period are the occupations of their fathers, but this is known for fewer than half the men discussed here. According to this evidence, the previous generation was divided between mechanics and small businessmen, with a scattering of farmers and professional men. Even more significant is a comparison of the occupations of father and son. With the exception of the Cooper brothers, John Frazee, and George Bruce, few sons seem noticeably to have moved up—or down—the social scale, although some were more successful than their fathers. One element difficult to assess in this connection is the relative position in the social hierarchy of public office, whether elective or appointive. Was a clerical position in the Custom House or a term as Alderman, for example, a step upward for a mechanic, or merely a payment for political services rendered? If this was one avenue toward higher social status, nearly half these men traveled it at least for a time.

The significance of other factors, such as education and religious denomination, is even more difficult to determine. Many of these men, of course, had little or no formal education other than that obtained during their apprenticeships. On the basis of incomplete evidence, fewer than one-third attended the equivalent of secondary school, the majority of these later entering medicine or the law. Moreover, this proportion is undoubtedly higher than that for the Workingmen as a whole, given the educational system of the time and the presumption that these men, being more famous and hence generally more successful than their fellows, were less typical of the movement than of its leadership. Religion is yet more evanescent as a factor; even the high ratio of anticlericalism and agnosticism among these men was not necessarily found throughout the entire movement.

These men for the most part, together with the labor leaders whose careers were described in the preceding chapter, were the leaders of the Workingmen's movement. Party wheelhorses, political gadflies, malcontents, ideologues—all made their contribution. These biographical vignettes not only add the dimension of personality to the flat surface of the political chronicle, but illustrate the variety and complexity of the movement. Yet there is a key to this variety: the high incidence of social and occupational mobility which characterizes these life histories. Disparate and diverse as their origins and careers might be, they seemed to share a desire for change, a striving for self-improvement. Many abandoned their vocations (some more than once) for others with seemingly greater potentialities or more possibility of personal gratification. Even those who followed only one profession or trade throughout their careers demonstrated this restlessness by changing their employment or residence, exploring and developing new techniques, or enlarging the focus of their activities into literary, forensic, or humanitarian areas. To some, politics became a career, while to others it was only an avocation. Nevertheless, for a few years these men and their followers endeavored through the Workingmen's movement to use political means to provide a matrix for the growth of individual opportunity and self-expression.

The Workingmen:
An Occupational Analysis

THE PRECEDING biographical study of selected Workingmen is enlightening but inconclusive in regard to the anatomy of the movement. Reliable and relatively complete biographical data are lacking for more than a handful of the Workingmen, most participants having gained immortality solely from the appearance of their names in newspaper accounts of party meetings. For this reason, further insight into the social and economic basis of the movement must be founded upon an analysis of its occupational structure.

A panel of Workingmen has been obtained for this purpose by a careful survey of newspaper accounts of Workingmen's meetings and party functions from 1829 to 1835; most fruitful, of course, were the *Working Man's Advocate,* the *Sentinel,* and the *Man,* with the *Evening Post* contributing in the later period. The Locofoco period, from 1835 to 1837, was more difficult to explore via the press, for with the virtual retirement of both Evans and Leggett there was inadequate journalistic coverage of Locofoco meetings. The principal source used for Locofoco membership, therefore, was Byrdsall's *History,* which is less complete in detailing party meetings than the press would have been. The panel of Workingmen is, as a result, heavily weighted toward the earliest period, 1829 to 1830, but an attempt has been made to take this into consideration in the study.

The complete panel chosen for investigation consists of 850 names, some of which are found in two or more of the three periods into which the study is divided. These men include chairmen and other officers of ward and general meetings, candidates for office, members of executive committees, speakers and resolutions committee chairmen, and at the bottom of the ladder members of ward vigilance committees; some men in these categories are excluded, especially party candidates like Edward Curtis, Anthony Lamb, and Frederick Tallmadge, whose connection with the movement was tenuous and temporary. Some names occurred only once in party rosters, while others played a prominent part in the history of the movement. After the establishment of the panel, their occupations were ascertained, principally from Longworth's *Directory*, supplemented or corrected by newspaper accounts or other sources. In some instances, a man may have had several occupations during the period, in which case an arbitrary choice was made of the one which he apparently followed for the longest time. Approximately 125 different occupations, organized for convenience into fourteen categories, were found listed for these men. A summary of this personnel study is contained in Table I.

TABLE I

WORKINGMEN BY OCCUPATION, 1829–1837

Occupation	Working-men 1829–30	Working-men 1831–34	Loco-focos 1835–37	Total 1829–37
Building trades:	103	27	12	118
Architect-builder	1	1	1	1
Builder	3	—	—	3
Carpenter	51	9	7	56
Glasscutter	2	—	—	2
Mason	13	6	—	15
Painter	24	6	2	28
Sashmaker	4	3	1	6
Sawyer	1	—	—	1
Stonecutter	4	2	1	6
House furnishings:	63	15	6	71
Bedstead maker	1	—	—	1
Blind manufacturer	2	—	—	2
Cabinetmaker	24	6	2	27
Carver and gilder	12	2	2	13
Chairmaker	13	2	1	15
Floor cloth manufacturer	1	—	—	1
Mahogany yard	2	1	—	2
Paperhanger	2	1	—	2
Turner	5	2	—	5
Upholsterer	1	—	—	1
Varnisher	—	1	1	2
Marine trades:	23	5	7	32
Block & pump maker	—	—	1	1

TABLE I (Cont.)

Occupation	Working-men 1829–30	Working-men 1831–34	Loco-focos 1835–37	Total 1829–37
Boat builder	2	1	1	3
Boatman	1	—	—	1
Engineer	4	—	1	5
Mariner	1	2	2	4
Rope maker	1	—	—	1
Sail maker	—	1	—	1
Ship carpenter	10	1	—	10
Shipmaster	2	—	1	3
Spar maker	1	—	—	1
Stevedore	1	—	—	1
Wharfinger	—	—	1	1
Metal trades:	60	13	9	70
Brassfounder	10	—	—	10
Coppersmith	1	—	—	1
Cutler	1	—	2	3
Engraver	2	1	—	3
Goldsmith	1	1	—	1
Grate maker	2	—	—	2
Gunsmith	1	—	1	1
Hardware	3	1	1	4
Jeweler	3	1	1	4
Locksmith	2	1	—	2
Mathematical instrument maker	1	—	—	1
Plumber	—	1	—	1
Portable furnace maker	1	—	—	1
Scale beam maker	1	—	—	1
Silversmith	8	2	1	9
Smith	10	—	2	12
Tinsmith	9	6	1	10
Watchcase maker	1	—	—	1
Watchmaker	3	—	—	3
Manufacturers, artisans:	31	10	6	38
Basket maker	—	1	1	1
Comb maker	8	—	1	9
Cooper	3	2	2	5
Glue manufacturer	1	2	—	2
Machinist	7	1	—	7
Piano maker	9	3	1	10
Plane maker	1	—	—	1
Soap factory	—	—	1	1
Stoneware manufacturer	2	1	1	2
Food and beverages:	83	16	19	109
Baker	7	1	1	8

TABLE I (Cont.)

Occupation	Working-men 1829–30	Working-men 1831–34	Loco-focos 1835–37	Total 1829–37
Boarding house	3	—	—	3
Butcher	3	1	—	4
Coffee house	1	2	—	2
Confectioner	1	1	—	2
Distiller	2	1	1	3
Farmer	2	—	—	2
Flour merchant	—	—	1	1
Grocer	58	9	14	75
Innkeeper	1	—	—	1
Porterhouse	4	1	1	6
Tavern	1	—	1	2
Clothing, dry goods:	34	14	12	47
Auctioneer	3	—	1	4
Dry-goods merchant	6	3	3	9
Dyestuffs	1	1	—	2
Furrier	1	1	—	1
Hatter	7	2	3	10
Tailor	15	6	5	20
Umbrella maker	1	1	—	1
Leather, shoemaking:	37	22	12	60
Blacking maker	—	—	1	1
Last maker, findings	1	—	1	2
Leather dresser	5	4	2	10
Pocketbook maker	1	—	—	1
Shoemaker	30	18	8	46
Merchants and tradesmen:	17	8	13	32
Bookseller	2	2	1	4
Coal dealer	—	1	2	2
Crockery dealer	2	—	—	2
Druggist	2	—	2	4
Feathers	—	—	1	1
Merchant	7	3	—	10
Oil merchant	1	—	1	2
Pedlar	1	—	1	2
Prints	1	1	1	1
Tobacconist	1	1	4	4
Printing, publishing:	17	17	11	36
Bookbinder	—	5	4	6
Editor	4	2	1	7
Printer	9	8	6	18
Stereotyper	2	—	—	2
Type founder	2	2	—	3

TABLE I (Cont.)

Occupation	Working-men 1829–30	Working-men 1831–34	Loco-focos 1835–37	Total 1829–37
Professional, clerical:	25	17	26	57
Accountant	4	2	—	4
Agent	1	1	—	1
Attorney	5	2	6	13
Broker	1	—	—	1
Clerk	1	—	—	1
Collector	—	—	1	1
Commission merchant	2	1	—	2
Conveyancer	—	—	1	1
Market man	—	—	1	1
Notary	1	1	—	2
Physician	7	9	14	24
Teacher	3	1	3	6
Transportation:	18	5	2	22
Cartman	13	3	1	16
Coachmaker	2	1	1	3
Livery stable	2	1	—	2
Wheelwright	1	—	—	1
Public employees:	2	1	1	3
City inspector	—	1	1	1
City weigher	1	—	—	1
Weighmaster	1	—	—	1
Miscellaneous:	2	1	2	5
Gas fitter	1	—	—	1
Hairdresser	1	1	—	2
Lamplighter	—	—	1	1
Paver	—	—	1	1
Unidentified:	118	35	7	150
Total	633	206	145	850
Total identified	515	171	138	700

Some observations on this compilation are in order. It is divided into the three periods used in the chronological narrative, but because some Workingmen were active in more than one period the total column, embracing the entire period 1829 to 1837, is not in all cases the arithmetical sum of the other three columns. Another factor requiring explanation is the unidentified category of 150 Workingmen, comprising about one-sixth of the panel, whose occupations could not be ascertained. Some of these men, although listed as active in the Workingmen's movement, either were not found in Longworth or were listed there with no occupation being given. In other cases several men with the same name were listed in the *Directory* and, other evidence being lacking, it was impossible to determine which was the man in question.* Numerically, most of the unidentified are in the first period, with about the same percentage in the second period, and only a handful in the third or Locofoco period.

When we examine the principal occupations of the identified Workingmen during the three periods of the study, we note furthermore that, as shown in Table II, more than half the panel is found

TABLE II

PRINCIPAL OCCUPATIONS OF IDENTIFIED WORKINGMEN

	1829–30		1831–34		1835–37		1829–37	
Occupation	No.	Pct.	No.	Pct.	No.	Pct.	No.	Pct.
Grocer	58	11.3	9	5.3	14	10.1	75	10.7
Carpenter	51	9.9	9	5.3	7	5.1	56	8.0
Shoemaker	30	5.8	18	10.3	8	5.8	46	6.6
Painter	24	4.7	6	3.5	2	1.4	28	4.0
Cabinetmaker	24	4.7	6	3.5	2	1.4	27	3.9
Physician	7	1.4	9	5.3	14	10.1	24	3.4
Tailor	15	2.9	6	3.5	5	3.6	20	2.9
Printer	9	1.7	8	4.7	6	4.3	18	2.6
Cartman	13	2.5	3	1.8	1	0.7	16	2.3
Mason	13	2.5	6	3.5	—	—	15	2.1
Chairmaker	13	2.5	2	1.2	1	0.7	15	2.1
Carver & gilder...	12	2.3	2	1.2	2	1.4	13	1.9
Attorney	5	1.0	2	1.2	6	4.3	13	1.9
Total	274	53.2	86	50.3	68	49.3	366	52.3

in only thirteen occupations, or about one-tenth of all occupations listed in Table I. As might be expected, nearly three-fourths of these leading occupations are skilled trades, only the grocers, physicians, cartmen, and attorneys not falling in that category. These skilled trades, moreover, obviously predominate from a percentage standpoint in all periods, with one noteworthy exception. This is

* Many such men were identified by a process of elimination; if it were known in what ward he resided, the use of a contemporary city map could identify the man by his address.

the 1835–37 or Locofoco period, in which grocers and physicians, and to a lesser extent attorneys, seem to have played a leading role. This indication is reinforced when we examine the complete panel of identified Workingmen by occupational categories, as summarized in Table III.

An examination of the leaders of the movement should provide further enlightenment, especially if they are compared with the Workingmen as a whole. For this purpose, a second panel was established, consisting of the most active men throughout the history of the movement. Qualifications for inclusion in the panel were

TABLE III
IDENTIFIED WORKINGMEN BY OCCUPATIONAL CATEGORIES

Occupational Categories	1829–30 Percent	1831–34 Percent	1835–37 Percent	1829–37 Percent
Building trades	20	16	9	17
Food and beverages	16	9	14	16
House furnishings	12	9	4	10
Metal trades	12	8	7	10
Leather, shoemaking	7	13	9	9
Professional, clerical	5	10	19	8
Clothing & dry goods	7	8	9	7
Manufacturers, artisans	6	6	4	5
Printing, publishing	3	10	8	5
Marine trades	5	3	5	5
Merchants & tradesmen	3	5	9	5
Transportation	4	3	1	3
Public employees	—	—	1	—
Miscellaneous	—	—	1	—
Total	100	100	100	100

determined by the combination of political activities ranging from membership on an executive committee to candidacy for political office and officiating at party meetings. Weighted totals* for approxi-

* The following points were given to various activities to obtain the weighted totals: 5 points—executive committee member, chairman of general meeting, delegate to party convention, candidate; 4 points—vice-president, secretary, or treasurer of general meeting; 3 points—chairman of ward meeting, nomination for political candidacy; 2 points—other officer of ward meeting, resolutions or other committee member; 1 point—listed as speaker at

mately two hundred Workingmen were computed for the entire 1829–37 period, and for each of the three periods into which the history of the movement is divided, and the top fifty men (this figure was chosen arbitrarily) were selected for the panel. These leaders, their occupations and activity totals, are listed in Table IV;

TABLE IV
Workingmen Leaders by Occupation and Party Activity

Name	Occupation	Activity Point Totals			
		1829–30	1831–34	1835–37	1829–37
Daniel Gorham	Tailor	35	22	46	103
Joel Curtis	Hardware	20	64	10	94
Robert Townsend, Jr.	Carpenter	24	—	40	64
Isaac Odell	Carpenter	42	10	8	60
Moses Jaques	Physician	—	2	58	60
Henry Meeks	Piano maker	40	20	—	60
George H. Evans	Printer	24	34	—	58
John Alwaise	Cabinetmaker	43	8	5	56
Ebenezer Ford	Carpenter	33	23	—	56
William Leavens	Mahogany yard	38	16	—	54
Alexander Ming, Jr.	Printer	—	—	52	52
John Windt	Printer	—	19	32	51
Edward J. Webb	Architect	15	18	17	50
Simon Clannon	Painter	47	1	—	48
Robert Walker	Shoemaker	28	18	—	46
John Commerford	Chairmaker	10	8	28	46
John Morrison	Merchant	24	22	—	46
Paul Grout	Cabinetmaker	30	9	—	39
Cornelius McLean	Sashmaker	34	5	—	39
Andrew Jackson	Sashmaker	27	6	5	38
Henry Walton	Shoemaker	25	10	—	35
Frederick Cozzens	Grocer	14	5	15	34
Job Haskell	Coal dealer	—	—	34	34
William F. Piatt	Physician	—	—	34	34
Barnabas Bates	Editor	—	27	3	30
John H. Bowie	Leather dresser	—	21	9	30
Paul Durando	Tailor	10	15	5	30
Henry G. Guyon	Carpenter	30	—	—	30

meeting. This system, admittedly, is not entirely satisfactory in obtaining a panel of the most influential leaders, for certain intangible leadership characteristics or activities cannot be measured in this way. Nevertheless, it is believed that few, if any, important political (as distinguished from intellectual) leaders are omitted.

TABLE IV (Cont.)

Name	Occupation	Activity Point Totals			
		1829–30	1831–34	1835–37	1829–37
Levi D. Slamm	Grocer	—	—	29	29
George Anderson	Umbrella maker	25	2	1	28
William H. Ball	Piano maker	26	2	—	28
Thomas Herttell	Attorney	5	14	9	28
Isaac Peirce	Grocer	11	17	—	28
Aaron L. Balch	Teacher	27	—	—	27
Fitzwilliam Byrdsall	(Unknown)	—	—	27	27
John Dean	Chairmaker	16	11	—	27
Robert Hogbin	Tinsmith	11	9	7	27
Ebenezer Whiting	Teacher	27	—	—	27
Edward C. Cooper	Physician	19	7	—	26
Benjamin Hallock	Coal dealer	—	—	26	26
Levi Prescott	Painter	26	—	—	26
John B. White	(Unknown)	20	6	—	26
P. C. M. Andrews	Printer	25	—	—	25
Thomas Cooper	Glue factory	20	4	—	24
William Froment	Turner	8	16	—	24
Robert Beatty	Bookbinder	—	19	4	23
Henry E. Riell	Tobacconist	16	2	4	22
John R. Soper	Grocer	17	5	—	22
Ralph Wells	Broker	22	—	—	22
Thomas Skidmore	Machinist	22	—	—	22
	Mean Activity Point Totals	24.0	13.8	20.3	38.8

it can be noted that more than half of them have been discussed biographically in previous chapters.

Further analysis of these leaders demonstrates that nearly one-half of the panel was active in two periods, one-fourth in one period only, and one-fourth in all three periods of the Workingmen's movement. A more detailed distribution of these leaders is shown in Table V, which contains a tabulation of the number who were active during any one year. While approximately three-fourths of the leadership panel was active in each of the first two periods, slightly more than one-half was active in the Locofoco period. This is somewhat surprising in the light of the comparative lack of information on the latter period, especially since no conscious effort was made to skew the panel by over-weighting the Locofoco leaders.

The compilation in Table V provides a justification for our

TABLE V

DISTRIBUTION OF FIFTY WORKINGMEN LEADERS BY YEAR AND
PERIOD OF ACTIVITY

Year	Number	Percent
1829	16	32
1830	39	78
1829–30	39	78
1831	34	68
1832	28	56
1833	25	50
1834	28	56
1831–34	36	72
1835	26	52
1836	20	40
1837	15	30
1835–37	26	52
1829–37	50	100

previous assumption of the essential continuity of the movement
from the organization of the Workingmen's Party to the full flowering of the Locofocos. Many early leaders, of course, dropped out
along the way, presumably into either the Tammany or Whig camp,
where a haven could be found from the stormy (and unrewarding)
sea of political heresy. Similarly, several Locofoco leaders, before
the great debate of 1835, had seen no necessity to revolt against the
doctrine of party regularity. Nevertheless, it is significant that such
a large proportion of the early Workingmen were found in positions
of leadership in the Locofoco Party.

When the leaders' occupations are compared with those of the
Workingmen in general, as in Table VI, we find both marked simi-
larities and differences. Looking first at the entire 1829–37 period,
60 percent of the leaders were drawn from four occupational categories: building trades, house furnishings, professional and clerical,
and printing trades. Furthermore, these categories are seen to dominate this panel in all three periods. Although the first two of these
categories show approximately the same percentage for both leaders
and Workingmen as a whole, the proportion of printers and professionals among the leaders is noticeably higher. On the other hand,

TABLE VI

COMPARISON OF LEADERS AND TOTAL WORKINGMEN BY
IDENTIFIED OCCUPATIONAL CATEGORIES

(By Percent of Panel)

Occupational Categories	1829–30		1831–34		1835–37		1829–37	
	Leaders	Total	Leaders	Total	Leaders	Total	Leaders	Total
Building trades	24	20	17	16	16	9	19	17
House furnishings	16	12	17	9	8	4	13	10
Food and beverages	8	16	9	9	8	14	8	16
Metal trades	5	12	5	8	8	7	4	10
Leather and shoe-making	5	7	9	13	4	9	6	9
Professional, clerical	14	5	9	10	12	19	15	8
Clothing, dry goods	8	7	9	8	12	9	6	7
Manufacturers and artisans	10	6	9	6	4	4	8	5
Printing, publishing	5	3	11	10	16	8	13	5
Merchants, tradesmen	5	3	5	5	12	9	8	5
Other	—	9	—	6	—	8	—	8
Total	100	100	100	100	100	100	100	100

metal craftsmen and the producers and sellers of food and beverages are in general found in a significantly higher proportion in the larger panel, while only slight differences can be found in the comparative percentages in the other four categories.

Comparing the principal occupations of the members of the two panels, as in Table VII, it is seen that they are nearly identical; in fact, slightly more than half of each panel, with only a few divergencies, is found in almost the same proportion in thirteen occupations. Excluding the two unidentified by occupation, the forty-eight leaders were found in twenty-eight occupations. Since no cartman, mason, or carver and gilder was included in the panel, the twenty-six men (or 52 percent of the total) listed were in only ten different occupations. Furthermore, nearly one-third of these men were in

TABLE VII

COMPARISON OF PRINCIPAL OCCUPATIONS OF LEADERS AND
WORKINGMEN

(By Percent of Panel)

Occupation	1829–30		1831–34		1835–37		1829–37	
	Leaders	Total	Leaders	Total	Leaders	Total	Leaders	Total
Grocer	7.7	11.3	8.3	5.3	7.7	10.1	8.0	10.7
Carpenter	10.3	9.9	5.6	5.3	7.7	5.1	8.0	8.0
Shoemaker	5.1	5.8	5.6	10.5	—	5.8	4.0	6.6
Painter	5.1	4.7	2.8	3.5	—	1.4	4.0	4.0
Cabinetmaker	5.1	4.7	5.6	3.5	3.8	1.4	4.0	3.9
Physician	2.6	1.4	5.6	5.3	7.7	10.1	6.0	3.4
Tailor	5.1	2.9	5.6	3.5	7.7	3.6	4.0	2.9
Printer	5.1	1.7	5.6	4.7	7.7	4.3	8.0	2.6
Cartman	—	2.5	—	1.8	—	0.7	—	2.3
Mason	—	2.5	—	3.5	—	—	—	2.1
Chairmaker	5.1	2.5	5.6	1.2	3.8	0.7	4.0	2.1
Carver and gilder	—	2.3	—	1.2	—	1.4	—	1.9
Attorney	2.6	1.0	2.8	1.2	3.8	4.3	2.0	1.9
Total	53.8	53.2	52.8	50.3	50.0	49.3	52.0	52.3

four occupations: grocer, carpenter, printer, and physician. The most obvious difference between the leaders and the Workingmen as a whole is the markedly higher proportion of printers among the former, a difference which exists in all periods of their history. This might be expected in any movement in which the press played such a dominant role.

But even taking into account the predominance of these occupations in the leadership panel, it cannot be justifiably concluded that the leaders had a higher socioeconomic position than their followers. It is difficult to determine whether leadership in the Workingmen's movement was a function of occupation—that is, whether these particular occupations were more sensitive to the social, economic, and political stresses of the times—or whether it was more fortuitous, dependent primarily upon individual personality.

As the preceding analysis demonstrates, the occupational approach is not sufficiently precise to permit the making of any well-defined class differentiation. The *Directory* contains no distinction, explicit or implicit, between master and journeyman, shop owner and wageworker. Of the 122 occupations listed in Table I, slightly more than half can be considered arts or crafts requiring varying degrees of skill, while the remainder are divided among the professions, retail trade and white-collar occupations. Since objective data are lacking on the relative socioeconomic positions of the occupations of the time, generalizations on this subject must be limited to the rather indefinite occupational categories used here, although tentative conclusions regarding social stratification can be drawn. With this in mind in analyzing these statistics, we see that the last period of this study, 1835 to 1837, included the highest percentage of professional and clerical occupations, retail tradesmen and merchants, while the two earlier periods showed a predominance of artisans and skilled craftsmen. From this we may conclude that the Locofocos appear to have had a somewhat higher socioeconomic position than the earlier Workingmen.

This must be qualified, however, by the realization that the Locofocos in our panel, upon whose occupations this conclusion is based, were not selected as a representative sample. Furthermore, the Workingmen of the 1829–30 period represent nearly three-fourths of the total number in the panel, so that a comparison of this group with the Locofocos may not be entirely fair. Not only is this the largest group numerically, it is the most complex in that it includes three warring factions, each bearing the Workingmen's Party label. For this reason, generalizations about the earliest period of our study should be predicated upon an occupational analysis of these factions. Table VIII contains a comparison of the faction led by Noah Cook, the coterie supporting Thomas Skidmore, and the *Sentinel* party, whose most vocal spokesman was George Henry Evans.

Here, again, no distinction among these factions can be made on the basis of occupational categories which would substantiate the invective of the period. The distribution of the three factions among the various categories neither proves nor disproves that the Cook faction was more "aristocratic" than the Evans faction, nor that the Skidmore group was truly a "Poor Men's Party." As Table VIII indicates, the panel used for the 1829–30 period includes a

TABLE VIII

FACTIONS OF WORKINGMEN'S PARTY, 1829–1830, BY
OCCUPATIONAL CATEGORIES

Occupational Categories	Evans		Cook		Skidmore		Total 1829–30	
	No.	Pct.	No.	Pct.	No.	Pct.	No.	Pct.
Building trades	49	17	17	24	—	—	103	20
Food and beverages	46	16	17	24	7	19	83	16
House furnishings	37	13	6	8	3	8	63	12
Metal trades	27	9	9	13	8	22	60	12
Leather, shoemaking	27	9	3	4	4	11	37	7
Professional, clerical	17	6	4	6	—	—	25	5
Clothing and dry goods	23	8	4	6	1	3	34	7
Manufacturers, artisans	25	9	2	3	2	6	31	6
Printing, publishing	10	3	1	1	4	11	17	3
Marine trades	9	3	5	7	3	8	23	5
Merchants and tradesmen	10	3	1	1	1	3	17	3
Transportation	11	4	2	3	2	6	18	4
Public employees	2	—	—	—	—	—	2	—
Miscellaneous	—	—	—	—	1	3	2	—
Total, identified	293	100	71	100	36	100	515	100

preponderance of the Evans faction. But we must not conclude from this situation that the Cook faction was in the indicated minority. The newspaper sources available, largely reflecting the *Sentinel* party viewpoint, were understandably incomplete as well as prejudiced in detailing the activities of the opposing factions, resulting in a panel heavily weighted in favor of the Evans faction. The Workingmen of the first period were therefore essentially the *Sentinel* party, although it must be realized that the relatively high percentage of Cook men in the building trades and Skidmore and Cook men in the metal trades modifies the pattern in these two categories.

The occupations of the Workingmen throughout the entire period of this study approximate an occupational cross-section of the general population of New York City during the 'thirties. This is evident from a comparison in Tables IX and X of the occupations of the Workingmen with the occupations listed in the *Directory* in 1833, the mid-point of the period under discussion. Several quali-

TABLE IX
IDENTIFIED WORKINGMEN IN THE TEN LEADING OCCUPATIONS
OF NEW YORK CITY

Occupation	Directory, 1833		Workingmen, 1829–37	
	No.	Pct. of Total	No.	Pct. of Total
Merchant	2,255	12.8	10	1.4
Grocer	2,106	11.9	75	10.7
Cartman	1,591	8.9	16	2.3
Carpenter	1,392	7.9	56	8.0
Shoemaker	1,113	6.3	46	6.6
Tailor	964	5.5	20	2.9
Mason	577	3.3	15	2.1
Attorney	573	3.2	13	1.9
Boardinghouse keeper ..	503	2.9	3	0.4
Physician	499	2.8	24	3.4
Total	11,573	65.5	278	39.7

fications must be made regarding these figures. It is obvious at a glance that the compilation from the *Directory* is incomplete and somewhat inaccurate. In the first place, this summary of occupations was taken from Longworth by a contemporary publication,[1]

TABLE X
PRINCIPAL OCCUPATIONS OF IDENTIFIED WORKINGMEN AND
LEADERS IN RELATION TO THE GENERAL POPULATION

Occupation	Directory Pct. of Total	Workingmen Pct. of Total	Leaders Pct. of Total
Grocer	11.9	10.7	8.0
Carpenter	7.9	8.0	8.0
Shoemaker	6.3	6.6	4.0
Painter	—	4.0	4.0
Cabinetmaker	0.9	3.9	4.0
Physician	2.8	3.4	6.0
Tailor	5.5	2.9	4.0
Printer	2.1	2.6	8.0
Cartman	8.9	2.3	—
Mason	3.3	2.1	—
Chairmaker	—	2.1	4.0
Carver and gilder..	0.4	1.9	—
Attorney	3.2	1.9	2.0
Total	53.2	52.3	52.0

and no effort has been made to check the totals against the names appearing in the *Directory*. Moreover, we may safely assume that painters and chairmakers, for example, lived in New York in 1833, even though these occupations were not listed in the compilation. The incompleteness of this volume is even more apparent when the total number of New Yorkers included is compared with the population of the city according to the 1835 State Census. The total population was 270,089, of which 43,091 were males eligible to vote.[2] The total listed by occupation in the *Directory* was 17,683, plus 2,963 widows. Only about 41 percent, therefore, of the males eligible to vote in the city were listed by Longworth.*

The comparison is useful, despite these flaws. The ten leading occupations as shown in Table IX included nearly two-thirds of the men listed in the *Directory*, with almost half of them in the first five. It is noteworthy that only two of these occupations—merchant and boardinghouse keeper—are not included among the principal occupations of the Workingmen as listed in Table X. Though less than half, the 40 percent of the Workingmen found in these ten occupations is significant, particularly since this group represented only 2 percent of the males eligible to vote in the city, or 4 percent of those listed in the *Directory*. As shown in Table X, the percentage of grocers, carpenters, shoemakers, physicians, and printers in the Workingmen's movement is remarkably similar to the employable population as listed by Longworth; the proportion of tailors, cartmen, and attorneys is much larger in the *Directory*, however, and presumably in the population as a whole. The fact that merchants comprise the largest occupational category in this compilation, and that such occupations as attorney, teacher, broker, and minister are found in a greater proportion than in the panel of Workingmen, would seem to place the latter as a group somewhat below the middle of the social scale. Yet, while the movement included a relatively high percentage of painters, carvers and gilders, cabinetmakers, and

---

* This explains many of the unidentified Workingmen. On several occasions during this study, moreover, a man could not be found listed in the *Directory* for several years, even though it was known from other sources that he was in the city during the entire period; also, a change in a man's occupation might not be shown in the *Directory* until two or three years had passed.

chairmakers, the number of tailors, cartmen, and masons—certainly no higher in the objective social scale—was comparatively smaller. Furthermore, such high-status occupations as physician and printer were found in a disproportionately prominent position among the leaders of the movement.

In spite of internal contradictions, the net result of this comparison is essentially to reaffirm the characterization of the movement as a microscosmic cross-section of New York City society. Reinforcing this hypothesis is the fact that virtually identical percentages of these groups were found in the thirteen principal occupations of the Workingmen. Even though the mercantile and menial pursuits at either end of the social scale were subordinated, the Workingmen's movement on the basis of this evidence was impressively democratic, representing and expressing the aspirations of significant segments of the multifarious occupational groups which formed the "producing classes" of Jacksonian New York.

The Program

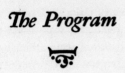

The Reformist Impulse

THE WORKINGMEN, incessantly urging that reform proceed further and faster, represented the radical fringe in New York City politics during the evolution of Jacksonian Democracy. Yet it is obvious that this movement must not be epitomized as the anti-capitalist striving of a submerged proletariat, nor can it be satisfactorily explained by the epithet "middle class." The source and nature of this radicalism, as demonstrated by the foregoing biographical and occupational analysis, is more complex, and can be further elucidated only with reference to the party platform. Varied and often visionary as were the Workingmen's demands throughout this period, they represented for the most part real grievances and offered concrete solutions. An analysis of this program, showing its relationship to the composition of the movement, provides a key to its socioeconomic orientation.

Because of the influence of Skidmore and Owen, the Workingmen's Party at its inception was tarred with the brush of "agrarianism" and "infidelity." The extent to which either panacea mirrored the desires of the party rank and file is impossible to assess, but it is probable that neither an equal division of property nor "National Rational Education" was primarily responsible for the support which the party received. Skidmore's scheme was based on the assumption that the "hereditary transmission of wealth," especially land, was "the prime source of all our calamities"; his speeches and writings outlined an elaborate plan to divide all property equally "among the adults of the present generation: and to provide for its equal transmission to every individual of each succeeding generation, on arriving at the age of maturity."[1] It is difficult to understand how he was able to dominate the Committee of Fifty and the early deliberations of the party, persuading them to adopt his scheme as a basic tenet of the movement; the most likely explanation is that an ideological vacuum existed, and Skidmore had a doctrine ready to fill it. The Workingmen lost little time after the election in ridding themselves of this incubus which, besides being impractical and too radical, ran counter to their hopes and aspirations. As the General Executive Committee of the party declared a few months later, "we expect the reward of our toil, and consider the right to individual property, the strongest incentive to industry."[2]

The demand for education, which rivaled and soon supplanted Skidmore's scheme as the principal plank of the party platform, was more fully in accord with the aspirations of the Workingmen. Through the medium of Miss Wright's lectures and Owen's articles in the *Free Enquirer,* education for all at public expense was urged as the basis of democratic prosperity, for "the most injurious species of inequality, is that produced by unequal education."[3] Of the approximately 52,300 children in New York City between the ages of five and fifteen, nearly half, or 24,200, attended no school.[4] This was the estimate of the Public School Society, a private institution founded in 1805, which administered all public schools in the city, its financial support coming partly from city and state appropriations but principally from private philanthropy.[5]

The existing educational system was deemed inadequate because schools were either private institutions with high tuition fees—which few could afford—or public schools based on charity—which were considered to be "degraded in the eyes of parents who know, that their wealthier neighbors would consider such an education as degrading to their children." Furthermore, schools were denounced for clerical influence, the Public School Society being characterized as "a secret engine of bigotry and aristocracy." Some criticized the subject matter and the teaching in the common schools, advocating manual labor schools to teach a trade instead of a "smattering of English, Latin, and Greek, an abridgement of geography and history, . . . [and] Arithmetic as far as the 'Rule of Three.'" Generally, however, the Workingmen's educational demands went beyond trade schools, which many feared would perpetuate their subordination to the educated "aristocracy," their program of "Equal Universal Education" being regarded as "the great lever by which the

Working Men are to be raised to their proper elevation in this republic."[6]

While little effort was made to agree on a proposed curriculum, their ideal was described as "a useful, solid, scientific, practical education, which will expand and strengthen the mind, and make our children enlightened and valuable members of the republic, who will know their rights and be able to defend them by the force of sound reason and argument."[7] The program, as elaborated by Wright and Owen in speeches and articles, would provide education "in every branch of knowledge, intellectual and operative," for all children between the ages of two and sixteen in boarding schools under "state guardianship"; parents would be permitted to "visit the children at suitable hours but in no case interfere with or interrupt the rules of the institution." Fanny Wright's ideal was the "educational equality" of ancient Sparta as exemplified by the Fellenberg schools in Europe, and she painted a picture of the "nurseries of a free nation" in glowing terms: "Fed at a common board; clothed in a common garb; . . . raised in the exercise of common duties, in the acquirement of the same knowledge and practice of the same industry, varied only according to individual taste and capabilities . . .— say! would not such a race, when arrived at manhood and womanhood, work out the reform of society, perfect the free institutions of America?"[8] A resolution of the Workingmen's General Executive Committee, declaring that "that education which is good enough for the rich, we consider not too good for the poor," reaffirmed this faith in the power of education: "We believe that you have but to satisfy the human mind, that virtue and happiness, vice and misery, are but cause and effect, and crime will cease. This can be done . . . by a proper training of the intellect, from infancy to manhood."[9]

The emphasis on state guardianship—and the avowed anticlerical and skeptical views of its principal advocates—led to factionalism and schism in the Workingmen's Party. Even after the debacle of 1830 the Evans group refused to modify its position, the *Working Man's Advocate* continuing through 1831 to fly the banner of Equal Universal Education from its masthead. As late as May 1834, Evans was demanding a "system of equal republican education," although money and banking received most of his attention; when admonished by a reader a few months later for neglecting this important subject, he replied: "We have made up our minds to believe that Universal Education is not to be obtained till another great reform is accomplished. . . . We must . . . elect men to office who will abolish monopolies, and by thus getting rid of the aristocracy they engender, remove the only obstacle to Universal Education."[10] The Locofocos virtually ignored the subject, except for the inclusion in their 1836 platform of a demand for a "more extended, equal and convenient system of public school instruction."[11]

By this time the center of gravity of the common school movement was shifting, as conservative educators and intellectuals began to urge universal education as a means of social control. Evans was conscious of the trend as early as 1831, when a public meeting sponsored by Lewis Tappan, the antislavery merchant and Presbyterian reformer, was called to salute the Oneida Institute. This school, although conducted on Fellenberg principles, had a pietistic atmosphere, its aim being the training of future missionaries. Evans commented ironically that the plan which "not a year ago . . . was denounced as 'the wildest dream that ever entered the brain of a visionary fanatic' " was now "openly advocated by reverend gentlemen."[12] As economic and social conflicts deepened after 1834, the campaign of the professional educators became intensified, culminating in the Common School Revival of 1837. A student of this movement concluded that the Workingmen's demand for education, although unsuccessful, was significant as a stimulus, for it "helped set in motion the ideas and acts of the educated and the wealthy which . . . were decisive for educational progress." Moreover, when common school legislation was finally passed, there was "far less clamor for it on the Left than before," which led him to question whether the "surface froth" of 1829–30 "indicated real stirring down below."[13] Education, though termed by the Workingmen "the pole star to which our efforts point,"[14] could hardly have been the sole motive force behind the movement, for the party platform even in the early months of its history listed many other grievances.

The spirit of anticlericalism charged to their educational program was apparent elsewhere in their creed, for the Workingmen attacked the tax exemption of church property as evidence of a union of Church and State.[15] This battle cry had earlier been raised by the Democrats on another issue, the attempt of Sabbatarians to prohibit the transportation of the mail on Sundays. The prospect of a "Christian party in politics" was denounced in Tammany meetings throughout 1829, and Richard M. Johnson's Congressional report denying the petitions of the orthodox was hailed as a masterly defense of the rights of conscience.[16] The Owenites used this issue as a springboard for attacks upon the Tract Society, the Sunday school movement, and other efflorescences of organized religion, later supporting Herttell's agitation against a religious test for jurors and pay for legislative chaplains.[17]

But, except for a few intellectual leaders and their coterie in the movement, the Workingmen do not appear to have been fundamentally committed to anticlericalism or skepticism. The original attack on church property was soon toned down to an ambiguous demand for "equal taxation on property" and even in this form was seldom included in the catalogue of Workingmen's measures. Early in 1834, when the Workingmen's Associations were reorganized in opposition to banks and paper money, the tax exemption question was revived along with education as an additional weapon in the arsenal of the movement.[18] It was quickly dropped, however, and was ignored by the Locofocos until their state convention in 1837 which proposed a new state constitution, providing among other prohibitions that "no exemption laws shall be passed or remain in force, exempting any person, class, order, kind, or description of persons or property, from any public duty, tax, or burden, to which the rest of the community is subject."[19]

The opposition press nevertheless continued to hurl the epithet of "infidelity" at the Workingmen, as well as at the Democrats on occasion, finding it a convenient issue at election time. While liberal religious views were more often held by the Jacksonians than by their opponents, the eighteenth-century deism of Jefferson and Paine was going out of style, evangelical Methodism being more typical of the religious climate of the 'thirties. Moreover, the economic issues which came to the fore with the Bank War could not easily be related to the First Amendment, as Colonel Johnson discovered to his sorrow, although Evans and a few others continued to see an alliance between the aristocrats of wealth and the oligarchs of organized religion.[20] To most Jacksonians, however, there was no inherent contradiction between democracy and religion; in fact, a marked similarity could often be found in a Tammany meeting and a Methodist "Love Feast."*

Another reform advocated by the Workingmen was abolition of imprisonment for debt. This anachronistic remnant of colonial law was first attacked in New York more than a decade earlier, when debtors were suffering from the effects of postwar inflation, and the result was the law of 1817 abolishing imprisonment for debtors owing less than twenty-five dollars. Four years later Kentucky, under the leadership of Richard M. Johnson,† became the first state to abolish all debtor imprisonment.[21] The movement for total abolition did not really get under way in New York until 1830, the Workingmen failing to list it as one of their grievances at the time of the 1829 election. It is difficult to discover how many debtors were actually imprisoned in the city at that time, most of them apparently being merely restricted to "gaol limits," a section of one thousand acres in the lower wards of the city;‡ as one student of the subject concludes, "imprisonment" for debt was largely a misnomer, "arrest" for debt being more correct.[22]

The Workingmen at first demanded only that the gaol limits be

---

* For an interesting instance see Richard A. E. Brooks, ed., *Diary of Michael Floy, Jr., Bowery Village 1833–1837* (New Haven, 1941), pp. 13, 76–77, 116–17, and *passim.* Young Floy was a devout Methodist and an abolitionist who voted the straight Tammany ticket in 1833 and 1834, and saluted "the *people's* triumph." "I am a Democrat," he wrote, "and they might as well try to make a new man out and out of my body, soul, and all as ever to beat any Aristocracy into me." By 1835 and 1836 he had apparently lost interest in politics, for he makes no reference to the Locofocos.

† Beginning in 1822 Johnson undertook a campaign in the United States Senate in favor of this reform; nominally, he proposed only the abolition of imprisonment for complaints of debt in federal courts, but his agitation had great propaganda value for the movement on the state level.

‡ Some debtors were actually in jail, however, for dinners were occasionally sent to imprisoned debtors by various organizations, even as late as 1835 when total abolition was supposedly an accomplished fact.

enlarged to include the whole county, since most of those affected
by the law lived and worked in the upper wards. Later a memorial
was sent to Albany calling for complete abolition which, it was
emphasized, would bring "increased business stability," would
"introduce wholesome vigor and caution in all business transactions," and would "mitigate and restrain those pernicious excite-
ments to speculation."[23] Agitation by both factions of the party
increased throughout the ensuing year. The efforts of the Workingmen were strengthened by a number of nonpartisan meetings of
influential men, and the Antimasonic Party soon joined in the
demand.[24] The result was that early in 1831 the legislature passed
an abolition bill, applying to all but fraudulent debtors, which was
hailed by Evans as a harbinger of further victories.[25]

Within two years a determined but unsuccessful effort was made
to repeal this law. Merchants unable to collect debts, charging that
too many debtors were taking fraudulent benefit of the law, were
in the van, supported by lawyers "interested in the emoluments
arising from litigation for small debts." Evans charged them with
an "attempt to confuse fraud with misfortune," adding pointedly:
"Their remedy is plain—let them refuse to give *credit*. They have
no right to apply for legislative aid to correct the evils of their own
mismanagement." He declared further that repeal of the law would
bring a demand to "abolish ALL *laws for the collection of debts*,"
which in effect would "almost entirely . . . abolish the *credit system*."[26] His prophecy was realized four years later when the Locofocos, meeting to protest against high prices, resolved that "in order
to put an end to the banking system, and the whole power of false
capital, we so alter our laws as to render all debts hereafter contracted, simply debts of honor, and thus give the advantages of
credit to honest industry, instead of allowing those advantages to
be monopolized by those best skilled in grinding the poor." This
principle was reiterated on other occasions, the party demanding a
new state constitution which would "perpetually prohibit the law
from ever interfering in any shape with any contract of debt, either
to enforce or to annul it."[27]

The movement to eliminate imprisonment for debt was obviously not limited to wage earners, for the master mechanic and the small retail tradesman doubtless suffered as much from the law; these entrepreneurs, in fact, had more occasion than the journeyman to face the perils of the credit system. "Given the exigencies of business," Dorfman concludes, "it was . . . the concern of the little businessman, and not infrequently the larger businessman, to ease this evil." A student of the parallel movement in Pennsylvania maintains that "the ideology of business came to the support of the ideology of democracy to condemn debtor imprisonment." The success of the movement can be attributed, not only to "the emergence to political consciousness and power of debtor groups relatively inarticulate during the earlier era," but to the fact that "the colonial attitude toward the debtor-creditor relationship could not survive the increasingly complex, uncertain, and depersonalized financial life of the nineteenth century."[28]

A further demand of the Workingmen was abolition or reform of the militia system. By law all citizens as members of the reserve militia had to turn out "armed and equipped" at least once a year for "military exercise" and a parade. Customarily, they were called out for a three-day period every fall, "at the most active time of the year, when every mechanic is in full employ." The only alternative to losing three days' pay or closing one's business for that period was to pay a fine of twelve dollars, a recourse often practiced by the well-to-do members of the community. It was generally agreed that as military training the "exercise" was a joke, and it was termed "baby play for baby men."[29]

Beginning late in 1829, the Workingmen continually attacked this system as unjust and unequal and demanded its abolition or amelioration.[30] Attempts to ridicule the law by appearing "dressed in motley" with "a loaf of bread for a cartridge box, a stock-fish for a sword, a cornstalk for a musket" were answered by courts-martial which meted out heavy fines or imprisonment.[31] The Workingmen were not alone in opposing the system, the Antimasons and many adherents of the two major parties joining in the attack. A nonpartisan meeting in 1831 memorialized the legislature to substitute for the three-day assembly a single muster annually throughout the state for inspection of arms—for "the right to bear arms must be kept"—and called for the abandonment of parades. Evans went further, insisting: "To make our militia system completely republican, the necessary arms and equipment for all the Militia should be furnished by the government, which should also pay every citizen for the time he might be on duty, according, as nearly as could be, to the average price of labor." He added that "on the present plan, the poor man is taxed as much as the rich for the expense of equipments," and "the man who owns no property contributes as much labor for the protection of property as the man who possesses a large accumulation."[32] Despite resolute attempts in the legislature to abolish or reform the system both in 1830 and 1831, it remained essentially intact until 1846, when the law was amended to prescribe only a nominal fee of fifty cents for absence. This in effect abolished the annual assembly, although in spite of its demonstrated inefficiency in military training the militia system survived until 1870 on the statute books.[33]

Similar in motivation to their attack on the militia system was the Workingmen's demand for compensation of jurors and witnesses.[34] This was never a major tenet of the party, although symptomatic of their more fundamental belief in the need for thoroughgoing political and legal reform. This demand stemmed in part from their disillusionment with the constitution of 1821. Although this momentous document, supplemented by an amendment four years later, removed all property restrictions on the suffrage and made most offices elective,* professional politicians still for the most part controlled the electoral machinery. This was demonstrated not only in local and state elections, in which "King Caucus" still ruled through a slate of candidates presented for *viva voce* nomination, but in elections for federal office as well. Both the Workingmen's Party and the Locofocos advocated the direct election of President

---

* The constitution made the paying of taxes, work on the public roads, or militia service a requisite for voting, but the 1825 amendment eliminated all requirements except age, sex, and residence; a property requirement was, however, retained for Negroes.

and Vice-President, the latter group demanding in addition that these officers be limited to one term.[35]

State and local politics, being more immediate, received their greatest attention and called forth their loudest cries for reform. The Workingmen's advocacy of direct election of the Mayor received support from other groups in 1831, the movement achieving success two years later.[36] Following New York's first experience with the new law in the bitter and violent election of 1834, Evans admitted that "something is necessary to prevent the delay, immorality, and confusion attendant on the present mode of voting in this city." The solution of the Whigs in the newly elected Common Council was compulsory registration of voters, but the Workingmen joined Tammany in denouncing this device as an unconstitutional curtailment of the right of suffrage. Evans objected that not only would it "cause a loss of time, which loss would be more burdensome to the poor than the rich, and would consequently deprive many poor men of their votes," but it would also be ineffective in eliminating illegal voting. "A man *disposed* to vote illegally," he argued, "would stand much less chance of detection, when registering his name, with few eyes upon him, than when liable to be cross questioned, surrounded by persons interested in detecting him, at the polls." Six years later, when the Whigs revived the registration plan, former Workingmen took a leading part in Tammany meetings called to denounce this "odious and unconstitutional law" for the "disfranchisement of hundreds of our most useful citizens."[37]

Although often finding allies in Tammany Hall in their attacks on the "aristocracy," the Workingmen more frequently denounced "the misrule of the dominant party in this state, and especially in this city." They especially cited the "general ticket" system of nominations as the principal means by which the "dominant corrupt party" maintained its power, and regarded the party convention as no more democratic than the caucus which it had supplanted. Demanding the establishment of election districts smaller than the senatorial district or the county, the Workingmen emphasized that this had worked well in the election of the Common Council; the nomination and election of Aldermen and Assistants by wards allowed "*all interests* to be represented" and resulted in a governing body seldom dominated by one party. In support of this proposal, Evans attacked the existing system for "the facility which it affords for combinations and parties to take the power of nominating candidates out of the hands of the people, and to confer it upon 'committees' and 'conventions' for their own special advantage." Furthermore, he declared, the nomination of candidates is left to "idlers, office holders, and office seekers; for the industrious citizen cannot afford to be absent from his business for a week to attend conventions."[38]

One of the principal reasons given in 1829 for organizing the Workingmen's Party was to elect representatives of "the industrious classes" to office. Yet it was apparent that this was impracticable in the case of offices, like the Common Council, for which no compensation was given. This situation led the Workingmen to advocate that Aldermen and Assistants be paid for their services, pointing out that under the system of gratuitous service "none but large property holders can be elected, . . . for poor men cannot afford to spend their time without receiving an equivalent for their labor." This reform, Evans believed, would also tend to decrease extravagance and corruption. Others, such as the *American,* an anti-Tammany paper, remarked on the "eager competition for places to which no compensation is attached," concluding: "Such places do afford, either by the patronage which results from them, or the opportunities of private jobs, abundant equivalents for the demands upon the time and ordinary avocations of those who occupy them."[39] But Evans disagreed with those who suggested increasing salaries in order to improve the quality of elected officials, declaring that "if *salaries* were not too high, office seekers would be less numerous." Such salaries, he asserted,

> should neither be so high as to make them an inducement for those engaged in useful occupations to *seek* for office, nor so low as not to compensate officials for their time as well as the majority of useful occupations compensate those who follow them. And one *qualification* for public officers of every description should be that they had been brought up to a *useful occu-*

pation, to which they might at any time return if the will of the people should require it.[40]

It was realized, however, that because of strict party control of nominations "the working people" generally choose for legislators men who "have not a single feeling in common with their constituents." To some extent, according to Evans, this could be ascribed to an inordinate respect for formal education, and he reminded his readers that "men who maintain our cause are entitled to our unqualified support at the polls, even though they should not be so well read, as those who *never work.*" The Workingmen expressed a special animosity toward lawyers, from whose ranks both major parties drew a high proportion of their candidates. Although a few men of this profession were enlisted in the movement, attorneys were generally denounced as lackeys of the aristocracy and "unceasing promoter[s] of strife" who were "educated, . . . if not in habits of idleness, at least in the habit of looking with contempt . . . upon all sorts of manual labor." As "A Working Man" argued: "The lawyers want office, power, patronage, sinecures, pensions. . . . To obtain distinction and emoluments of this sort, they very naturally unite with men of wealth, and give them banks, monopolies, etc., and with priests and other literary men, to endow colleges and universities for the benefit of a class of men separate and distinct from the working men."[41]

A more fundamental criticism of the legal system was the attack on the "unintelligible and unmeaning jargon" of the courts and the unnecessarily complicated laws "introduced, interpreted, and put into execution" by men "who have assumed an authority which the people never gave them." The Workingmen's Party went no further than to call for a simpler law code and a less expensive legal system, but the Locofocos, partly in reaction to the labor conspiracy cases, demanded the election of judges for a limited term and an end to "judicial legislation" or reliance on precedents. Their 1836 state convention in its Address to the People declared that "the practices of our courts of law are as aristocratic, arbitrary and oppressive as they were in the dark ages of feudalism," and reiterated the leading principle of the Equal Rights Party: "In a Republic but few laws are necessary, and those few plain, simple, and easy of comprehension." The proposed new state constitution drawn up at the 1837 convention, in addition to prohibiting capital punishment for any crime, provided that all judges be elected and that "no court of law or justice shall hereafter practice judicial legislation, by adopting or admitting the laws, precedents, decisions, or legal authorities of other nations or states into the jurisprudence or courts of this state. When our own laws provide no special act or provision for a case, the jury shall determine according to the principles of natural right and justice."[42] This attitude toward the role of law in society was a reaffirmation of the view generally held by the early Workingmen, as expressed by Evans six years before, that "law, like medicine, if a necessary evil, is an evil still . . . to be dispensed with whenever it safely can be."[43]

The Workingmen were not completely consistent in their adherence to this laissez-faire philosophy, for there were some areas in which they urged positive state action. One of these, as has been shown, was education, and another was the demand for a mechanics' lien law. This was an important part of their program from the beginning, both Skidmore and Owen revealing its popularity by including it among their demands.[44] In fact, the election of a carpenter on the Workingmen's ticket in 1829 and the high proportion of men in the building trades during the early period of the movement, as revealed in the preceding occupational analysis, can undoubtedly be attributed to the Workingmen's stand on this issue.

As early as 1823 mechanics in the building trades had asked for a law giving a lien on the building to all those employed in erecting it. Maryland had passed a limited law in 1791 to encourage building in the new federal capital, and in 1803 Pennsylvania enacted a provision, applying only to Philadelphia, subjecting buildings to the payment of debts contracted by the owner for any work done or materials furnished in their erection.[45] In New York the increase in building construction that characterized the period following the depression of 1819–22 brought with it many abuses. Instances were cited of foremen or overseers pocketing a part of the wages due their workmen and, at the other end of the scale, of contractors and builders suffering from a building owner's insolvency in the course of construction. Some of the most flagrant abuses were charged to building contractors. A letter from "A Builder who is a friend to the poor working man" described the situation:

> In many instances persons of notorious character, calling themselves builders, take contracts at from 10 to 15 per cent below what any honest man could undertake to fulfill them for, they employ workmen, and under various pretences . . . they pay the poor workman off on Saturday night with one or 2 dollars, and a promise to pay the balance *next* week (a week that never comes). . . . When the contractor has paid about 25 per cent, the remainder he pockets; the workmen are cheated out of their wages, and those who have furnished materials, fare no better— while the contractor . . . takes the benefit of the insolvent act yearly, or at least once in 2 or 3 years, consequently it is impossible to collect money from him. . . .[46]

The results of the 1829 election convinced Tammany politicians that "the mechanics have a justified grievance," and efforts were made to pass a lien law in order to win back their allegiance to the Democracy. But the *Courier and Enquirer,* "organ" of the Tammany Society, cautioned that the law must not only protect the mechanic but "preserve the capitalist" who invests in houses. "Nine tenths of all the houses put up," it was pointed out, "are contracted for by mechanics of small means, who receive advances as the work progresses. They are willing to work for a small profit, and the competition thus created, forces the wealthy builder to conform to their prices, thereby inducing the capitalist to invest his money . . . [and] giving employment to the mechanics and labourers of the city." Moreover, the law urged by the Workingmen, giving the journeyman as well as the contractor a lien on the building "for the price of his labor," would, it was feared, allow "a few master builders of large property" to monopolize the business, for they alone could give sufficient security for the payment of their workmen. The law favored by this journal, therefore, would provide that "master builders only shall have a lien on buildings." The *Working Man's Advocate* replied that such a law not only would virtually guarantee a monopoly but "would be highly injurious to the capitalist, the poor builder, and all journeymen and laborers, and only benefit the *rich* builder." Both the contractor and the journeyman should be protected, but Evans saw no necessity for extending a lien to materials furnished, for unlike the laborer "the owner has the power of retaining his material till paid for."[47]

The law passed by the legislature on April 20, 1830, although it did not in fact impose any lien upon real property, established a procedure by which "every mechanic, workman or other person" engaged in the building trades in New York City, whether as "journeyman, laborer, cartman, sub-contractor, or otherwise," could stop payments due from the owner to the general contractor until his account was satisfied.[48] The Workingmen as a party henceforth ceased their agitation on this subject, a large number of them undoubtedly returning to Tammany Hall on the strength of this legislative concession, but Evans continued through 1831 to carry on his masthead a demand for "an effective lien law."[49] In 1832 the act was amended to give the same protection to material men, being broadened in addition to apply to "verbal or parol contracts or agreements" as well as written contracts. By the acts of 1844 and 1851 contractors and workmen were enabled to obtain an actual lien on the building by recourse to the Court of Common Pleas, but it was not until 1885 that a statewide lien law was passed.[50]

The Workingmen's movement for mechanics' liens was anomalous in view of their often reiterated principle that "the only legitimate objects of legislation are the defence of the lives, liberties, and *equal individual* rights of the governed."[51] It revealed a dualism in their position on the debtor-creditor relationship, which combined the advocacy of strict legal enforcement of contract obligations in connection with lien laws with a struggle to loosen the legal sanctions in regard to debtor imprisonment; in the first instance, of course, they were speaking as creditors and in the second as present or possibly future debtors.[52] Furthermore, support of this demand was not unanimous, some Workingmen urging caution in embracing self-styled "friends" who would willingly sacrifice National Education and other "true" principles of the party to obtain "one of the party trifles which aristocracy would readily give to purchase the continued submission of the working classes, to the present system of oppression and unwise legislation."[53]

Although this plank was instrumental in bringing party victory in 1829 by enlisting the adherence of the building trades and material men, this warning seemed to be justified during the following year when it was seen that the Cook faction, containing a large representation from the building trades, was calling a halt to further reform.* As demonstrated by this cleavage, support of mechanics' liens came not alone from journeymen, although they were an influential segment of the movement; one student of the subject emphasizes that the law "was introduced, not so much for the benefit of the 'proletarian' as for representatives of the great middle class."[54]

Here, as in their other reformist demands, the Workingmen represented an amalgam of skilled mechanics and small businessmen struggling to improve their lot by removing or mitigating social, economic, and political disabilities. While the agitation for enactment of a lien law, like their attack on specific monopolies, was directly related to the interests and aspirations of a particular occupational element in the movement, the other issues discussed here had a more general appeal. The emphasis upon free public education, abolition of imprisonment for debt, and legal and electoral reform was part of the humanitarian impulse of the times, expressed in equally uncompromising terms by "aristocratic" reformers intellectually descended from the Enlightenment. But for the Workingmen these demands were both based on principle and rooted in experience. Few of them had been able to acquire more than a rudimentary education, and all had been subject to the nuisance of a militia muster; furthermore, though refusing to be cautious or conservative about the future, most of them were intimately acquainted with the dangers of debt. Probably most important was their experience with the legal and political machinery of the Republic, their disillusionment leading them to view it as a denial of justice and democracy. The Workingmen reflected the hopes and fears, as well as the discouragement, of the first

* See Tables I and VIII in Chapter 6, above.

generation of enfranchised commoners. Yet they endeavored to exercise this power, not only to gain an effective voice in their own government, but to use political means to break down the barriers standing in the way of their social and economic betterment. That they largely succeeded in these reformist objectives, and in a relatively short time, demonstrates the broad base of the movement and indicates the respect that the evidence of this power engendered in the major political parties.

The War Against Monopoly

"The world is governed too much" was the slogan of the Washington *Globe,* principal spokesman of the Jackson administration. This became the rallying cry of Jacksonians, North and South, and especially of those party radicals, like the Locofocos, who scolded their more conservative fellow Democrats for departing from the guiding principles of Jefferson and Jackson. Meanwhile, they saluted the President for his forthright statement in the famous 1832 veto message: "There are no necessary evils in government. Its evils exist only in its abuses. If it would confine itself to equal protection, and, as Heaven does its rains, shower its favors alike on the high and the low, the rich and the poor, it would be an unqualified blessing."[1] George Henry Evans, more than a year before this, had denounced "government intermeddlings" for invading the rights of citizens, declaring that "when government has effectually protected the lives and properties of the citizen from violence, it has done *almost* all that government can advantageously do."[2] William Leggett, restricting the "true functions of government" to "the making of *general laws,* uniform and universal in their operation," maintained further that "governments have no right to interfere with the pursuits of individuals . . . by offering encouragements and granting privileges to any particular class of industry or any select bodies of men, inasmuch as all classes of industry and all men are equally important to the general welfare and equally entitled to protection."[3]

It was on this basis that the Workingmen attacked monopolies, although they seldom paused to define the object of their wrath, assuming that their adherents would easily recognize the enemy in its manifold guises. But early in 1835 the Democratic-Republican Young Men of the Fifteenth Ward, meeting to organize for the coming contest, found it expedient to define the term. Monopolies, they asserted, are "all exclusive privileges, or powers, or facilities, for the accumulation of wealth, or the exclusive use and enjoyment of the bounties of Providence secured to individuals or combinations of men by legislative enactments, the free and uninterrupted enjoyment of which are denied by laws to other members of the same community." Later that same year Theodore Sedgwick, Jr., Leggett's intimate and a regular contributor to the *Evening Post,* wrote an influential pamphlet entitled *What Is a Monopoly?* in which he agreed essentially with the above definition, but stated it more concisely: "Every grant of exclusive privilege, strictly speaking, creates a monopoly; it carries on its face that the grantee has received facilities of making pecuniary or other gains from which the mass of his fellow citizens are excluded. This is the very substance of a monopoly."[4]

These definitions reveal no conception of an economic monopoly, developing from the interaction of production and the market situation. To the Jacksonians, the source of monopoly was to be found in the statutes, in legal privileges created and protected by legislative enactments; moreover, these monopolistic privileges, while generally found on the state level, could also originate in city ordinances and Congressional acts. For example, agitation for land reform was expressed, not as an indictment of landlords who had monopolized the soil, but by the demand that the law should be changed to give the potential settler free access to the public lands. Although this was not a significant tenet of the Workingmen's platform, Evans was increasingly coming to believe that "the land monopoly" was more important than the monetary question, "because there is a surplus of mechanical laborers, and . . . the wages of mechanics must continue to be reduced unless that surplus can be employed upon the land.[5] During this period, of course, the banking system received the brunt of their attack, but the Workingmen singled out other "exclusive privileges" as well and called for their elimination. As in the case of the mechanics' lien law, each one of these demands appealed especially to one or more occupational groups whose "equal rights" were being infringed, although all could be included under the rubric of "abolition of chartered and licensed monopolies."

The auction system was one such target during the early history of the Workingmen's movement. Dating essentially from 1815, when the British chose New York as the main funnel for the "dumping" of their surplus manufactures, sales by auction had become the rule in the import trade, especially in textiles. In order to maintain New York's advantage over her rivals in this lucrative business, the legislature in 1817, at the instigation of auctioneers, passed a measure to reduce the scale of duties collected by the state and to enforce final sales of all goods put up for auction. Importing merchants following traditional business methods were unable to compete with the violent price fluctuations of the auction rooms, and were consequently deserted by New York jobbers and country merchants looking for bargains. Moreover, the right to sell at auction was a licensed monopoly restricted to a small group appointed by the Governor; although they usually numbered about fifty, the business was dominated by fewer than a dozen men.[6]

The system was strenuously attacked throughout the next decade, its opponents maintaining that auction sales "destroy everything like fair and honorable competition, and . . . originate the most scandalous frauds." Congress was memorialized to tax or otherwise mitigate the monopoly, and in 1828, after auction sales had reached a peak of twenty-four million dollars, nearly two-thirds of the total imports, the anti-auction movement entered politics.[7] A number of prominent merchants, demanding a national tax of 10 percent on auction sales and stricter regulation to eliminate fraud, met to denounce two of New York's Congressmen, Cambreleng and Verplanck, for refusing to take action to regulate the monopoly. It was acknowledged that merchants were most affected by the system, but an appeal was also directed to "mechanics" whose interests "are closely bound up with ours." Meetings of "mechanics and tradesmen" and merchants' clerks endorsed the movement, and a slate of Congressional candidates was nominated.[8] Although politically unsuccessful,* this group remained active during the following year, making an effort to induce Governor Van Buren to restrict auctions while continuing their agitation for realistic federal regulation.[9]

The Workingmen's Party had been organized in the meantime, and included among its demands the suppression of the auction monopoly, even Owen's Association passing resolutions against it. But the emphasis differed somewhat from the earlier movement, as shown by the resolution approved at the December 29 general meeting of the party:

> The present auction system . . . operates as a means of oppressing the producing classes, by introducing large quantities of the products of labor of foreign countries, which otherwise would be furnished by our own mechanics. . . . This system is . . . injurious to the mechanics' interest, . . . compelling them in many cases, to abandon their business or dishonestly manufacture very inferior goods for the competition of the auction room.[10]

Despite this official stand Evans was not entirely convinced by the argument, asserting that "the mechanics are in favor of a more effectual remedy for the present evils than a *restriction* to the auction system"; this he believed would merely "throw monopoly out of the hands of the auctioneers into those of the merchants." But he urged support of the movement "as far as they go," though warning the Workingmen to remember that "we wish no 'entangling alliances.'"[11]

An alliance of sorts was made, however, for a few men conspicuously associated with the 1828 movement became affiliated with the Workingmen; most prominent were Abijah Mathews, a furniture dealer who served on the General Executive Committee, and Joseph Curtis, a jeweler who was offered the party's nomination for the Assembly.[12] The *Sentinel* faction of the party generally

---

* Their only successful candidate was Campbell P. White, previously nominated by Tammany; he polled 18,000 votes as compared with the 11,000 received by their other nominees, David B. Ogden and Thomas C. Taylor.

ignored the issue, only once including "exclusive auctioneering" in their attacks on monopolies, and Evans failed to list the abolition of auctions among the "Workingmen's Measures" carried on the masthead of his paper.[13] The Cook faction was primarily identified with this reform, its resolutions linking the attack on auctions with a demand for "the protecting and fostering of our own industry." Many of them had supported Adams and the high tariffs of the American System in 1828, which explains their coalition with the Clay Republicans in the 1830 election; moreover, several were active in the American Institute, organized in 1828 to foster protection and encourage native manufacturers, and participated in meetings and conventions during 1831 and 1832 which opposed all efforts to reduce the tariff.[14]

But the tariff issue was of minor importance in New York City politics, largely dominated by a mercantile community and a belief in free trade; representatives of the metropolis in Congress voted against the 1832 tariff and the 1833 compromise act.[15] For this reason, the Workingmen seldom discussed the issue except to dismiss as specious the "pauper labor" argument advanced by proponents of protection. "We fear," wrote Evans, "that the cant phrase 'protection of American industry' blinds many *industrious Americans* to their true interests, and prevents them from ascertaining the cause which has occasioned the wages of *journeymen* to be reduced with every successive *increase of the tariff duties.*" They also tended increasingly to regard the tariff from the viewpoint of consumers rather than producers, the Locofocos holding it to be one cause of high prices and at one point advocating repeal of all customs duties on "the prime necessaries of life," especially foreign coal.[16]

One student of the anti-auction movement concludes that it was supported mainly by proponents of Clay's American System and anti-English merchants.[17] While this may be true of the 1828 movement, the basis of the Workingmen's attack on auctions was more complex. The issue was undoubtedly responsible for the adherence of a number of "merchants" and dry-goods dealers, as well as retailers of other commodities imported and sold at auction;

these included teas, silks, chinaware, hardware, groceries, drugs, wines, and liquors.[18] But here antagonism was directed as much against the violent price fluctuations and the speculative nature of the business as against the existence of a licensed monopoly. Furthermore, some mechanics whose products had to compete with imported merchandise, like hardware and furniture, doubtless were easily convinced that restriction of auctions was a desirable step in the direction of protecting their industry. While this would account for some of the occupations enlisted in the Workingmen's ranks, the existence of three auctioneers in the party of 1829–30 can only be explained by the fact that these men gained comparatively little profit from their appointment; hence they may have hoped to improve their situation from a reform of the system, which would mainly penalize their most successful competitors.[19] At any rate, the auction issue was of only brief importance in the development of the Workingmen's movement, though nonetheless significant in revealing its heterogeneous composition. After 1830 auctions steadily declined from their preeminent position in the import trade—whether because of the agitation is difficult to say. The number of importing merchants increased, and with the ending of the appointment monopoly in 1838 the auction system virtually came to an end.[20]

The attack on the New-York & Harlem Railroad was indicative of the Workingmen's attitude toward monopolies created by legislative charter. Although no formal opinion was expressed on this subject, the question arising during the relatively inactive period between 1831 and 1833, the views of several influential spokesmen of the Workingmen can be regarded as typical. The company was chartered by the legislature early in 1831 and given the exclusive privilege for thirty years to construct and operate a railway from the Harlem River to Twenty-third Street. Ground-breaking ceremonies were held the next year, after which an amendment was passed allowing extension of the rails to Fourteenth Street; in January 1833 a second amendment permitted construction through any street in the city. Since most of the incorporators were prominently associated with Tammany, the initial outcry against the project came primarily from the New York *American*. Formerly the organ of the "high-minded" Federalists and consistently anti-Tammany, it denounced the scheme as "mischievous, unjust, and founded alone in private speculation." Within a few months Evans joined the attack, characterizing the plan as an "aristocratic device." "If a railroad is necessary," he asserted further, "it is not necessary that, to obtain it, we should give a regiment of rich aristocrats the exclusive privilege of increasing their wealth by the profits of it. We have already too many laws to favor *capitalists*. . . . We are opposed, as every *true* republican must be, to the Harlem Railroad, as a chartered monopoly."[21]

With the threatened extension of the rails into the heart of the city in 1833, Leggett began an editorial campaign against the company. He charged that the railroad was "essentially injuring Broadway as a great public thoroughfare, and changing it, instead, into a field for the operations of a joint stock institution," and argued that "an even and durable pavement" would be of greater advantage and less harmful to property values. He also objected "to the privilege being given or sold to any individual or private company, believing that every citizen has an inalienable right to the free use of the streets—a right which would be essentially impaired by acquiescing in the wishes of the Harlem Railroad Company."[22] A number of meetings were held on the subject and remonstrances by "the most respectable and substantial citizens" sent to Albany. Supporters of the company felt constrained to publish a pamphlet defending their course, and Ely Moore, not yet a famous labor leader, prepared a reply. Presented at a meeting in Tammany Hall (the Democratic organization was now divided on the question), this "triumphant answer" to the company was printed and copies sent to the legislature. Echoing many of the arguments put forward by Leggett, Moore added that there would have been little opposition to the railroad if it had stopped at Twenty-third Street, allowing omnibuses to continue to serve the city instead of driving them from the streets, and he feared widespread unemployment would result from its competition with cartmen. This agitation was unavailing, however, and soon ceased;

the tentacles of the Harlem Railroad continued to spread southward during the succeeding years, and in 1839 a double track extended to City Hall.[23]

As the antimonopoly movement developed, chartered monopolies were usually attacked with special reference to the banking system, but railroads, canals, and other similar corporations also received attention. A controversy arose on this issue following the 1834 election, when Leggett demanded that "manufacturing business, railroad speculations, bridge speculations," as well as banks, be "left to the free competition of capital and enterprise." The *Times,* speaking for the Tammany conservatives, replied that, because individuals seldom had sufficient capital, chartered companies were often necessary to build railroads and canals, that "without legislative facilities, no turnpike, railway, nor canal can be constructed." Evans, however, characterized as "the height of folly" the belief that "there would be no public improvements, of any consequence, without Chartered Monopolies," maintaining:

> To us it appears that whenever a bridge, a turnpike, canal, or rail road, is *needed* by a town or county, or by the State, there is ample provision for its construction without granting exclusive privileges, and thus infringing on the Equal Rights of the people. . . . All that the Monopolies do, is to go far enough ahead of the public wants to ensure themselves a profitable speculation.[24]

He differed, moreover, from Leggett's emphasis on "a system of perfect free-trade in all things," insisting that "it is the granting of those 'facilities' to companies or individuals *alone* that is objected to, not the use of them for the benefit of the whole people." Opposing the recommendation by the *Post* that joint-stock partnerships be authorized by a general law for these purposes, Evans argued that this would invade the province of the state, for it was "wrong for government to farm out its legitimate and appropriate duties as privileges to any portion of the people."[25]

The antimonopoly argument took another form in the Workingmen's denunciation of the contract labor system in the state prisons, which they denominated the "State prison monopoly." Though not a monopoly in the strict sense of the term, this system was attacked for extending a law-created privilege to the contractors and purveyors of prison-made goods, offering unfair competition to "honest mechanics." The Auburn plan of prison discipline, used in the two state penitentiaries at Auburn and Sing Sing, had been adopted in 1823 as a solution to the ill effects of solitary confinement. Congregate contract labor, silently performed, was the basis of the system; one of the principal arguments in favor of the plan was that receipts from contractors easily covered all administrative expenses and occasionally returned a profit to the state. Inmates with no special skills were taught a trade which, it was emphasized, not only defrayed the cost of imprisoning them but provided them with the means for an honest livelihood after their release.[26]

The first protest against this system was recorded as early as 1823 by a group of cabinetmakers, shoemakers, brushmakers, and comb makers, who warned: "Let no . . . mechanic think himself safe, because his business is not conducted in the prison; for he knows not how soon an attempt may be made to wrest from him . . . the labor of his hands and the profit of his trade."[27] The agitation was revived in 1830 and 1831, particularly by stonecutters protesting the use of granite and marble from Sing Sing in the construction of several New York buildings. Declaring that the "inferior price" and quality of such stone would either drive one thousand stonecutters from the city or force them to work for lower wages, they resolved not to work with prison-made materials and to "use all just and proper measures in our power" to persuade other journeymen to do the same. Shoemakers and blacksmiths also testified to their distress from convict competition, and a memorial, signed by several politicians from both major parties, was sent to the legislature.[28]

The furor did not reach its height until 1834, when it became a major political issue. This was undoubtedly due in part to the distress resulting from inflationary pressures, the same climate which saw the flowering of journeymen's associations. The societies affiliated with the Trades' Union, especially the Stonecutters and Marble Polishers, protested loudly against the competition of convict labor, urging a boycott of all employers dealing with prison agents and the expulsion of journeymen who refused to comply. The first convention of the National Trades' Union approved a resolution against prison labor, and the newspaper of the same name proclaimed in its prospectus: "The subject of the STATE PRISON MONOPOLY, in particular, will receive . . . the examination which its importance to the whole community, and particularly the mechanic branches demands." A letter in the Whig *Evening Star* declared in support of this stand that "the regular mechanic, (I mean the journeymen only) have, during the last year . . . been deprived by this . . . Monopoly of $400,000, calculated at fair and regular wages."[29]

It was not only journeymen who opposed the system, for master mechanics complained that the products of convict labor "compete with and lessen the fair price and amount sold of the mechanical products of honest citizens," and as a result "master mechanics lose a part of their business, and journeymen their employment." They maintained furthermore that because convicts were taught mechanical trades, "the occupation of mechanics in general is degraded in public estimation, and a class of bad men are turned out to seek . . . employment in the business they had learned in prisons." Mechanics exposed to "the association of convicts," they concluded, were liable "to be corrupted in morals." These employers, assisted by merchants and small tradesmen, took the lead in the public agitation on the subject, their memorial to the legislature being signed by more than 12,000 mechanics and "merchants of the first standing."[30]

Politics became involved when Whig mechanics denounced Governor Marcy and the Democratic administration in Albany for refusing to abolish or revise a system in which they had a vested interest, while Tammany spokesmen replied that the most notorious prison agents in the city were prominently associated with the anti-administration party.[31] The Workingmen, recently reorganized, essentially stood with Tammany on this issue, noting that the proposed state convention of mechanics opposed to prison labor was dominated by Whigs; for this reason, Evans warned: "It would be a great error for the Mechanics . . . to elevate men to office on the strength of a professed opposition to the state prison system and to find out after their elevation, that they were in favor of other and greater monopolies."[32] The result of this agitation by different groups was the introduction of a bill in the legislature early in 1834, followed by the appointment of Ely Moore as one of three commissioners to investigate the state prisons. Many of the New York mechanics were disappointed upon learning of the deletion of one section of the bill enabling the Governor to prohibit any labor found to offer "injurious competition" to any mechanical trade, and asserted that nothing would be accomplished "but the appointing and paying of three Commissioners." Their disappointment turned to resentment and recrimination when Moore informed them that the section had been stricken out at his suggestion, because he believed that Marcy's unwillingness to take the required responsibility would endanger passage of the entire bill.[33]

The commissioners' report, published in January 1835, added fuel to the flames of their discontent. Although admitting that "in *some articles,* and to some extent," the mechanics' complaints were justified, the commissioners argued: "Common humanity requires that the lives, bodily health, and mental sanity of confined convicts should be preserved . . . by active employment. Common justice requires that convicts should contribute by their labor to their own support." Declaring further that mechanics had "erroneous impressions" of the extent of "injurious" competition from prison labor, the report recommended changes in the method of letting contracts in order to eliminate "the errors in the practice of the present prisons." Legal limits should be placed upon the number employed in any branch of business, and more publicity should be given before contracts are let, "so as to allow full and free competition, and to produce such prices that the contractor could not afford to undersell the market." Dismissing as impracticable the suggestion that convicts be employed on state public works, for not only would they compete with "honest laborers" but "there are no State works of permanent continuance to be done," the commissioners' principal solution was the introduction of crafts from foreign countries in order to manufacture products supplied chiefly by importation, such as fine cutlery and "the manufacture of silk goods from cocoons."[34]

The reaction to the report was immediate and vitriolic, directed chiefly against Moore. Evans in the *Man* and Leggett in the *Evening Post* denounced the report as "a weak, inaccurate, shuffling document," and Moore's approval of it as "a barefaced piece of treachery." The *Times* as the spokesman of Tammany took a more moderate attitude, characterizing the report as "sound and just" on a "subject . . . of some difficulty." The Albany *Argus,* organ of the Albany Regency, defended Moore's course in approving the report, publishing a letter from the Speaker of the Assembly which stated that he had dissuaded Moore from submitting a minority report, suggesting that his alternate plan of employing convicts on the construction of a macadamized road and a railway from New York to Lake Erie be placed separately before the legislature. This disclosure failed to placate the opposition, Evans declaring that Moore had not only neglected his "plain duty" to submit a minority report, but had also offered a specious plan, for "the laborer must no more be interfered with than the mechanic." The *National Trades' Union,* on the other hand, found merit in the proposal and minimized the potential competition with "the common laborer," emphasizing that unless a road or railroad were built by convicts *"it would not be made at all;* unless made by a *chartered company,* which would be highly objectionable."[35]

The members of the General Trades' Union were not convinced, and numerous attacks on their president were made by representatives of the stonecutters, chairmakers, locksmiths, and leather dressers. John H. Bowie, a delegate from the latter society, urged Moore's resignation, but a committee appointed to study the report could not agree on a resolution and was finally discharged. Bowie and John Commerford of the Chairmakers also played a prominent part, along with Edward J. Webb, one of the original Workingmen, in an assemblage of "mechanics opposed to the State prison monopoly." Denominating the projected introduction of silk manufacture "ridiculous and absurd," the address adopted by the meeting charged that "the sympathies of the Commissioners . . . are so completely exhausted on the convicts that . . . not a tear remains for the mechanics and their families who are beggared and broken down by this infamous system." Furthermore, the Workingmen's General Committee, of which Bowie was chairman, passed a strong resolution questioning Moore's "political honesty" and "moral courage."[36] Within a few months the outcry had subsided. The legislature passed an act remedying some abuses, although opponents felt that "it only made the system stronger," and a state mechanics' convention called to take action on the question was sparsely attended. In succeeding years the Locofocos continued to attack the system, resolving that "the time or labor of convicts shall not be bargained to contractors" and proposing that "all articles manufactured in the prisons . . . shall be appropriated to the use of the poor." The question was briefly revived in the electoral campaigns of 1838 and 1839, but generated little enthusiasm.[37]

This issue was of great importance in the history of the Workingmen's movement, and its agitation during the campaign of 1834 explains in large measure the success of the radical wing of the Democratic Party in New York, as well as the nomination and election of Ely Moore to Congress; as Leggett commented, "an excitement was produced among the mechanical classes so strong and general, that it swallowed up almost every other question." Reference to Table XI, showing the occupations of convicts in the state prisons during this period, explains the adherence to the Workingmen's cause of several significant occupational groups.* The prominence, both in the Locofoco Party and the Trades' Union, of John Commerford, a chairmaker, John H. Bowie, a leather dresser, and Levi Slamm, nominally a locksmith, can also be explained in part by relation to the prison labor issue. The importance of this question is apparent, even though both Evans and Leggett belittled its significance as a fundamental cause of the ills of society. As Leggett wrote, while at the same time denouncing Moore and the commissioners' report, "we are as decidedly opposed

* See also Chapter 6, Table I, above.

TABLE XI

CONTRACT LABOR IN NEW YORK STATE PRISONS, 1833–1834*

Occupations	Number of Convicts Employed		
	Sing Sing 1833	Auburn 1834	Total
Coopers	196	55	251
Stoneworkers[a]	136	18	154
Weavers and tailors	56	96	152
Shoemakers	99	48	147
Blacksmiths, etc.[b]	56	52	108
Locksmiths	46	15	61
Comb makers	—	41	41
Furniture makers[c]	—	33	33
Saddle and harness makers	—	26	26
Clock makers	—	22	22
Cooks and bakers	18	—	18
Machinists	—	17	17
Silk hatters	11	—	11
Miscellaneous[d]	15	28	43
Total	633	451[e]	1,084

* Adapted from October 1833 report of prison inspectors, quoted in *Man*, March 6, 1834, and "Report of the Commissioners," p. 19.

[a] Includes masons, stonecutters, quarry men, and tenders.

[b] Includes coppersmiths, brassfounders, platers, and planemakers.

[c] Includes cabinetmakers, chairmakers, bed makers, and turners.

[d] Includes painters, glaziers, polishers, matters, and laborers.

[e] Of this total, 315 learned the trade in prison.

to the principle of state prison labour as any person can be; yet we believe that the *practical* evil of the present system, on any branch of productive industry, is exceedingly trifling, and indeed almost below computation while the result to society at large is decidedly beneficial."[38] But to the Workingmen the actual competition of prison labor did not have to be proved. The system served as a satisfactory scapegoat to be blamed for the decline of their business or their loss of employment and, moreover, as a "monopoly" was open to attack for providing "exclusive privileges" and invading "equal rights."

The state government was not the only malefactor in granting monopolies, for the city government was similarly attacked as the creator of licensed monopolies. The practice of regulating markets and related activities by inspection and licensing was a heritage from colonial times, designed to prevent fraud and promote commerce, and was exercised to some extent throughout the nation.[39] In New York City the Common Council appointed or licensed butchers, grocers, tavern and porterhouse keepers, cartmen and hackney coachmen, pawnbrokers, market clerks, as well as various inspectors, weighers, measurers, and gaugers of such items of merchandise as lumber, lime, coal, grain, and flour; it was asserted in 1828 that the city patronage included nearly seven thousand persons, more than three-fourths of whom were included in these categories.[40]

Demanding the abolition of "all licensed monopolies" in 1830, the Workingmen submitted a memorial to the Common Council specifying their dissatisfaction with the market laws, which they held largely responsible for high prices and rents. Their eight-point program requested the sale of all city-owned property in the markets, elimination of market taxes and reliance on property taxes for revenue, abolition of nonenforceable laws against forestalling, permission for butchers and hucksters to sell anywhere in the city, establishment of tax-free country markets with adjacent taverns to encourage farmers to come into the city, and exemption of market produce from ferry or bridge tolls. The "evil" received greater emphasis in 1835, and in succeeding years the Locofocos echoed the appeal, calling for "the abrogation of all inspectorships over articles of commerce" and "the repeal of all laws under which the Common Council . . . restrain or prohibit the freedom of trade; and all other laws by which they levy indirect taxes on the people."[41] Evans, summarizing the indictment of the system, declared:

> Perhaps there is no law known to our civil statutes more unconstitutional, more tyrannical, more aristocratical and obnoxious to Equal Rights, nor one by which the hard earned substance of the poor is more extensively and cruelly wrenched from them, for the benefit of the rich, than this . . . law for Licenses. By its operation, taxes and fines are collected by our city government equal to the whole necessary expense of its maintenance,

. . . the whole of which is drained from the pockets of the hard working operatives. Almost every article necessary to their existence, from the meat at the butcher's stall to the twopenny macharel [sic] of the grocer, is encumbered with an indirect tax, levied through the agency of this license humbug.[42]

The *Democrat* put it more succinctly, objecting that "we cannot pass the bounds of the city without paying tribute to monopoly; our bread, our meat, our vegetables, our fuel, all, all pay tribute to monopolists."[43]

It was not only as consumers but as producers and entrepreneurs that the Workingmen reacted to this regulation, attacking "the whole system of licensing and favoriteism [sic] which now palsies the energy and enterprize of humble industry." Denouncing the state laws and city ordinances "requiring licenses to prosecute lawful business," grocers and butchers in particular found the license fees and market taxes onerous.[44] Restricted to specified public markets, butchers in order to receive a license first had to purchase the "good will" of their stalls at auction and pay a yearly rental to the city; the auction price of each stall ranged from one to five thousand dollars, and the rental from forty to two hundred dollars per year depending on its location. Fine or imprisonment punished any attempt to practice this occupation without a license or outside the markets, despite protests that this "odious monopoly" was "preventing competition and raising the price of meat."[45] Moreover, according to one member of the trade,

the Corporation [of the city] are indifferent to whom they sell; in consequence of which, not only butchers, but drovers, grocers, carters, and other trades people who possess the means, take stalls and practise a business which should properly belong to the regularly bred butcher. . . . The poor butcher finds that the *rich one,* assisted by the Corporation, has *monopolized all the business.* . . . Is it not time . . . that the markets should be thrown open to all who are qualified to exercise the trade there to be pursued?

Because of this artificial restriction, it was further charged that "there were not a sufficient number of markets to conveniently supply the wants of the citizens," and it was urged that the monopoly could at least be mitigated by granting licenses to sell meat under adequate regulations elsewhere in the city.[46]

Grocers and tavern keepers, besides agitating against regulation in general, protested the necessity of paying a license fee to sell ale, porter, or liquor, as well as the prohibition of its sale on Sunday, which they insisted was "violated with impunity by some."[47] Evans asked somewhat captiously:

> If the sale of liquors is a good and proper business, why should it be prohibited on the Christian Sabbath any more than on the Jewish Sabbath, and why on either any more than on any other day of the week? And if it is *bad* to sell liquors, why do our worshipful Common Council allow every grocer to do it who will pay 12 dollars for the privilege? Again, if it is right and good to sell liquors, where did our Common Council get the power to *restrict* the right to grocers and tavern keepers? And . . . with what justice can they make those persons pay 12 dollars a year for the privilege, and thus indirectly tax the citizens with that amount, *those who do not drink the liquors as well as those who do!*[48]

Other merchants and tradesmen from tobacconists to flour dealers denounced the system of inspection and weighing, urging that these lucrative offices be abolished. Even when the law was amended to permit the weighing of some goods by merchants, it was asserted that this provision "is rendered entirely nugatory by the band of weighers, who, whenever they find a person weighing his own goods, immediately prefer a complaint against him for encumbering the street," and as a result, the merchant who hopes to avoid the weighmaster's fees pays equally as much in fines.[49]

The agitation of this issue undoubtedly accounts for significant segments in the occupational alignment of the movement. While only four butchers were numbered in the ranks of the Workingmen, the seventy-five grocers made that the leading occupation. Other groups in the movement subject to the licensing and inspection system included cartmen, tavern and porterhouse keepers, tobacconists, and flour and coal dealers—in all more than one hundred of the Workingmen whose occupations are known. The adherence of three weighers and inspectors is inexplicable on this basis, as is the fact that at least eleven former Workingmen later accepted appointments to offices against which they had inveighed a few years before.* The attack on licensed monopolies should not be viewed solely as the reaction of those protesting against restrictions upon free enterprise, for, as has been indicated, it also reflected the concern of consumers with the cost of subsistence. It was believed that market laws inevitably meant higher prices, which worked a particular hardship on the mechanic, not only because of his low income but because his "family"—including apprentices and dependent relatives—was generally larger than that of the "non-producing classes."[50]

The Workingmen often linked their indictment of the licensing system with an attack on the ferry monopoly. Regarded as recipients of an unconstitutional grant of "exclusive privileges," the ferries serving Long Island, Staten Island, and New Jersey were leased as franchises by the Common Council. The tolls of four cents for pedestrians and thirty-seven and one-half cents for horse and gig, providing an annual revenue of about ten thousand dollars for the city, was condemned as oppressive and exorbitant, responsible in part for the high price of foodstuffs. It was asserted, moreover, that these charges helped to keep rents high in the city, for it was argued that a reduction of tolls would "furnish to those who do not hold land easy outlets to where they can get cheap rents."[51]

As enunciated by Evans, the Workingmen proposed "ferries at the public expense and for the public benefit" on the same principle as streets and roads. Additional ferries, he feared, would not be a guarantee of lower rates through competition, for

> we could no sooner think of giving the control of those ferries to any man or any set of men, other than public officers, than we could think of chartering a company with the privilege of putting up a tollgate in Broadway. . . . We think that additional Ferries ought to be established by the joint means of the people of New York and Brooklyn; that the Ferries ought to

* See Chapter 6, Tables I and II, above. Robert Townsend, Jr., was one who served as city weigher in the 1840's.

be *free;* and that the expense ought to be paid out of taxes levied on the property of both cities.[52]

William Leggett, the other leading spokesman of the antimonopolists, disagreed with this view, advocating as a solution the enactment of a general law to provide "free trade" in ferries. He viewed free ferries at municipal expense as an "agrarian" invasion of property rights, bestowing a valuable gratuity on those using the ferries at the cost of those who had no occasion to ride them.[53] "Every taxpayer in New York *does* use the Ferries," Evans maintained in rebuttal, "if not directly, *indirectly,* through the means of those who supply him with his marketing. . . . We have no doubt that the making of roads, streets, canals, ferries and bridges is one of the few powers that belongs to the public authorities, and one which they cannot delegate consistently with the public rights and interests."[54]

Another licensing provision challenged by the Workingmen was that which created "the medical monopoly," attacked by the patient as well as the professional. The debate within the latter group was probably more significant and certainly more traditional, dating back to the turn of the century when the State Medical Society was incorporated. The licensing of physicians by the state was first provided by the law of 1760, reenacted in 1792 and 1797 with increasingly stiffer penalties for unlicensed practice. In 1806 the legislature delegated regulation of the profession to the State Society, consisting of delegates from the various county societies. This law was amended seven years later, as the result of remonstrances by the growing body of botanic physicians, to permit the practice of "using or applying for the benefit of any sick person, any roots, barks, or herbs, the growth and produce of the United States." Meanwhile, agitation against the educational monopoly of the two medical colleges (including the College of Physicians and Surgeons in New York) recognized by the State Society culminated in 1826 with the organization of the Rutgers Medical Faculty, led by the eminent Dr. David Hosack. But this institution after a four-year struggle was forced to dissolve, its diplomas being held invalid for purposes of licensing.[55]

These controversies formed the basis for the agitation, largely within the profession, that continued during much of the ensuing decade. By the Revised Statutes of 1828 it became "the duty of every physician not already admitted, to become a member of the medical society in his county, under pain of the forfeiture of his license," and unlicensed practice was made a misdemeanor. Spokesmen for the New York County Society defended this step as a necessary regulation of "ignorant and rash practitioners," but many physicians attacked it for giving too much power to the societies. Some also demanded the establishment of a second medical college in the city to mitigate the "exclusive privileges" of the College of Physicians and Surgeons.[56] The requirement of the County Society that membership certificates be purchased before licenses were issued also elicited protests. Sixty-five practitioners refusing to abide by this rule were listed in the press for failure to comply with the law, after which the nonconformist physicians held meetings and published notices in newspapers denouncing the regulation as "unjust, arbitrary, and wholly in defiance of the inalienable rights of man." Many practitioners, it was emphasized, with "every testimony of their having regularly studied medicine" were being stigmatized for failure to comply with "a certain bye law of the Society requiring of them a Bonus for the privilege of enjoying their own property." For this reason, they expressed the hope that "the public will not form . . . any opinion injurious to the professional character of the gentlemen whose names are mentioned . . . nor consider them as Medical outlaws." The issue was finally carried to the State Supreme Court, which ruled that "the county medical societies might legally impose a tax or contribution on the admission of members."[57]

In 1830 the law was modified, unlicensed practice being no longer a penal offense. Not only did botanic physicians begin to flourish once again, but an even stranger breed emerged, exemplified by the advertisement of a "Professor of Medical Electricity," whose "electric shower bath and ball" would cure afflictions ranging from nightmares to the king's evil.[58] But some members of the profession were less concerned about quackery than with the extent of medical ignorance among licensed practitioners. The New York County Society took the lead in pressing for reform in medical examinations, against the opposition of the faculty of the College and the State Society. The reformers emphasized that

> the present mode of examination . . . does not afford the people any good voucher that justice has been done to them, in the recommendation of men to whom they are to entrust their health and lives, nor does it afford any check to favoritism, the influences of consanguinity and pupilage, the recommendations of powerful men . . . and personal animosities, these examinations being conducted in private, and often by interested individuals, whose word alone must be taken as evidence of the qualifications of the candidates.

At their instigation a bill was introduced in the Assembly by Dr. Philip Milledoler providing for public examinations, both oral and written, for medical diplomas and licenses, to be conducted by a board of examiners appointed by each county society.[59]

The remonstrances of the leading physicians in the state, primarily the faculty of the College of Physicians and Surgeons and the officers of the State Society, expressed the fear that the society in the metropolis, "consisting of three or four hundred individuals, of different views and jarring interests," was not well fitted to select an examining board with high standards, for "the young and unemployed will always have the numerical ascendancy, and will consequently be more likely to appoint a board, . . . not from the prominent and most distinguished members of the society, but from the more active and managing portion of their own class."[60] It was further objected that this proposal would remove the "very just distinction . . . between the license to practice physic and surgery, and the diploma of the doctor in medicine." The usual procedure of obtaining a license and then continuing study toward the degree would be curtailed by the reform, enabling "certain young aspirants to burst the bonds by which they conceive themselves . . . bound, and emerge into full-blown professors."[61] The reformers, denying the charge that "free competition . . . will be detrimental to the advancement of sound knowledge," replied that the bill by diminishing "the undue influences and pecuniary gains of present established medical schools" would "open a fair field of competition among the learned and talented of the medical profession," which would in turn "be productive of greater endeavor to excel in teaching, and to promulgate sound knowledge."[62] The State Society was denounced for acting "totally in the interest of the two colleges" in the state, having acquired "a monopolizing character . . . at variance with the real interests of medical societies in general," and contrary to its original charter.[63] The powerful opposition to reform was strengthened by the support of seventy-six members of the County Society, and the bill was defeated by an unfavorable committee report, attacking the "levelling doctrine" which it feared would lead only to "anarchy and confusion."[64]

The act of 1830 was repealed in 1834, botanic practice being prohibited with penalties of fine and imprisonment for the collection of fees by unauthorized physicians.[65] It was at this time that the Workingmen first took cognizance of the medical question, although more than half the physicians affiliated with the movement had participated in the earlier controversies,* and Evans had supported examination reform when it was first proposed.[66] Denouncing the new law "by which a man is prevented from making choice of his physician," the antimonopolists warned that "every man's health is placed at the disposal of a particular school of medical practitioners." As Evans asked: "Why, in the name of Republicanism, should a society of men be organized with the exclusive privilege of practising medicine, or of granting *licenses* to practise medicine? Why should those who have the misfortune to be sick be compelled to swallow the doses of men who dare not bring their knowledge and skill into the field of fair competition?"[67] A strong effort was

* Fifteen of the 24 physicians included in Table I above were listed as taking part in these controversies, the most active of whom were Alexander F. Vaché, John F. Gray, and Philip E. Milledoler, the latter introducing the 1832 bill in the Assembly. A few were found with the opposition on occasion, Cornelius Blatchley urging stricter regulation in 1828 and Stephen Hasbrouck joining in the 1832 remonstrance against Milledoler's bill. Of the Locofoco leaders who were physicians, only Moses Jaques and John W. Vethake appear to have taken no part in these controversies. One Workingman, Adrastus Doolittle, was listed in the 1833 *Directory* as a botanic physician.

made in the Assembly to repeal or modify the obnoxious law, and
Job Haskell (later a Locofoco standard bearer) was hailed as a
hero by the botanic physicians for his efforts in their behalf. On
the other hand, Dr. Christopher Rice, another Assemblyman from
New York who opposed any reform, was castigated by Evans as
"a man pledged to oppose '*all* monopolies' actually voting to uphold
a monopoly benefiting a chosen *few,* of whom he himself is one!
a man *licensed* to physic people after a particular fashion voting to
compel the people to be physicked after his fashion, or to go *without*
physic!"[68]

While the prohibition of botanic practice was repealed, discrimination was continued with the provision that only licensed physicians could sue for the collection of debts in the state courts. Some
antimonopolists, interpreting "the voice of the people," called for
the repeal of "all Law in regard to Physic and Surgery," maintaining that "all Laws conferring exclusive privileges on the faculty
will serve to enkindle strife, confusion, anarchy and death." The
Locofocos indulged in little specific agitation on the subject, but did
make a blanket declaration that "every profession, business, or trade,
not hurtful to the community, shall be equally open to the pursuit
of every member of the community, without charter, license, im-
pediment, or prohibition."[69] The rivalry within the medical profession, based partly on jealousy and envy of income and position,
continued for another decade, the struggle against monopoly intensified by the attacks of irregular physicians and the popular
feeling that the profession had failed to justify its favored position
by its works. In 1844 the wave of reform reached its height with
the repeal of the regulatory functions of the State Medical Society,
and thereafter physicians could be prosecuted or penalized only for
malpractice or gross ignorance.[70]

Though receiving comparatively little emphasis in the program
of the Workingmen, repeal or reform of the "medical monopoly"
was undoubtedly a significant factor, as revealed by the number of
physicians supporting the movement and playing an important part
in its deliberations. Moreover, as in the case of the other "exclusive
privileges" regarded as monopolistic restrictions upon "equal rights"

and free competition, the interested occupational groups could obtain support for their stand from a sizable segment of the general public, on the basis of principle. And these groups could also join enthusiastically in the condemnation of "chartered monopolies" like banks, canals, railroads, and bridges as "direct and palpable infringements on the true spirit and genius of our institutions."[71]

The significance of the Workingmen's movement, therefore, can be fully understood only in the light of their entire program, even though the demand for education in the early period and later the attack on banks and paper money received their greatest emphasis. These issues, particularly the banking question, served as a solvent for numerous discontents, but the movement would not have mustered the strength it manifested without the support of members of all these various groups—whether professionals, merchants, tradesmen, master mechanics, or journeymen. Each had his own grievance against existing institutions and vested interests, and each was convinced that his own advancement, and that of society as a whole, could only be obtained by the abolition of all monopolies and privileges and the triumph of "equal rights."

The Banking Question

FROM THE organization of the Workingmen's Party in 1829 to the dissolution of the Locofocos eight years later, a basic issue in the movement was the complex question of money, credit, and banking. Although subordinated in the earlier period, first to Skidmore's "agrarian scheme" and then to the demand for education, banking was even then emphasized as a major "cause of [our] present unhappy condition." Banks were denounced for their "exclusive privileges" and for their unconstitutional emission of bills of credit, while bankers were characterized as "the greatest knaves, impostors, and paupers of the age" because they had "promised to pay to their debtors 30 or 35 millions of dollars ON DEMAND, at the same time that they have . . . only 3, 4, or 5 millions to do it with." Not only were frequent bank insolvencies cited as a prime cause of distress, but also the necessity of borrowing from the banks to obtain credit led the Workingmen to demand that the community should "destroy banks altogether."[1]

These charges were reiterated and elaborated throughout the later history of the movement, although primary emphasis was placed upon opposition to banks as "chartered monopolies" with many arguments similar to those employed against other monopolies. As the monetary issue was, however, both more fundamental and more complex, the Workingmen's grievance was not limited to the simple existence of a monopoly infringing "equal rights." Their denunciation of the monopolistic features of banking incorporated other demands than the abolition of the chartering system, and included the substitution of a specie currency for small notes, security for the noteholder, and easier access to credit. Moreover, in spite of general agreement in regard to the existence and identity of the enemy, a difference of opinion was manifested in the movement concerning both the reform objectives desired and the means which should be pursued to attain them. In part, this reflected the confusion and misapprehension concerning the nature and function of banking which was characteristic of the age. But the economic ideology of the Workingmen was also an outgrowth of monetary developments and controversies during the preceding four or five decades in New York and the nation.

The first bank incorporated in New York was the Bank of North America in 1782, but since it never domiciled itself in the state, Alexander Hamilton's Bank of New York was the first actually to be organized there. This institution opened for business under articles of association in 1784, but was unable to secure a legislative charter until 1791. In that year a branch of the First Bank of the United States was also established in New York City.[2] Many New York bankers and businessmen, led by John Jacob Astor, showed considerable hostility toward the branch bank during its two decades of existence, for the local banks resented the "unreasonable" practice of sending their notes home for redemption instead of keeping them in circulation. Also, the growing rivalry between New York and Philadelphia was fed by indignation that the branch was allotted only about one-third as much capital as that possessed by the Philadelphia bank; whenever a prospective borrower was unsuccessful in obtaining a loan in New York, he was likely to blame it upon a conspiracy to keep his city in subordination by making loanable capital scarce.[3] Similar objections were made in New York against the Second Bank of the United States in a later period.

Although not so specified in the legislative act, it was taken for granted that the charter of the Bank of New York conveyed a monopoly. The legislature incorporated two upstate banks within the next two years, but the first real impairment of the city-wide monopoly did not come until 1799, when Aaron Burr secured a charter for the Manhattan Company by his notorious subterfuge of promising to supply the city with "pure and wholesome water." The original monopoly was further impaired by an increasing number of private banking associations owned by individuals or partnerships. By 1804, after six banks had been chartered by the state, an effort was made to prevent further competition and guarantee to the existing banks "a monopoly of the rights and privileges granted to them, which had been encroached upon or infringed by private associations." The Restraining Act of that year declared it illegal for any person to become "a proprietor of a bank or a member of a banking company" unless authorized by law. Restated and strengthened in 1813 and 1818, this law despite strong opposition was not seriously modified until passage of the Free Banking Act of 1838, and was not effectually repealed until the constitution of 1846.[4]

While saving the state from a possible flood of wildcat banks, the Restraining Act, by allowing further incorporation by legislative enactments, did not maintain an absolute monopoly for the Bank of New York and its fellows, but instead legalized the existing practice of a divisible monopoly. At the same time it introduced large-scale political corruption, as lobbyists for hopeful bankers offered inducements to hesitant legislators in order to obtain valuable charters. This became increasingly apparent after 1811, when the end of the Bank of the United States brought a banking mania which was expressed by a flood of charter applications. Between 1811 and 1818 the legislature approved the charters of twenty-three new banks, mostly upstate, thus authorizing an increase of banking capital from seven million to nearly twenty-five million dollars. The most flagrant scandal was the lobbying in 1812 for the Bank of America charter. This bank was to be capitalized at six million dollars, and its promoters hoped that it would enable New York to wrest financial leadership from Philadelphia now that the national bank was no more. Bonuses of more than one-half million dollars were offered to the state, plus two million more in loans, and the charter was approved by the legislature despite the strong opposition of Governor Tompkins.[5]

The constitutional convention of 1821 attempted to prevent further corruption by providing that each charter must be approved by two-thirds of the members elected to each branch of the legislature. But this only increased the evil, as a contemporary writer put it, "by rendering necessary a more extended system of corruption." Moreover, the provision did not noticeably decrease the number of bank charters granted, for ten applications were approved in the four years after the adoption of the new constitution.[6] Following a grand jury investigation of legislative corruption and the frequent use of bank charters for speculation and stock manipulation, the Revised Statutes of 1827 attempted for the first time to provide strict regulation of chartered banks. The law forbade the declaration of dividends except from actual surplus, made stockholders doubly liable for all debts of the corporation, deemed every bank insolvency fraudulent unless disproved by bank records, and required annual reports to the state comptroller. Although embodying several needed reforms, the law was felt to be so severe that no charter applications were received by the legislature while it was in force.[7]

A compromise on regulation was reached in 1829 when the Safety Fund law supplanted the unpopular legislation. This act, vigorously supported by Governor Van Buren, made no attempt to eliminate political corruption or limit the number of bank charters granted. But it did recognize for the first time in New York legislation that protection of the noteholder was a proper function of government. Each bank chartered under the law contributed to a state "safety fund" an annual tax of one-half of one percent of its capital until a total of 3 percent was paid in. From this fund all debts of insolvent banks, except capital liabilities, were to be paid, the fund being replenished by the same annual tax. In addition, three state bank commissioners were appointed, one by the Governor and two by the banks, to make quarterly inspections. In an attempt to mitigate the evil of overissue by country banks, note issue was restricted to twice the amount of capital, and the whole capital stock had to be paid in before a bank opened for business.[8]

Many city bankers were hostile to the plan, asserting that it was unfair to tax the better banks to bolster the credit of the unsound country institutions. They maintained that the assessment should be based upon the amount of outstanding notes, for their capital was almost four times greater than the total amount in the country banks while the total of outstanding notes was almost equal in the two areas. Some opponents declared further that the fund would encourage new banks to issue notes recklessly because they would be secured by the whole banking capital of the state. As the anti-administration New York *American* declared shortly after passage of the act, "the purpose seemed to be fixed and immoveable, of imposing upon the City of New York the forced guarantee of each and all the mismanaged banking institutions of the State," warning that no bank in the city "will accept a renewed charter under such conditions." Despite these attacks the law operated with comparative success until serious failures began in 1840. During the legislative session of 1829 sixteen old banks and eleven new ones were chartered under the act, and by 1837 ninety state banks, including eighteen of the twenty-three banking institutions in the metropolis, had been brought into the system.[9]

While New York was moving toward modified regulation of state banks, the federal government had returned to Hamilton's belief in the efficacy of a central bank, chartering the Second Bank of the United States in 1816 following suspension of specie payments by the state banks functioning as government depositories. This institution, under the direction of Nicholas Biddle, performed its deposit services efficiently and furnished a sound and uniform currency. Nevertheless, its control over the extension of credit by local banks was widely resented, especially in the West, and fear was expressed of its monopolistic power. In spite of the Bank's real contributions to the commercial and financial life of the nation, it also encountered unexpected animosity in the New York business and banking community. The rivalry with Philadelphia for economic leadership of the nation was an important factor, expressed by the desire to replace Biddle's Bank with a local institution. Since customs duties, most of which were collected in New York and deposited in the local branch bank, were the chief source of federal revenue, some businessmen in that city believed the situation should be recognized and the dominance of Philadelphia ended.[10]

Yet more specific grievances were present to account for the hostility to the Bank of the United States. Since 1825 this institution had gradually secured a virtual monopoly of foreign exchange dealings, supplanting a number of large New York mercantile houses. The chartered banks also had reason to oppose the Bank, for although state law permitted them to charge 7 percent interest, the competition of the New York branch bank forced them to take no more than 6 percent or lose business. In addition, as the inflationary boom and the speculative mania gathered momentum, many New York bankers visualized the tremendous profit to be made from additional funds and desired their reinstatement as government depositories.[11] These hopes were realized in 1833 with the Treasury Department order removing government deposits from the Bank of the United States, three of the newly designated state depositories being in New York City. The effect of this added incentive was seen almost immediately; these three banks increased their loans and discounts by more than half—from eight million to more than twelve million dollars—in the six months after the removal was ordered, a time of year when they would normally be contracting their loans as other banks in the city were doing.[12]

The Workingmen during these years were generally more concerned about the "evils" of the state banks than the dangers of the "Mammoth Monopoly," although their emphasis tended to change as Jackson's veto was succeeded by removal of the deposits and Biddle's retaliatory policy. The program adopted by the party late in 1829 ignored the Second Bank, while denouncing the chartering system and attacking "Wall Street" for monopolizing capital through bank bills.[13] No stand was taken against the Bank of the United States until the late summer of 1830, when it was coupled with the state banks in a resolution on chartered monopolies. Little more was said on the subject until early the following year, when Evans stated that the country was faced with a choice between "an Oligarchy or a Despotism," concluding: "We prefer the former; because, whether the *immediate* effects would be more beneficial or not, the ultimate fall of the Banking Monopoly would be hastened. Besides . . . the U. S. Bank might become an American Bonaparte, ruling with a rod of gold."[14] Within a few months he had changed his opinion, asserting that "a single despot is a curse; but a host of petty tyrants is often a greater." He added:

Local Banks, *with* a U. S. Bank, are bad enough: *without* one, it may be, they would be still worse. . . . A blow that reaches the U. S. Bank, and reaches *not* the Local Banks, may be only a blow in favor of the Wall Street Brokers. . . . Thus, while our legislatures madly persist in granting charter after charter to private companies . . . we take little interest in how the U. S. Bank question is settled. . . . We oppose the U. S. Bank as a monopoly, and the local Banks as monopolies.[15]

With the virtual end of the power of Biddle's Bank in 1834, this confusion was brought to an end.* Henceforth the full force of the Workingmen's attack could be concentrated upon the state banks. These were rapidly multiplying in response to the speculative fever which swept over the state after the short-lived 1834 recession. The legislature was besieged with demands for bank charters, ninety-three applications being filed during 1836 alone when the madness was reaching its peak. The bank commissioners appointed under the Safety Fund Act were submitting annual warnings of the dangers of overissue and loan expansion, courting unpopularity in many areas by opposing the creation of new banks. In order to furnish banking capital to the community without greatly increasing circulation, the commissioners recommended increasing the capital of established banks; since two of these men were appointed by the chartered banks, the petitioners viewed this proposal with suspicion. Many of them, of course, were more interested in investing in bank stock than in receiving loans from new banks. Ever since the beginning of the speculative boom, dividends had been at a high level, especially those received by stockholders of country banks. This fact also accounts for the continuation of widespread political corruption, legislators generally being eager to approve a bank charter if given stock in the new institution. The commissioners continually warned that the majority of new banks were demanded because of the profits to be gained from stock speculation, not from a desire to furnish needed capital to the community. They also recommended the prohibition of the prevalent practice of hypothecating bank

---

* See Chapter 2, above, for a more detailed account. The Bank of the United States continued in existence after Jackson's veto and the removal order, obtaining a Pennsylvania charter and exercising considerable financial influence until 1839.

stock—pledging one's stock as security for loans from one's own bank—which was declared to be equivalent to withdrawing capital.[16]

The demand for the opportunity to gamble continued unabated as resort was had to numerous expedients to obtain shares in new banks. William Gouge, one of the most influential and respected opponents of chartered banks, cited the common practice by would-be investors of hiring draymen and other "huskies" to jostle their way to the subscription windows. Another method was to "subscribe a much greater amount than the nominal capital, and then clamor for a *pro rata* division"; Gouge gave an instance in New York in which the capital of a new bank was fixed at $100,000, but the total subscriptions amounted to eight millions.[17] Even some of the antimonopolists were cognizant of the benefits which flow from the possession of bank stock. Theodore Sedgwick, Jr., advanced as one argument for the adoption of free banking that "persons of the most moderate means might make investments." William Leggett, while admitting that stock gambling was bad, defended the business of dealing in stocks as respectable and useful, and declared his opposition to any plan prohibiting the use of credit in stock-exchange operations.[18] Evans, deploring the fact that "a good many professing democrats . . . subscribed for stock, not for the purpose of making a permanent investment, but with no further object than present speculation," admitted that these securities were an "inducement to every man who has saved a few dollars." He saw this "thirst for speculation" resulting in "the blunting of the public moral sense," for "it has made of many an honest industrious man a lazy speculator and *worse,* and many a small rogue it has made a great one. Every new bank that has been put in operation has added supporters to the Banking system in proportion to the amount of its *Capital.*" Speculation, he concluded, is undesirable because it combines "the creation of a distaste for the steady pursuit of those modes of business by which wealth is gradually acquired" with "the awakening of a desire for enterprises which hold out the dazzling prospect of sudden riches."[19]

The Workingmen, and New Yorkers in general, had more experience with bank notes than bank stock, so a major part of their program through the years was (in Leggett's words) "restricting banks in their issues of small notes and in the amount of notes they are permitted to put into circulation."[20] Criticism of paper money, particularly in the smaller denominations, had long been prevalent in the United States, as well as in England, where all notes below five pounds were prohibited in 1829. The most frequent objections to small notes were those advanced by Adam Smith seven decades earlier; that is, they are received with less caution than those of higher denominations, they pass mainly into the hands of the poor, and they displace specie from circulation.[21] President Jackson delighted the Workingmen in 1834 when he announced his intention to forbid the new state depositories to issue small notes and to refuse such notes in payment of government dues; he hoped ultimately to eliminate from circulation all notes under twenty dollars, thus providing "a metallic currency . . . for all the common purposes of life, while the use of bank notes would be confined to those engaged in commerce."[22] Although the hard-money advocates won a victory in 1835 when the New York legislature prohibited the circulation of bills under five dollars, the Locofocos continued to agitate for a minimum denomination of ten dollars; after the onset of the Panic they went further, demanding "the speedy prohibition of all bank notes under the denomination of one hundred dollars."[23]

It was the belief of the Workingmen and other hard-money advocates that the suppression of small notes would "infuse" more specie into the circulation and restore the "constitutional currency of gold and silver." Yet a careful student of American monetary history maintains that "there was a scarcity of coins in regions where notes were not common, and the scarcity existed after small notes were suppressed."[24] This scarcity was due primarily to the failure of the American coinage system to supply a satisfactory retail currency during its first forty years of operation. The Coinage Law of 1792, by establishing a bimetallic ratio of fifteen to one, soon undervalued gold, thus preventing its importation. As a result, gold was not a general medium of circulation after 1800, and after 1825 it entirely ceased to circulate. Silver was little better as a circulating medium during this period. Few silver dollars were coined, and most of these were exported in exchange for Spanish dollars which had a higher silver content. Coinage of quarters, dimes, and half-dimes was also negligible; the total minted before 1830 was less than one piece for each person in the United States at that time. The only denomination coined in relatively large amounts was the half-dollar. But these coins were regarded as bullion and did not circulate widely; instead, they soon found their way to the vaults of the Bank of the United States and other banks, or to brokers who exported them. Copper coinage was also unsuccessful, the coins, unpopular because of their size, often being sold by the cask as metal by enterprising government officials. A further complication was the presence of foreign coins, especially Spanish silver, estimated at five million dollars' worth in 1830. These were generally clipped or debased, but circulated under the aegis of the regularly renewed Legal Tender Act. It is understandable, then, why bank notes were issued to fill the void, for there was no domestic coin between the half-dollar and the two and one-half dollar gold piece, and no coin in general circulation larger than the Spanish dollar.[25]

The credit contraction of 1833–34, resulting from Biddle's pressure upon the business community, led to an increased importation of specie, mainly silver, estimated to total twenty million dollars in slightly more than a year. This development was adduced by the Workingmen as proof of their contention that "as the paper went *out* of circulation the specie would come *in*; that the moment we might begin to *want* specie, it would come from abroad as readily as any other article in demand."[26] Meanwhile, the Jacksonians in Congress, led by Campbell P. White of New York, introduced and obtained the passage of a new coinage law designed to provide a hard-money currency by increasing the bimetallic ratio to sixteen to one, overvaluing gold. In part the result of political pressure to hasten the destruction of the Bank by supplanting its notes with gold coin, this measure was also urged by Southerners hoping to encourage gold mining in that region, and Eastern commercial interests desiring the restoration of gold for general business purposes as well as foreign trade.[27] Although hailed by spokesmen of the Workingmen as "an important measure" toward the restoration of a metallic currency, the law was criticized by most banking theorists, regard-less of their stand on the Bank question, who viewed the ratio as too high and predicted that silver would be driven out of circulation.[28]

It seemed for a time that this prediction would be borne out, for during the last half of 1834 gold coinage amounted to four million dollars, or ten times the average annual coinage during the previous decade. Moreover, foreign debtors now sent gold in payment instead of silver, and the free coinage of silver was discouraged by the ratio. But a series of somewhat fortuitous circumstances postponed for about a decade the complete realization of this calamity. Except for a temporary demoralization during the Panic of 1837, the United States for the first time in its history had a fairly satisfactory frac-tional currency. The mint increased its coinage of pieces under the half-dollar, most of which remained in circulation, rather than being hoarded or exported, because the disparity between the legal and market ratios was not great until after 1844. In addition, silver was released into circulation from bank vaults and replaced by gold. Despite the unfavorable ratio which caused a steady flow of silver to England, the metal was imported extensively from Mexico, ex-ceeding the amount exported by twenty million dollars in the decade after passage of the Coinage Act. This measure, therefore, relieved the former scarcity of specie, although bank notes remained a major element in the currency until the Civil War.[29]

The improvement resulting from the Coinage Act of 1834 did not halt the attack on paper money, the Workingmen maintaining that "while bank notes continue to be issued without stint, no efforts of legislation on coinage can bring back the precious metals into cir-culation."[30] Most banking theorists of the time agreed that the best currency would be composed wholly of specie or of a mixture of specie and bank notes issued against an equivalent amount of hard money, although many were skeptical of ever achieving this ideal. Concurring with Adam Smith's contention that the principal ad-vantage of paper money was the provision of an inexpensive sub-stitute for specie, which could then be exported in exchange for productive goods, these writers emphasized the ease with which bank notes could be issued in such quantity as to cause "perpetual fluctuations and alarms." Overissue, they maintained, depreciates the monetary standard, since, in accordance with the quantity theory of money, banks cannot provide a larger amount of effective purchasing power by issuing notes than they have previously received from stockholders and depositors.[31]

Following this reasoning, Evans saw no objection to the use of paper "as a real representative of specie . . . to facilitate exchanges of property."[32] But generally the Workingmen had an instinctive aversion to paper money and a constant fear of its depreciation. One of their chief complaints concerned the practice followed by some employers of paying wages in "uncurrent bills"—small notes issued by distant and often insolvent banks, selling at a discount by brokers and bank agents. This device was characterized as "aiding and abetting robbery" in order to defraud workmen of a portion of their pay. It was emphasized, moreover, that since "the wealthy and intelligent are too well acquainted with their value to be imposed upon, . . . it is only the poor and the inexperienced upon whom they can be successfully palmed." These notes were kept in circulation by various subterfuges even after passage of the prohibitory law of 1835, for it was charged that "the rich and influential bank aristocracy . . . in total disregard of the laws of their country, force the trash on their workmen, and those whom they consider their dependents."[33]

Aside from this specific grievance, the Workingmen seemingly were divided on the merits of paper money, although a sizable segment agreed with Evans in condemning bank notes without qualification, even though issued by reputable and solvent local banks. The prevalent attitude was expressed in a letter signed by "Hard Money" in 1834: "It is idle to talk to mechanics and farmers about currency, and finance, and exchange, and other like mysteries. They want a *specie currency* and *no* monopolies."[34] The effusions of other correspondents in the columns of the *Working Man's Advocate* attacked "the principle of *commercial expediency*" as a justification of note issue. "The greatest enemy of the working men is paper money," declared "A Journeyman Printer," and without it "banking would not be profitable." Evans' definition of banking as "the power

to receive interest on more money than is possessed by the receivers"
was accepted by most of his readers. They agreed that the banker
in issuing paper money, instead of loaning only his capital, is enabled
to "pocket money as *interest* when in fact he . . . advanced no
principal."[35] Characterizing this operation as receiving double and
triple interest, Evans and his supporters declared: "We are not
contending against capital, or the interest on capital, but against
fictitious capital, and the interest upon that which is neither of any
intrinsic value . . . nor the representative of value."[36] "A Working Man" quoted Hamilton to the effect that "bank notes are not
capital, but merely evidences of debt, and therefore have no right
to draw interest as a matter of justice."[37]

To these hard-money advocates, convertibility was no protection
against the dangers of overissue and depreciation, for "the *constant
tendency* of banks is . . . to lend too much, and put too many notes
in circulation." As "A Working Man" insisted, the only check on
note issue is the bankers' own discretion.[38] Furthermore,

> was every bank note certain of being redeemed in specie, when
> presented, one of the greatest evils of the system would still be
> left, . . . for besides the uncertainty of ascertaining how much
> paper a bank issued on its securities, they would be drawing
> double and triple compound interest on their property—first in
> the shape of rent, and then in the shape of interest on discounts
> of their own paper, thus absolutely *receiving interest* on their
> own debts!![39]

Skeptical of all systems purporting to give security to the noteholder, these men denounced the Safety Fund at its inception as "a
cunning device of the bank gentlemen, not likely to produce an
adequate security." After five years' experience with it Evans concluded: "The Safety Fund has prevented bank failures, by holding
out an idea of security which did not and *does not now exist,* and
the consequence has been that the banks have *doubled in number*
under the operation of that wily scheme, and consequently the tax
upon the industry of the people has *doubled*."[40] Several writers
during this period believed that the only effective way to prevent
overissue and depreciation was to require that bank capital be in-

vested in permanent securities, like government bonds, and that note issue be restricted to the amount of capital.[41] Although at first receptive to this plan, some of the Workingmen later denounced "the specious but delusive idea of ultimate redemption" and viewed it as "quite as atrocious as the present Banking system."[42]

The Locofocos viewed all banks as "legally authorized banditti, levying contributions and indirect taxation from every honest business," and encouraging speculation, forestalling, and extortion.[43] With their precursors in the movement, they held bank notes largely responsible for high prices and the consequent decline in real wages. As "A Journeyman Printer" maintained:

> Paper money enables bankers to make advances to farmers on their grain or wool, and thereby causes these articles to be stored instead of coming into the market; an advance in prices is the consequence. . . . Banks, by increasing their issues, sometimes cause an augmentation in the prices of commodities; trade then becomes brisk, labor is plenty, and *perhaps* wages may advance. . . . [But] the quantity of false money in circulation . . . makes bread and meat dearer also, and thus the working man loses in one way, as much as he may obtain in another.[44]

"A Working Man" agreed, asking, "of what use would it be to the working man to receive the 'high wages' of 10 dollars a day, when for everything he wanted he would have to pay at the same high rate?" Evans went further, insisting that "the Credit System" depresses wages* by enabling "a privileged class . . . to obtain from the laborer his products for that which is no equivalent."[45] If paper money were completely abolished, he explained, "specie no doubt would . . . supply the place of the small notes; but it is not probable that it would, or desirable that it should, equal them in nominal amount." This decrease in the amount of the circulating medium would be beneficial in large part, he believed, for although wages would inevitably be reduced, the prices of most commodities would decline even more.[46]

---

* Evans also argued that "turnouts," or strikes, were ineffective, giving only temporary relief, since low wages made it impossible for mechanics to afford the period of unemployment necessary to win their demands.

That this view of money and banking was not held unanimously by the Workingmen is revealed by numerous letters from "A Mechanic" published in the *Working Man's Advocate*. He disagreed that paper money in itself is always an evil, for without it there would be "complete stagnation in the market for labor" and society would retrogress. If restricted and easily convertible into specie, note issue "facilitates the intercourse of business," since "gold and silver is but the representative of labor, and solvent paper money the representative of them."[47] Citing Thomas Cooper as an authority, he emphasized further that "true paper money is . . . issued in consequence of the real demands of commerce, and it is or ought always to be . . . redeemable in national currency when demanded."[48] In contradiction to Evans he argued that the diffusion of convertible or "solvent" paper money increases business and creates a greater demand for labor. Although admitting that wages tend to lag behind prices, he maintained: "If left free and unfettered, they will soon find their level. . . . [Moreover] we would find, that the more capital employed in our country, so would the wages of labor be higher and the produce in general cheaper."[49]

This controversy on the merits of paper money was extended to the Workingmen's discussions of proposed remedies for the existing evils—even "A Mechanic" was no defender of the chartered banks. Evans and his supporters emphasized that a specie-based economy, less expansive and more stable than one resting on paper, would operate without dependence on banks; that it would be essentially static and even primitive, reinforcing economic stratification, did not deter these hard-money advocates. In fact, they welcomed such an eventuality as a means of eliminating all banks, except those institutions confining their operations to the simple functions of deposit and transfer.[50] "The banking system," Evans insisted, "would be a great evil . . . if it was not a monopoly, . . . but as a monopoly, it is a greater evil still."[51] Even savings banks, originally approved enthusiastically by the Workingmen, by 1834 were viewed with suspicion; because of their practice of investing deposits in chartered banks, which had led to an occasional failure, Evans denounced them as "mere cloaks for those . . . who wish to speculate on the industry of the useful classes."[52] Unremitting hostility to all banks resulted in the demand for an end to bank chartering so that these institutions would gradually disappear as their charters expired. A more radical solution, although criticized by Leggett as an invasion of vested rights, was on occasion suggested by this group. "The working men," Evans declared,

> are opposed to chartering *any other* bank, and are in favor of getting rid of those already chartered as soon as it can be done without producing more evil than good; and they are in favor of getting rid of them without reference to the terms of their charters, they having been obtained upon unjust principles, and of course being as liable to be taken away by the people, as *stolen property* is liable to be taken away at any time, and wherever found, by its owner.[53]

Although many of the early Workingmen accepted Evans' attitude toward banks, others regarded their monopolistic features as the greatest evil and urged the legislature to "grant the privilege of banking to every one who can give security for his fidelity and honesty." Even Fanny Wright, while insisting on a specie currency, saw a need for banking operations, if reduced to "those of private citizens acting on individual responsibility"; in this way, "a fair, useful and simple business would gradually arise to facilitate honest trade" and a "convenient means of transfer, exchange, discount and deposit" would be provided.[54] The chief indictment of the banking system advanced by "A Mechanic" was that it was "based on principles of unequal rights," for "we find a favored few exclusively chartered . . . with privileges denied to others."[55] Some legislators, including Thomas Herttell, a spokesman of the Workingmen on many questions, attempted to obtain repeal of the Restraining Law and, when this failed, recommended approval of all proposed bank charters in order to "diminish the monopolistic influence of those now in operation, and . . . weaken the effects" of the law. Although denounced by "A Working Man" for "advocating the doing of evil that good might come," Herttell was praised by "A Mechanic" for his "moral courage" in the face of "the censure of those who only look at one side of the question on banking."[56]

From 1833 to 1835 the pressure for repeal of the prohibitory legislation constantly increased, and Leggett's editorials placed the *Evening Post* at the head of the antimonopoly forces. "Either the Bank system . . . must be put down," he declared in 1834, "or the days of democracy are numbered." This was to be done by refusing to grant new bank charters or extend existing ones, and by opening banking to the free competition of all who choose to enter into that pursuit.[57] This idea, of course, was not original with Leggett, since Adam Smith, after observing the Scottish banking system, had concluded: "If banks are restrained from issuing and circulating bank notes . . . for less than a certain sum; and if they are subjected to the obligation of an immediate and unconditional payment of such bank notes, as soon as presented, their trade may, with safety for the public be rendered in all other respects perfectly free."[58] In 1827 John McVickar, a respectable political economist, had recommended free banking as a panacea to eliminate the evils of fraud and corruption under the chartering system, further suggesting bond-backed notes to maintain a sound circulating medium; other banking theorists, dissatisfied with the Safety Fund system, later repeated and elaborated this plan.[59]

To replace the obnoxious Restraining Law and the equally obnoxious corporations which it protected, Leggett and his followers in the movement proposed a general law enabling joint-stock partnerships to engage in the activities formerly limited to chartered corporations. These would be "voluntary associations of men, possessing no privileges above their fellow citizens, and liable to the same free competition which the merchant, the mechanic, the laborer, and the farmer are, in their vocations."[60] Some went further, notably Theodore Sedgwick, Jr., writing as "Veto" in the *Evening Post*. He advocated enactment of "a general law providing for the creation of *Corporate Partnerships*" with "all the powers now enjoyed by corporations," including limited liability. This was justified by his assertion that the "corporators will . . . have no advantage over the public at large, because any individual can become a corporator, when and for what purposes he pleases."[61] Leggett expressed reservations on this point, but Evans used stronger language, condemning the entire concept. " 'Veto' either carelessly neglects to take EQUAL RIGHTS for his guide, or worse, wilfully," he wrote, for

> he would give *privileges* to business or other associations . . . and he would allow associations for purposes which, in themselves, would be privileges of the most aristocratic character.
> . . . We want no new law. Let wealth associate, if it please, under the present laws of ordinary partnerships. It is quite powerful enough without privileges. . . . We believe the proposed law would be an infringement on the honest doctrine of "free trade" so ably maintained by the *Evening Post* itself.[62]

"Anti-Monopoly" writing in the *Working Man's Advocate* accused "Veto" of being misled by the "doctrine of expediency," finding little difference between the system of special charters and the proposed general law, except that "it would save the time and expense of special legislation on the subject." Moreover, he asked, "of what use is a special or general law of incorporation to a poor man? and is not the majority of every community composed of men whose capital consists in their skill or labor?"[63]

As the controversy between the two wings of the movement continued, Evans and his cohorts were charged with waging "an indiscriminate war of extermination upon banking as an ordinary branch of business." Replying to this accusation, the editor advised "the utmost caution on the part of the democracy" in regard to the "many plausible schemes of banking proposed as a substitute for the present, which . . . will be quite as bad, or worse."[64] But late in 1835, as the schism in the New York Democracy became irreparable, the antimonopolists subordinated their differences in the struggle against the common foe, the Tammany defenders of the chartering system. The "doctrine of anti-monopoly," as expounded by John W. Vethake a few weeks before the election which brought the Locofoco Party into being, linked restoration of "the constitutional currency of gold and silver" with the enactment of "a general law by which any two or more individuals may declare themselves in business partnership, as well for wood-sawing . . . as for manufacturing or banking." Denying that such a program would result in either economic stagnation or unbridled speculation, Vethake asserted:

We are confident that a wholesome system of general business on this scheme would grow up gradually amongst us, infinitely more favorable than the present to the small capitalist. . . . An unprecedented activity on equitable principles would thereby come to pervade all occupations, and . . . the advances of society would be comparatively uniform and in mass; and, instead of observing as now nought but rapid and destructive fluctuations of prosperity and adversity, . . . the *money market* would be relatively stable and the public mind settled and serene.[65]

The Locofocos, although essentially following Leggett in opposing the monopolistic features of banking rather than banking itself, adhered to Evans' hard-money principles in advocating a specie currency and the abolition of small notes. Their Declaration of Principles reaffirmed an "uncompromising hostility to bank notes and paper money," to "any and all monopolies by legislation," and to "the dangerous and unconstitutional creation of *vested rights* by legislation." Within a few months, however, the principal tenet of the party had become repeal of the Restraining Law "to permit offices of deposit and discount, but not of issue."[66] Led by Colonel Samuel Young, an upstate Democrat and political veteran, an unsuccessful attempt was made in 1835 to abolish the law.* Two years later, financial collapse increased the unpopularity of the chartered banks, inducing the legislature to follow Governor Marcy's recommendation that the restrictive act be modified along the lines demanded by the Locofocos; "individuals" were authorized henceforth to receive deposits and make discounts, with unlimited liability for all debts.[67] With the passage of the Free Banking Act of 1838, success finally rewarded the efforts to "authorize associations for the purpose of banking,"[68] the Whig legislative majority receiving credit for this antimonopoly measure.† The act permitted individuals or joint-stock associations with a minimum capital of $100,000

* Colonel Young was offered the Locofoco nomination for Governor in 1836, but declined because of his opposition to a third party.

† Although Governor Marcy had recommended enactment of a general banking law in his 1838 message to the legislature, most Democrats voted against the bill, some showing resentment that the Whigs had made capital of this popular issue.

to issue an equal amount of notes. This capital was to be invested in federal and New York State bonds, or certain types of mortgages, deposited with the state comptroller; provision was also made for a 12½-percent specie reserve. In the eighteen months following passage of the act seventy-six banks were organized, with a note circulation of about six million dollars.* The comparative success of the system led to its adoption during the ensuing two decades by fifteen other states, and it contributed much to the National Banking Act, which operated from 1863 to the establishment of the Federal Reserve System.[69]

The faith of the dominant wing of the Locofocos in the efficacy of free banking to provide a remedy for all monetary evils hardly seems consistent with their contention that banks supplied an excess amount of the circulating medium. The roots of this anomaly can be found in the widespread demand for long-term credit, insufficiently provided by the existing banking structure. While such a demand was understandable in the West and the recently opened rural areas of the East where farmers and small enterprisers felt they needed permanent capital in the form of long-term, easily renewable loans on landed or personal security, this desire was equally strong in the metropolis. Mercantilist writers had earlier drawn a distinction between "banking on private credit" and "banking on mercantile credit," preferring the former because it was based on tangible assets rather than on the success of the borrowers. The belief that banks should advance credit "to all who can give good security for it," and not demand repayment as long as the interest is regularly paid, persisted into the Jacksonian period. This was true even after the Bank of England, and the American commercial banks created in its image, broke with tradition by specializing in short-term, self-extinguishing mercantile credit. Some of these in-

* The Safety Fund banks continued as a parallel system, the act remaining on the statute books until 1866, although essentially abolished in 1854 when the fund became insolvent. Because the Free Banking Act had not been adopted by a two-thirds majority of the elected legislators (as the 1821 constitution provided for banking legislation), and because some courts held that banking "associations" were "corporations" in fact, its constitutionality was in doubt for more than a decade, the issue finally being resolved by the constitution of 1846 and subsequent court decisions.

stitutions, such as the two Banks of the United States and the Bank of New York, made exceptions in favor of long-term advances to the state and to large-scale enterprise, but credit on land and personal security to farmers and small enterprisers was scrupulously avoided. As these groups could not, as corporations were beginning to do, turn to Europe for capital, and as their credit demands were increasing enormously, economic and political pressure was exerted against the only available resource, the banks. As a result, long before 1840 this specialization had broken down and most banks, many even in the commercial centers, were serving in the main the interests which had been refused fifty years before; even when the short-term principle was verbally professed, it was often circumvented by frequent renewals.[70]

The contest between these two banking principles was demonstrated in the New York money market. During this period the state bank commissioners continually reiterated the contention of sound-money advocates that "the legitimate function of banks is not loaning capital but furnishing a sound currency" and negotiating short-term loans, pointing warningly to the prevalence of "accommodation paper" or promissory notes over "commercial paper" or trade acceptances. Although stocks and bonds, as well as mortgages, were often used as collateral for accommodation loans, the most common practice was for the borrower to secure one or two endorsers known to the bank, after which the board of directors approved or disapproved the loan. As was to be expected, in prosperous times the banks grew lax both in extending credit and approving renewals, but in the late 'twenties, in 1834, and from 1837 to 1845 credit was tightened. Until its dissolution the Second Bank of the United States brought trade acceptances into wider use and, by maintaining a market for them, encouraged other banks to follow its example. But while its discounts of acceptances increased from one and one-half million to eighteen million dollars between 1820 and 1833, its loans on promissory notes increased from twenty to forty million dollars in the same period. As these figures indicate, even this sound-money institution was unable to assuage the thirst for long-term credit, while at the same time its resolute attempt could not fail to decrease its popularity with the small enterpriser and mechanic.[71]

It is understandable, then, that the hard-money Workingmen, to whom the banks were anathema for many reasons, shared this desire for credit. While demanding restriction or abolition of note issue, this group throughout its history generally agreed in indicting the chartered banks for failing to provide adequate borrowing facilities for "industrious farmers and mechanics, and plain dealing merchants and storekeepers." Not only were most bank loans made for too short a period to be adapted to any other use than speculation, it was asserted, but most banks discriminated against these classes of prospective borrowers. In this belief, they echoed William Gouge, who contrasted the ease with which Franklin had been able to establish himself in business by means of credit with the existing situation in which "capitalists deem the chances of re-payment not sufficient to justify lending to young mechanics: and the embryo Doctor Franklins who are among them are left to contend with adversity, without assistance from their richer neighbors." The result, he added, is that

> men having no capital of their own, and unable to borrow, must unless employment is afforded them by others, remain in absolute idleness. It is now, indeed, possible for such men to borrow from the Banks, if their indorsers please the Directors. But the loans of the Banks are for 60 to 90 days, while months, and even years, are required for bringing the enterprizes of the farmer and the mechanic to successful completion.

Instead, "facilities are . . . afforded to many men for borrowing, to whom no man ought to lend"—those who "are led by Bank loans to engage in business for which they are not fitted by either nature or education"—and by the failure of their enterprises "the wealth of the community is diminished."[72]

Even the early Workingmen demanded easier access to credit. Evans, writing in 1829, declared that "the workingmen of this city are determined to . . . [obtain] a fair participation of bank favors," since even "the most prudent and industrious working man" cannot borrow fifty dollars from any bank, "unless he happens to have a

friend at the board of directors." According to the *Evening Journal,*
"Mechanics of slender means were seldom accommodated with loans
necessary to render their business profitable or extensive, in consequence of the moneyed institutions being generally under the control
of rich merchants . . . [with] little sympathy for the wants or
pursuits of the honest and industrious Mechanic." Moreover, on the
few occasions when a loan was granted, the mechanic was "obliged
to appear cap in hand, with an unbecoming self-abasement, before
the aristocratic money-lender."[73] Others remarked on the rudeness
of bank employees, even at the savings banks, toward members of
"the laboring classes." "If a working man should want a dollar,"
wrote one correspondent in the *Working Man's Advocate,*

> and apply to one of the banks . . . for a loan to that amount on
> the security of his next coming week's wages, he will have a
> refusal from the principals, and be quizzed . . . by the clerks,
> *because he is poor.* If a full-pursed, well-dressed, white-handed
> monopolizer apply at the bank for the loan of 1000 dollars for
> six months, and offer his promissory note, he will be "accommo-
> dated," *because he is rich.*[74]

Furthermore, as "A Journeyman Printer" emphasized, the banks
"assist great wealthy employers to compete with and crush little
ones—and prevent honest industrious journeymen from becoming
employers." He cited the example of Peter Plane, a journeyman
carpenter, who

> by great economy and industry has saved 200 dollars, and be-
> comes a Boss upon a small scale. Peter learns that there is a lot
> of timber for sale cheap *for cash,* the price of which is $100.
> Peter has only $50 in hand, being unknown at the Bank cannot
> get his note discounted, and therefore is obliged to go round
> among his customers to collect a few small debts. In the mean
> time Ichabod Log, a Boss builder . . . by chance sees the tim-
> ber, buys and pays for it *immediately* by a check . . . on his
> Banker; the Banker honors the check . . . although Log is al-
> ready indebted to him for several hundreds of dollars. . . . The
> Banker likes that kind of business and becomes *liberal* in assist-
> ing men already wealthy, like Log, but would decline having any
> dealings with men of small capital like Peter Plane.[75]

Evans agreed with this interpretation, maintaining that "the merchant who borrows can get a better assortment of goods than his neighbor who *cannot* borrow, so that he can undersell him"; similarly, "the master mechanic who borrows paper money, by being enabled to do more business, can underwork his neighbor . . . and still make a greater aggregate profit . . . after paying the interest." The result is not only business failure and unemployment for mechanics and working men but decreased competition and higher prices for the community.[76] In replying to Evans' objections to paper money, "A Mechanic" argued that it "enables the *poor* to compete . . . with the rich," for "if the credit system were abolished, those possessed of capital would be able to monopolize as they please." The Workingmen, instead of demanding the abolition of banks and paper money, he concluded, should work for repeal of the monopolistic Restraining Law in order to improve their position in society.

> Do away with paper money, and you at once paralyze [*sic*] the operations of machinery, for you withdraw the facilities of obtaining credit; and consequently all owners of machinery, who are not capitalists, would be driven from competition, and . . . those they employ would be driven out of employment. . . . It would operate alike on every business that requires capital; and what business is it that can be conducted without it? . . . You are *warring* with that which enables those who are not capitalists, to compete with, and keep in check those very capitalists.[77]

This difference in emphasis became more acute as chartered banks multiplied and inflation spiraled. "In the midst of a flood of paper," declared one writer, "more cash is required to do business; but then it is obtained on loan with greater proportionate ease." As credit became more readily available, even to the "working classes," Evans and his cohorts became increasingly suspicious and their strictures against the spirit of gambling and speculation more vehement. "I know," wrote "A Working Man" in obvious disappointment, "that it is not every mechanic who would wish the banking monopoly destroyed—many have grown rich by its facilities—many are at present amassing fortunes by the advantages it

gives them over their humbler competitors." Credit was regarded
as an insidious influence by these advocates of a hard-money economy. Even though young mechanics and farmers are enabled to
become their own masters, they maintained, "were it not for the
decoying influence of the bank," they "would *earn* their capital instead of borrowing it, they would lean upon industry and not upon
the proffered aid . . . of these shaving mills. . . . [Although]
nine out of ten of the working men who 'set up for themselves in
business' do so without the aid of these banks, . . . engaging in
them in after time has too frequently proved fatal to their business."
As "A Journeyman Mechanic" explained, "the necessity produced
by this system of *giving* credit to customers" was a further reason
for the failure of many of these enterprises.[78] This attitude was
summarized in a resolution approved by the 1834 Workingmen:

> We consider the present mode of extensive *business credit*
> . . . highly injurious, and productive of far more evil than
> advantage to the reputable merchant and trader; for, by it, they
> are subject to long credits and uncertain receipts from cus-
> tomers, while bound to Banks short credits and liable to uncer-
> tain "accommodations"; . . . but under the cash business gold
> and silver would produce, they would transact a safe business
> with a fair profit.[79]

The Locofocos, while joining in the denunciation of the evil
effects of paper money, were less suspicious of the credit system.
Leggett, in fact, showed little concern for the almost universal desire
for credit, even though he condemned the chartered banks for invading equal rights and abrogating the principles of free trade. To
him,

> the great majority of the laboring classes can never become
> stockholders nor directors, nor can they share the loans of the
> banks, simply because they have no money to invest in stocks,
> and no real property to offer as a security for repayment of the
> imaginary loan. The privilege, therefore, is a monopoly, con-
> fined strictly to a meagre minority. . . . The men who do
> business on their own little capital, or on the most solid of all
> capitals, their own labor, are unable to exist.

To remedy this situation he recommended that the legislature "should repeal their laws imposing restraints on the free exercise of capital and credit."[80] His friend Sedgwick, while admitting that chartered banks "have caused a rapid circulation, and have stimulated enterprise," maintained that they have at the same time "caused great public and private injury to the community." The banking system should be a means for "idle capital" to be "freely invested in the hands of needy and industrious borrowers," but, Sedgwick asserted, *as compared with what would have been effected under a free trade system,* the banks have been a clog upon the industry of this country."[81] Vethake, expressing the views of the early Locofocos, agreed. He declared,

> If incorporated banks were at once suppressed, not a cent of money would be lost to the business community. The evolutions of capital and of credit, in all abundance, would be conducted by active and intelligent individuals under a measure of competition and a degree of personal responsibility to society which, when compared with incorporated institutions, would be vastly great and vastly advantageous to the humbler circles of business men.[82]

Even the ensuing period of untrammeled credit expansion which culminated in financial collapse did not seriously modify this view. In 1837 the Locofocos, while ascribing the cause of distress to an "undue expansion of credit," concluded that

> the best mode of completely destroying both the curse of paper money and the curse of usury would be, simply *to let credit alone;* to leave each man's credit to stand solely on its own bottom, without any attempt to strengthen or weaken it by legislation. . . . It would prevent the man of doubtful honesty, whatever might be his wealth, from obtaining very extensive credit; and it would enable the honest man, however poor, to obtain as much credit as he ought.[83]

In common with many of their contemporaries, the antimonopolists, with few exceptions, did not fully understand the principles of commercial banking. In their attack on note issue and their demand for easier credit they failed to realize that the two aspects of banking—providing a medium of payment and lending purchasing power—could not be separated except abstractly, for it was in placing purchasing power in the hands of entrepreneurs that banking brought media of payment into existence. The monetary controversies of the Jacksonian period, as Bray Hammond emphasizes, demonstrated this confusion, for the "legitimate demand for long term credit was regularly translated into a political attack on the objectivity and stability of the medium of exchange, and the equally legitimate defense of the medium of exchange was regularly translated into an attempt to strangle agriculture and small enterprise."[84] The would-be borrowers formulated their demands politically in terms of the monetary system, and their success resulted in "a fatal hybridization of function." Banks on the one hand issued "evidences of liability which constituted the country's means of monetary exchange" to be redeemed on demand, and simultaneously provided "capital for fixed investment." By providing "equal opportunity to borrow," free banking was a victory for this group, making credit more accessible to more people. The Act of 1838, according to Gallatin, "bears internal evidence that it was prepared by speculators"; as a proponent of sound money, he viewed bank credit as a means to facilitate trade rather than an instrument for the exploitation of capital resources.[85] The New York legislation contained safeguards against monetary abuses, but Gallatin's fears were borne out by banking practices in several states in the Upper Mississippi Valley, especially Michigan, where the notorious "wildcat" banks were created by a similar act.[86]

The Locofoco pattern, exemplified by many state banking systems, was also evident in the development of the federal financial organization. In 1837 the universal suspension of specie payments by the banks, including the federal depositories, brought the operations of the Treasury to a standstill. While it was no longer lawful for the public deposits to remain in the suspended banks, it was almost impossible to remove them because the government was prohibited from accepting depreciated paper and there was little specie in circulation. It was at this juncture that President Van Buren called Congress into special session and proposed that the public funds be kept exclusively by public officials in subtreasury offices and that nothing but specie be received for government dues.[87] This so-called Independent Treasury system manifested another element in the Locofoco creed, "divorce of Bank and State," and embodied the proposal made in 1833 by William Gouge.[88] Two years earlier Evans and the hard-money Workingmen had endorsed a plan for "a National Bank of *Deposit and Transfer*." This was modified a few months later when Evans, foreshadowing the Workingmen's 1834 resolution in favor of "Sub-Treasury offices . . . to receive and disburse the revenue," wrote:

> If Banking *is* necessary, it ought not to be carried on in a republic but by the *whole people*. . . . Although we believe that Banking should be carried on by the Government, *if at all,* we believe that Government Banking would be attended with danger to our republican institutions; and we think that Banking would be rendered totally unnecessary . . . by the establishment of an institution with a branch or branches in each state, to receive specie on deposit, and to issue notes therefor, thereby to facilitate the exchange of property by the citizens of distant parts, and accomplish the *only* useful object now accomplished by *Banking* Institutions.[89]

Since Congress refused to approve Van Buren's plan in 1837, it was fortunate that federal income was not large during the ensuing years of depression, for until 1840 the government had no fiscal system other than leaving revenues on deposit with collecting officials. In that year the first Subtreasury Law, sponsored by the hard-money Democrats, finally went into effect. Albert Gallatin, now the financial leader of New York because of his role in bringing about resumption in 1838, opposed the new system, complaining that it failed to provide a channel for the distribution of government funds throughout the nation, thus separating governmental finance from the financial existence of the rest of the country. But the Democrats, interested primarily in protecting the Treasury

against another bank suspension, ignored the fact that the specie
they demanded came from the banks. Despite Gallatin's criticism,
the subtreasury system produced few changes during the year of
its operation, before the Whig victory resulted in its repeal; banks
were still in use to some extent as depositories and bank notes were
still receivable for government dues. The Whig administration
restored the state banks as sole depositories, but the redeposit of
public funds had little deleterious effect, since economic conditions
were not propitious for inflationary practices. Although an attempt
was made to recharter the Bank of the United States or a similar
institution, Biddle's wildly expansive policies in Pennsylvania, culminating in the Bank's failure, made him a less influential figure,
and President Tyler's stubborn states' rights views prevented
passage of any such law. So Polk's victory allowed the Democrats
to reenact in 1846 a slightly modified version of their earlier Sub-
treasury Act, which remained the basis of the federal financial system
until the Civil War.[90]

Thus, in following the Locofoco philosophy, the Jacksonians,
while incorporating their hard-money views into the federal fiscal
organization, at the same time provided, consciously or uncon-
sciously, a system with little or no effective control over the activities
of the state banks, the chief source of credit for an expanding
society. The Workingmen's movement in its struggle with the
banks had successfully, though often illogically, cooperated in eradi-
cating the restrictions upon enterprise which both the Bank of the
United States and the monopolistic state banks had imposed. While
credit was thereby made more accessible, there was concurrently a
definite realization among many Jacksonians, including the Workingmen, that an unrestricted monetary system contained evils which
were detrimental to the pursuit of sound business. Evans and his
followers saw the elimination of paper money, especially small notes,
and the restoration of a specie currency as the only salvation; to
this group, any currency other than that issued by the federal government was an unconstitutional "emission of bills of credit."[91]
Others were less doctrinaire, demanding only that the banks should
provide security for the noteholder and arrest depreciation. This

was essentially accomplished by the Free Banking Act, but at the expense of elasticity.*

Yet the problem of security for the depositor, or even the realization that deposits played a part in the expansion of credit, was ignored in this legislation, as it was largely throughout the period. The general conception was that bank deposits formed "an auxiliary to its capital" rather than a "component part" of a bank's credit. As banking was usually identified with the function of note issue, it was recognized that the banker in his discounting operations created liabilities against himself that formed part of the currency, but only a small minority saw that discounting could create deposit credits which were also demand liabilities. So the Workingmen, ascribing most evils of banking to note issue, urged that these institutions be deprived of that privilege, but saw little need to place restrictions upon deposit banking. It is especially strange that the role of deposits was so long unrecognized in New York City, where the banks seem to have had a larger proportion of deposit liabilities than circulating notes, and where by 1840 checks had become a common device among the merchants. The crisis of 1837 demonstrated their importance, for the New York City banks were forced to suspend specie payments, not as a result of the volume of notes presented for redemption, but because of the demands of their depositors. The lesson was not learned until the Panic of 1857 when bankers came to realize, and to act upon their realization, that in a crisis deposits are usually withdrawn before notes are presented for redemption, and hence must be guarded by a specie reserve.[92]

While the banking system did not become the stable mechanism that the Workingmen had hoped to create, the elimination of monopolistic privilege and the greater accessibility of credit helped to break down the stratification of economic power in American society. This occurred in spite of the controversy regarding the nature and uses of credit within the ranks of the heretofore unprivileged.

* Most banking theorists of the early nineteenth century regarded an inelastic currency as desirable, so this characteristic of the act was not seriously criticized for more than a decade.

Manifested not only in New York but throughout the nation, banking development in the antebellum period demonstrated the conflict, and eventual compromise, between the "no-bank" and "anti-bank" factions, between the hard-money opponents of all bank notes and bank credit and those opposing only the corporate features of banking. The struggle on occasion became a three-cornered contest as proponents of sound money and short-term mercantile credit advocated either the creation of a state-wide central banking system or a stricter regulation of free banks.[93] The New York Workingmen, moreover, shared the general confusion concerning the nature of speculation, disagreeing among themselves as well as with others on where to draw the line between credit for legitimate investment and credit which encouraged unwholesome speculation.[94] It is unquestionable that most of those in the movement desired easier access to credit, while strenuously opposing the existing system for fostering "gambling and forestalling." Although dedicated to the spirit of enterprise, they were generally more conservative in both their demands and their expectations than those who later espoused their cause, whether in the East or the West. But in struggling against the banking monopoly they were consistent in their avowed objective, similarly apparent in their struggle against other monopolies, of advancing the "democratization of business." Bray Hammond's characterization of the "age of Jackson" as "an age of triumphant exploitation" is an apt summation of the contribution of the Workingmen's movement, for they "put forth the promise that anyone could be a capitalist, an investor, or a speculator; and . . . made banking a form of business 'free' and open to all."[95]

The Working Class and the Democracy

L IKE MOST third parties in our history, the success of the Workingmen's movement cannot be measured by election returns.
Of greater significance was its leavening influence upon the New
York Democracy, modifying both the personnel and the program
of the Tammany party. Its impact upon politics in the Empire
State was echoed by political developments elsewhere, and by the
1840's the Locofoco strain had come to permeate the national party
organization.[1] A survey of elections from 1828 to 1838 is valuable,
nevertheless, in elucidating this relationship between Tammany
and the Workingmen, and the concomitant effect upon the evolution of Jacksonian Democracy in New York City. Furthermore,
an effort to delineate the economic basis of New York politics by a
comparison of the wealth and party allegiance of the electorate
supplements our investigation of the Workingmen and their program and aids in determining the character and purpose of the
movement.

The decade following the War of 1812 saw New York City
outstrip its commercial rivals in both population and prosperity, a
situation which became even more marked during the Jacksonian
period. As shown in Table XII, its population continued to grow,
nearly doubling in the fifteen years between 1825 and 1840. The
metropolis had become a magnet to the ambitious and enterprising
in the hinterland, drawing young men especially from nearby New
England and New Jersey. In addition, immigrants from Europe
contributed to this growth, nearly sixty thousand entering in 1836
alone, many of whom remained in the city by choice or necessity.[2]
While the city was expanding northward, five new wards being
created during this period, the lower wards at the tip of Manhattan
were gradually losing population as many old merchant families
moved uptown, mainly to the new Fifteenth Ward.[3] The age-group

TABLE XII

Population of New York City by Wards, 1825–1840*

	Population				Eligible Voters	
Ward	1825	1830	1835	1840	1835	Pct.
1	9,929	11,331	10,380	10,629	2,208	21
2	9,315	8,203	7,549	6,406	1,477	20
3	10,801	9,599	10,884	11,581	2,211	20
4	12,240	12,705	15,439	15,770	3,159	20
5	15,093	17,722	18,495	19,159	2,813	15
6	20,061	13,570	16,827	17,199	2,216	13
7	14,192	15,873	21,481	22,985	3,511	16
8	24,285	20,729	28,570	29,093	4,245	15
9	10,956	22,810	20,618	24,795	3,122	15
10	23,932	16,438	20,926	29,093	3,684	18
11	7,344	14,915	26,845	17,052	4,137	15
12	7,938	11,808	24,437	11,678	3,288	13
13[a]		12,958	17,130	18,516	2,606	15
14[b]		14,288	17,306	20,230	2,444	14
15[c]			13,202	17,769	1,970	15
16[d]				22,275		
17[e]				18,622		
	166,086	202,949	270,089	312,852	43,091	16

* New York State Census of 1825 and 1835, and Federal Census of 1830 and 1840; cited in Williams, *Annual Register* (1835), p. 72; (1837), p. 345; D. T. Valentine, *Manual of the Corporation of New York* (1841), p. 49.

  [a] Constituted in 1826 from Tenth Ward.
  [b] Constituted in 1826 from Sixth and Eighth wards.
  [c] Constituted in 1831 from Ninth Ward.
  [d] Constituted in 1836 from Twelfth Ward.
  [e] Constituted in 1837 from Eleventh Ward.

composition of the various wards is indicated by the percentage of males eligible to vote at this time, the maturity of the established merchants in the lower wards contrasting with the younger families farther uptown.*

Population growth was most rapid in the five years from 1830 to 1835, when the wealth of the city was increasing in proportion. As Table XIII reveals, the assessed valuation of real and personal property nearly doubled between 1833 and 1836, reaching a peak

* See Table XII. The distribution of Negroes, only a handful of whom could vote, and aliens is an important factor in explaining the varying percentages, the proportion of both groups being much less in the lower wards.

TABLE XIII

Assessed Valuation of Property by Wards, 1833–1840*
(Thousands of Dollars)

Ward	Total of Real and Personal Property				
	1833	1834	1835	1836	1840
1	$46,501	$50,532	$55,950	$64,032	$59,779
2	13,822	14,532	16,264	21,631	16,856
3	16,521	17,731	18,876	23,016	17,261
4	9,419	9,777	10,930	12,395	10,416
5	12,417	11,870	13,150	18,621	12,506
6	8,525	9,985	10,721	14,280	9,998
7	8,440	10,823	12,398	16,791	15,292
8	8,306	10,904	11,451	16,081	13,249
9	5,316	6,032	7,326	12,365	9,777
10	4,721	5,162	5,834	8,399	6,858
11	6,007	6,998	9,796	20,149	14,462[a]
12	8,115	10,262	18,185	42,539[b]	30,284[c]
13	2,696	3,041	3,445	4,986	4,554
14	6,439	7,027	8,076	10,221	8,762
15	9,247	11,872	16,323	23,995	22,783
	$166,492	$186,549	$218,724	$309,501	$252,837

* Williams, *Annual Register* (1835), p. 311; (1837), p. 343; Valentine, *Manual* (1841), p. 184.

[a] This figure represents the valuation of the Eleventh and Seventeenth wards, the latter created in 1837; the breakdown is: Eleventh—$3,897,591, Seventeenth—$10,564,699.

[b] This figure represents the valuation of the Twelfth and Sixteenth wards, the latter created in 1836; the breakdown is: Twelfth—$17,817,622, Sixteenth—$24,721,464.

[c] This is the sum of: Twelfth Ward—$12,365,350, Sixteenth Ward—$17,919,139.

of more than three hundred million dollars in the latter year, just before the economic collapse. By 1840, after three years of depression, the amount was still considerably higher than it had been five years before in the midst of an inflationary period. The lower wards, especially the aristocratic First Ward, contained the greatest wealth, although the Twelfth and Fifteenth offered an increasing challenge.* More significant was the wealth per capita in each ward, shown in Table XIV, which furnishes an indication of the socioeconomic distribution of the population. The first three wards were the wealthiest, followed by the Twelfth and Fifteenth in the

* The assessed valuation was largely based on real estate, which ranged from 65 percent to 75 percent of the total during these years; the exception was the First Ward, where personal estate equaled or exceeded real estate.

TABLE XIV
Approximate Wealth per Capita by Wards, 1830–1840

Ward	1830–33[a]	1834[b]	1835[c]	1836[d]	1840[e]
1	$4,104	$4,868	$5,390	$6,169	$5,623
2	1,685	1,925	2,154	2,865	2,631
3	1,721	1,629	1,734	2,115	1,490
4	741	633	708	803	660
5	701	642	711	1,007	652
6	628	593	637	849	580
7	532	504	577	782	665
8	401	382	401	563	455
9	638	292	355	600	404
10	287	247	279	401	235
11	403	261	365	751	222
12	687	420	744	2,119	1,059
13	214	177	201	291	245
14	451	406	467	591	432
15		899	1,236	1,818	1,282
16				1,542	804
17					567
	$820	$691	$810	$1,146	$808

[a] Computed from 1830 population and 1833 valuation of property; the figure for the Ninth Ward is based on the sum of the valuation for the Ninth and Fifteenth wards.
[b] Computed from 1835 population and 1834 property valuation.
[c] Computed from 1835 population and 1835 property valuation.
[d] Computed from 1835 population and 1836 property valuation.
[e] Computed from 1840 population and 1840 property valuation.

later years of the period; lowest on the scale were the Tenth and Thirteenth, joined by the Eleventh after its division in 1837.

These factors are useful for an analysis of the party vote in New York during the Jacksonian period, providing an index to the social and economic basis of political affiliation.* An examination of representative political contests in the principal elections from 1828 to 1838, summarized in Table XV, demonstrates the declin-

* This technique was first used in 1919 by Fox in *Decline of Aristocracy*, pp. 430–49, although no attempt was made to evaluate the vote distribution in each ward; instead, wards were classified on the basis of which party received the majority vote, and then compared with per capita wealth. For a criticism of this method see Robert T. Bower, "Note on 'Did Labor Support Jackson?: the Boston Story,'" *Political Science Quarterly*, LXV (September 1950), 441–44.

TABLE XV
New York City Vote by Parties, 1828–1838*

Year	Elective Contest	Total Vote	Percent of Total Vote[a]		
			T	A	W
1828	President	25,117	62	38	
1829	Assembly	19,516	55	12	31
1830	Congress	20,494	53	36	11
1832	State Senate	30,388	59	41	
1834	Mayor (April)	34,969	50	50	
	Assembly (November)	35,591	53	47	
1835	Congress[b]	22,518	44	40	16
1836	Congress (November)	33,973	48	48	4
	Assembly (December)[c]	19,795	45	51	4
1837	Mayor (April)	34,999	39	49	12
	Assembly (November)	35,131	46	53	1
1838	Governor	39,486	49	51	

* Computed from election returns in the following: *Evening Post,* November 10, 1828; *Courier and Enquirer,* November 12, 1829; *Working Man's Advocate,* November 13, 1830; *Sentinel,* November 14, 1832; *American,* April 18, 1834; *Working Man's Advocate,* November 15, 1834; Williams, *Annual Register* (1836), p. 317; *Evening Post,* November 26, 1836; *New-Yorker,* December 31, 1836; Williams, *Annual Register* (1837), p. 348; *Evening Post,* November 14, 1837; Williams, *Annual Register* (1840), pp. 224–25.

[a] T—Tammany. A—Anti-Tammany, especially National Republican and Whig. W—Workingmen and Locofocos; Rump Locofocos in 1837.

[b] Election to fill vacancy.

[c] Special election to fill vacancy.

ing fortunes of Tammany during these years and the balance-of-power role played by the Workingmen's and Locofoco parties. The Democratic majority of 1828 revealed the bankruptcy of the National Republicans in New York, seeming to promise Tammany a long period of political hegemony. The threat posed by the Workingmen the following year* was countered by Democratic concessions, and the 1832 election showed a large majority for the Tammany ticket. But the Bank War led to more serious defections, and by 1834 the inchoate opposition had been molded, largely by the astute Thurlow Weed, into the Whig Party. This group offered a more serious challenge to Tammany domination, losing the

* The Antimasonic Party, which polled the remaining 2 percent of the vote in 1829, was never a serious challenge in the city, although its adherents constituted an element of the "Coalition" of 1830, joining with the Cook Workingmen and the remnant of Clay men.

mayoralty by a minute margin but capturing the Common Council. Although the 1834 fall election showed a Democratic gain, it was short-lived. During the ensuing two years the Locofoco secession, followed by their coalition with the Whigs, undermined the Tammany majority, even though the Democracy succeeded in electing most of its candidates in 1835 and 1836. With the Panic, the "ins" suffered as Tammany went down to defeat in 1837 and 1838, foreshadowing the Democratic debacle of 1840.*

A closer examination of these election results in relation to the distribution of wealth should reveal the extent to which the voting pattern was a product of the socioeconomic structure, and, conversely, the degree of lower-class support for the Workingmen's movement in comparison with the major parties.† The 1828 election for Presidential electors, as indicated in Table XVI, demonstrated great Democratic strength throughout the city, even the three lower wards giving Adams only a slight majority. Gaining the support of former National Republicans, Tammany carried these wards by a wide margin the following year, but its city-wide majority was reduced by the emergence of the Workingmen's Party.‡ Although this new group received its principal support from the

* The Democrats carried New York City in 1840, giving Van Buren a slight majority, and increased their margin in 1842.

† Lacking more reliable indices, real and personal property can be accepted as an indication of the socioeconomic stratification in New York City during this period. But it must be realized that the assessed valuation of real and personal property is not the most accurate index to wealth or economic class, for it cannot be truly equated with income. Much of the real property in the city was owned by absentee landlords, like John Jacob Astor, and a large proportion of the mechanics and laborers lived in rented dwellings. Yet, in so far as property values determine rentals, they can be considered an index to the income and class of the inhabitants of a given locality. Moreover, as Fox points out (*Decline of Aristocracy*, pp. 431, 436), other available data tend to substantiate the validity of this criterion as a basis for classification of the wards according to the wealth of the inhabitants. For example, a comparison of the population per occupied lot in 1834 (see Williams, *Annual Register* [1835], pp. 312–13) with property valuation per capita shows an inverse correspondence in most wards (the Ninth and the Eleventh are the most obvious exceptions).

‡ The vote in 1829 was about 5,600 less than in 1828; the Workingmen's ticket received approximately 6,000 votes, while the Tammany vote decreased about 5,000 and the National Republicans by more than 7,000.

poorest wards, it cannot be determined from this tabulation whether its appeal was to former Adams or Jackson adherents. The Workingmen were split in the 1830 election, the Cook faction forming a coalition with the Antimasonic and National Republican parties. While the Tammany vote showed little change from 1829, the other parties exchanged positions, as former Workingmen seemingly supported the anti-Tammany coalition in several wards. Some of them maintained this allegiance in 1832, as is shown in Table XVII, although the over-all pattern was markedly similar to the contest in the previous Presidential year.

The 1834 elections revealed a strong anti-Tammany sentiment, channeled through the new Whig Party. This was especially prevalent in the wealthier localities, notably the three lower wards and the Fifteenth, but the Whigs demonstrated surprising strength

TABLE XVI

COMPARISON OF VOTING AND WEALTH IN THE ELECTIONS OF
1828, 1829, AND 1830*

Ward	Wealth per Capita 1830	Percent of Total Vote by Parties and Elections[a]								
		1828		1829			1830		
		T	A	T	A	W	T	A	W
1	$4,104	49	51	73	17	10	50	44	4
2	1,685	44	56	51	35	11	45	48	7
3	1,721	49	51	66	15	16	46	46	8
4	741	57	43	66	16	16	50	41	8
5	701	60	40	59	17	24	49	32	19
6	628	67	33	64	10	25	52	38	10
7	532	69	31	58	13	28	60	32	8
8	401	64	36	42	11	46	44	41	15
9	638	66	34	50	9	36	55	32	12
10	287	66	34	46	6	48	56	38	12
11	403	69	31	48	3	49	60	26	14
12	687	67	33	74	4	21	65	28	7
13	214	65	35	40	5	55	50	44	6
14	451	64	36	55	7	35	61	29	10
	$820	62	38	55	12	31	53	36	11

* Wealth per capita from Table XIV; percentages computed from election returns in *Evening Post*, November 10, 1828; *Courier and Enquirer*, November 12, 1829; *Working Man's Advocate*, November 13, 1830.

[a] T—Tammany vote. A—National Republican vote. W—Workingmen's vote.

elsewhere as well. The Democracy, on the other hand, found its principal support in the poorer wards in the northern and eastern sections of the city and in the reliable Sixth Ward, virtually a pocket borough of the Tammany politicians in and around City Hall. Between April and November, while the brief recession was succeeded by renewed prosperity, about 3 percent of the electorate shifted their political allegiance. This gave Tammany a comfortable margin of victory, the gain being spread fairly uniformly over all wards. But the Democratic split in 1835 again threatened the dominance of the Wigwam, the Locofocos with 16 percent of

TABLE XVII

COMPARISON OF VOTING AND WEALTH IN THE ELECTIONS OF 1832 AND 1834*

| Ward | Wealth per Capita 1832 | Percent of Total Vote[a] | | | | | | Wealth per Capita 1834 |
| | | 1832 | | 1834[b] | | 1834[c] | | |
		T	A	T	A	T	A	
1	$4,104	43	57	28	72	31	69	$4,868
2	1,685	39	61	32	68	36	64	1,925
3	1,721	45	55	36	64	41	59	1,629
4	741	56	44	45	55	51	49	633
5	701	62	38	47	53	48	52	642
6	628	66	34	58	42	57	43	593
7	532	66	34	53	47	54	46	504
8	401	57	43	49	51	53	47	382
9	400	63	37	55	45	59	41	292
10	287	64	36	56	44	59	41	247
11	403	72	28	63	37	67	33	261
12	687	74	26	65	35	68	32	420
13	214	67	33	60	40	60	40	177
14	451	63	37	54	46	58	42	406
15	972	63	47	40	60	40	60	899
	$820	59	41	50[d]	50	53	47	$691

* Wealth per capita from Table XIV; percentages computed from election returns in *Sentinel*, November 14, 1832; *American*, April 18, 1834; *Working Man's Advocate*, November 15, 1834.

[a] T—Tammany. A—National Republicans and Whigs.

[b] April election for Mayor and other city officials.

[c] November general election for Congress and legislature.

[d] The Tammany candidate won the Mayoralty election with 50.3 per cent of the vote cast.

the vote holding the balance of power. Because about 13,000 fewer
votes were cast in this off-year election, it is difficult to determine
whether the Locofoco votes came from disgruntled Democrats or
hopeful Whigs, but the compilation in Table XVIII indicates that
the dissidents received support from all wards.

The 1836 general election is even less subject to analysis because
of the Locofoco alliance with the Whigs and their support of some
of the Tammany candidates. Stephen Hasbrouck, the only Congressional nominee of the insurgents not endorsed by a major party,

TABLE XVIII

Comparison of Voting and Wealth in the Elections of
1835 AND 1836*

Ward	Wealth per Capita 1835	Percent of Total Vote[a]									Wealth per Capita 1836
		1835			1836[b]			1836[c]			
		T	A	W	T	A	W	T	A	W	
1	$5,390	27	69	4	33	67	1	28	72	—	$6,169
2	2,154	28	61	11	29	69	2	25	72	3	2,865
3	1,734	39	55	6	34	65	2	31	67	2	2,115
4	708	34	40	26	47	50	4	39	56	5	803
5	711	41	41	12	45	53	3	46	52	2	1,007
6	637	52	35	13	61	36	3	59	39	2	849
7	577	53	34	13	50	47	4	43	53	4	782
8	401	41	39	20	48	47	5	44	50	6	563
9	355	61	32	7	57	41	3	59	38	3	600
10	279	32	32	36	49	44	9	51	40	9	401
11	365	59	27	14	56	40	4	51	43	6	751
12	744	80	10	10	75	22	2	80	18	2	2,119
13	201	42	36	22	50	47	4	49	48	3	291
14	467	41	40	19	49	46	5	42	54	4	591
15	1,236	30	54	16	36	63	2	33	65	2	1,818
16	—	—	—	—	55	39	7	47	44	9	1,542
	$810	44	40	16	48	48	4	45	51	4	$1,146

* Wealth per capita from Table XIV; percentages computed from election returns in
Williams, *Annual Register* (1836), p. 317; *Evening Post*, November 26, 1836; *New-
Yorker*, December 31, 1836.

[a] T—Tammany. A—Native American and Whig. W—Locofoco.

[b] November Congressional election. The vote in each ward does not invariably total
100 percent because of the complex voting pattern in this election. Of the ten candidates
nominated on a general ticket for the four Congressional seats, three were endorsed by two
parties. The three candidates cited in the table were Cambreleng for Tammany, Hoffman
for the Whigs, and Hasbrouck for the Locofocos; percentages were computed on the total
vote for State Senator, for which only two candidates were nominated.

[c] December special election for Assemblyman.

TABLE XX

CORRELATION BETWEEN PROPERTY AND VOTING IN
NEW YORK CITY, 1828–1838*

		Coefficients of Correlation by Parties[a]		
Year	Elective Contest	T	A	W
1828	President	−.71	+.71	
1829	Assembly	+.55	+.50	−.68
1830	Congress	−.30	+.47	−.51
1832	State Senate	−.73	+.73	
1834	Mayor (April)	−.78	+.78	
	Assembly (November)	−.79	+.79	
1835	Congress	−.45	+.75	−.50
1836	Congress (November)	−.46	+.52	−.59
	Assembly (December)	−.42	+.49	−.49
1837	Mayor (April)	−.35	+.54	−.59
	Assembly (November)	−.63	+.63	−.41[b]
1838	Governor	−.74	+.74	

* Computed from data in Tables XVI–XIX.
[a] T—Tammany. A—Anti-Tammany parties. W—Workingmen and Locofocos.
[b] Rump Locofocos.

paratively high degree of support from the lower economic orders, the pattern in other years is less well defined, indicating support from a broader economic cross-section of the population. The anti-Tammany vote on the other hand manifested in general a significant degree of support from the wealthier classes in the city, although here again the relationship is indefinite in some instances. The analysis of the electoral support of the Workingmen during this decade reveals a consistent negative correlation of voting and wealth, but their vote cannot be fundamentally attributed to the lower economic stratum. Only in 1829 can it be said that the Workingmen's movement was truly a manifestation of lower-class voting, primarily by comparison with the vote for the two major parties. In 1830 the Workingmen had a higher negative correlation than Tammany, but not significantly so, and the relatively low positive correlation for the anti-Tammany coalition indicates considerable lower-class support here also. The economic base of the Locofoco vote is revealed as remarkably similar to that of Tammany, with a slight modification in the 1837 Charter election. The reunion with the Democracy the following November apparently added some lower-class support, while the small vote received by the Rump Locofocos revealed no clear-cut class basis in this diehard remnant of the movement.

The Workingmen, therefore, did not receive their sole electoral support from the lower class. Although their followers on the average possessed less tangible wealth than the supporters of the major parties, it is difficult to assert from this analysis that this was a class movement in any sense. In general, the difference in the property basis of Tammany and the Workingmen was slight, indicating that these parties appealed largely to the same socio-economic elements in the population. The Workingmen, like the Democracy, were broadly based, gaining support from a loose alliance of skilled mechanics and unskilled laborers, businessmen and professionals. Because they both drew upon essentially the same segments of society, the Workingmen, whenever they entered the lists, diluted the power of Tammany and impelled the New York Democracy to fall back upon the support of a more narrowly based electorate, where they could compete less successfully with the opposition party.

In representing the radical wing of the Jacksonian movement in New York, the Workingmen differed from Tammany principally in the democratic character of their leadership. Though including some disgruntled politicians, the movement for the most part was led by men who had emerged from the ranks. The Tammany leadership on the other hand included many members of the "privileged aristocracy"—bank directors, leading merchants, lawyers, and prominent physicians. Their main problem during this period was to maintain their power and prestige with a minimum of concessions to a party rank and file drawn from a broader cross-section of the populace. Journeymen and master mechanics, small tradesmen and apprentice clerks, immigrant laborers and transplanted Yankees faithfully attended Tammany rallies and cast their votes for the Democracy. Some eventually became disillusioned by the failure of victory to alleviate specific grievances or grew disenchanted by oligarchical tendencies in the party organization. Many of these sought temporary refuge with Whigs, Nativists, or Workingmen, often returning to the fold after one election. This tendency not only resulted in a fluid political situation, but induced the Tammany Sachems to dilute both their platform and their personnel. Campaign promises were made—and often kept—to aggrieved factions, and political preferment or a share of the party patronage offered to their leaders. Learning from this example and capitalizing on economic distress, the New York Whigs achieved success toward the end of the decade; the inherited National Republican nucleus was augmented by coalitions with emergent third parties, and disgruntled Democrats were gradually weaned from their traditional allegiance. But, with only an occasional exception, the Whigs were unable to maintain their advantage in New York City as economic conditions improved, the politics of the 'forties being dominated once again by the Democracy. Furthermore, Tammany for the most part succeeded during this decade in retaining the allegiance of former Workingmen.*

The constitution of 1846, essentially a Democratic instrument, revealed the influence of the Workingmen and their permanent contribution to the New York Democracy. Many of the major reforms which they had urged during the preceding decade were now embodied in the fundamental law of the state. Although the educational ideal of Robert Dale Owen, Frances Wright, and the early Workingmen was not realized, the state recognized an obligation to establish a fund to support common schools and academies. Sectarian influence was minimized and liberty of conscience guaranteed by the provision that "the free exercise and enjoyment of religious profession and worship, without discrimination or preference, shall forever be allowed in this state to all mankind; and no person shall be rendered incompetent to be a witness on account of his opinions on matters of religious belief."[4] Most state offices were now elective instead of appointive, including the canal com-

---

* This conclusion is based, not on a quantitative analysis of party personnel in the 'forties, but on the role played in Tammany politics by a number of the most notable former Workingmen; for some examples see Chapter 5, above.

missioners and state prison inspectors. In accordance with the Locofoco demand, judges were also elected, and for short terms.[5] Furthermore, a commission was to be appointed to reform and simplify the rules of legal practice and judicial proceedings, and an effort was made to decrease the influence of common law precedents. Providing that all parts of the common law "as are repugnant to this constitution, are hereby abrogated," the document stipulated that "the whole body of the law" be reduced "into a written and systematic code."[6]

Of even greater significance were the provisions regarding "monopolies" and corporations. Governmental licensing functions were curbed by the abolition of "all offices for the weighing, gauging, measuring, culling or inspecting any merchandise, produce, manufacture or commodity whatever," though this blanket abrogation was modified by the assertion of the state's obligation to protect the public health and to supply correct standards of weights and measures.[7] Article VIII, repealing the traditional special chartering system for all but municipal corporations, gave constitutional sanction to the practice, embodied in the Free Banking Act, of creation by general act. Moreover, all doubt of the constitutionality of that pioneering legislation was removed by the statement that "the term corporation . . . shall be construed to include all associations and joint-stock companies having any of the powers and privileges of corporations not possessed by individuals or partnerships." An effort to protect the community against a recurrence of financial distress was envisioned by the denial of legislative recognition to any future suspension of specie payments; in addition, all banknotes were to be fully secured and registered, noteholders were given preference over all other creditors in case of insolvency, and stockholders were made individually liable to the extent of their holdings for all corporation debts and liabilities.[8]

This document, when compared with the constitution of 1821, reflects the changes, social and economic as well as political, which had occurred in New York in a quarter-century. "We stand," Federalist James Kent had warned his fellow delegates at the earlier convention, "on the brink of fate, on the very edge of a precipice." He, as a stalwart defender of the old Federalist order, believed sincerely that "the tendency of universal suffrage is to jeopardize the rights of property and the principles of liberty." Predicting the imminent danger of an "agrarian law," Kent saw as the aftermath of mass enfranchisement "the oppression of minorities, and a disposition to encroach upon private right—to disturb chartered privilege—and to weaken, degrade and overawe the administration of justice."[9] One need not share Kent's prejudices to maintain that part, at least, of his prophecy had been borne out by 1846. And much of the responsibility for this transformation could be imputed to the Workingmen and their allies and proselytes among the Democracy.

Yet it is inconceivable that this small band of political dissidents could have effected such a revolution unaided. The reforms accomplished during the 'thirties and 'forties, and the 1846 constitution in particular, could not have been enacted into law but for the acquiescence—indeed, the active cooperation—of a significant segment of the population upstate. Participation in this liberalizing movement, moreover, was not necessarily limited to nominal Democrats, as demonstrated by the Whig role in passage of the Free Banking Act. Democrats, in fact, were often the most steadfast opponents of reform and the most resolute defenders of vested rights. Jacksonian Democracy, therefore, as it developed in New York was the product of the interaction of diverse groups whose common denominator was not loyalty to President or Party, but the desire for social change and individual amelioration. The Workingmen represented an important and at times influential element in this movement. In turn goading and persuading the regular party organization toward acceptance of their principles, they largely succeeded in converting the Democracy into an instrument dedicated to the protection and enlargement of freedom of opportunity and "equal rights."

Conclusion

"THE EIGHTEENTH century closed in 1821," concluded Dixon Ryan Fox; "its problems, most of them, had now been settled."[1] While the constitutional debate of that year breached the last bastion of aristocratic republicanism in New York, enabling reformist energies to be diverted to other fields, new problems arose as the enfranchised masses and their political leaders wrestled with the issues created by social and economic developments. It was in this period, more than a decade before the election of Andrew Jackson, that the seedbed of the Jacksonian revolution was planted. The coming of peace in 1815 opened a new era in the United States as well as in Europe. The beginnings of the Industrial Revolution, increased immigration, commercial expansion—even the brief but severe economic recession—all served as essential prologue to the dramatic events of the 'thirties. Now politically liberated, the urban middle class moved into the economic sphere in an effort to remove restrictions on individual enterprise. Because these restrictions were buttressed by law-created "privilege" and vested rights, the battle was of necessity fought primarily in the political arena. With Tammany and the Albany Regency controlling the governmental machinery, a dominant group within the New York Democracy, by successive grants of "exclusive privileges," had become the new aristocracy. Determined to consolidate their position, they joined Jackson's war against the Bank of the United States to eliminate the most effective check on their growing power; it was, as Bray Hammond maintains, "a blow at an older set of capitalists by a newer, more numerous set."[2]

The lower orders of society, the "labouring classes," had discovered meanwhile that the right of suffrage alone was no panacea for their political, social, and economic disabilities. The New York Workingmen's movement represented an effort on the part of these mechanics and small businessmen to further the democratization of this capitalist society, making more of its fruits available to all. Though often stating their demands in radical language, these men were expressing, not a proletarian animosity to the existing order, but the desire for equal opportunity to become capitalists themselves. Disillusioned with Tammany, because its democratic pretensions were seldom matched by accomplishments, they relied upon independent political action by the "producing classes" to democratize the Democracy. First advancing universal education as a nostrum, they then focused on the banking system as both symptom and cause of their social ills. Yet aversion to banking is no more the key to the Equal Rights Party than is faith in education to its precursor; whether as Workingmen or Locofocos, opposition to "monopoly" and "exclusive privileges" came to be the basis of their indictment of the social order. And, as Tammany had become the chief defender of vested rights, no effort was spared—including alliance with the "aristocratic" party—to punish the Democrats for forsaking the "correct principles" expounded by Jefferson and Jackson.

The resultant political agitation in New York during this period was symptomatic of the changes occurring in the class structure of the nation's greatest commercial city. New avenues of social mobility had been opened by the defeat of the Monster Bank, each charter approved by the legislature being a means of recruiting additional members to the economic aristocracy. But at the same time the position of the journeyman mechanic was worsening, for he was beset both by the fear that his craft was being debased and by consciousness of the increasing difficulty of setting up his own shop. Though many supported the objectives of the Workingmen, their motives were related less to their present position than to their future expectations. Like their employees, master mechanics were increasingly concerned with their social status. Blaming the merchant capitalist and the credit situation for keeping them in a subordinate position, they too were fearful of slipping back irrevocably into the proletarian ranks. As industrial stratification and the division of labor had not yet come to characterize New York manufacturing, skilled wage workers and their employers were more often united than divided on political issues. Some began to rely on journeymen's combinations and the strike weapon, but to the majority this was a temporary expedient resulting from the exigencies of the immediate situation. Although politicians became labor leaders, and labor leaders politicians, the link between this labor movement and the Workingmen was tenuous; the organized journeymen were generally successful in avoiding the pitfalls of politics, and the political movement had broader objectives than the improvement of wages and working conditions.

Because the socioeconomic situation in New York City was increasingly dynamic during this period, the stratification of society was not well defined. It is obvious from the preceding biographical and occupational analysis that the New York Workingmen represented more than journeymen or wage earners. But the pattern otherwise seems heterogeneous, with neither a common denominator nor clearly delineated class limits. The diversity of these life histories and occupational groups begins to take form with reference to the specific issues in the party program. Each occupation represented significantly in the movement had a specific economic grievance. The building trades and suppliers of building materials demanded a mechanics' lien law; dry-goods merchants and other mechanics and tradesmen competing with imported goods asked for restrictions on auctions; the convict labor system was denounced by aggrieved mechanics and manufacturers ranging from stonemasons to shoemakers; grocers and butchers were joined by consumers and other retailers in demanding repeal or reform of municipal licensing; physicians and patients denounced the "medical monopoly." Moreover, many occupational groups in Jacksonian society could agree on such social and political demands as public education, repeal of imprisonment for debt, and judicial and electoral reform. All these issues could be agitated in terms of the demand for "equal rights" through the abolition of the monopoly system, the banks serving as a familiar and convenient scapegoat for their real or imagined distress. In agitating these issues, these men were the spokesmen of the urban working class of pre-industrial America, a class so broadly conceived that it included large elements of the bourgeoisie, yet delimited from the drones and parasites in the privileged commercial and financial aristocracy. To indicate it complexity, the Jacksonians continually referred to this segment of society in the plural, as "the working classes," "the industrious classes," "the producing classes," or "the useful classes." All members of this group, it was believed, had a community of interests, based on their common devotion to useful and productive work; they shared a common relation, not to the means of production, but to its end, for each contributed in his own way to the creation of tangible goods of value to society.

As representatives of this working class, the Workingmen were struggling against law-created privilege, rather than attacking the business community of which they considered themselves actual or potential members. For this reason their struggle took the form of a campaign to transform government into an impartial arbiter among free individuals, each pursuing his own economic self-interest. Even when this view of the role of the state was modified in the case of education and mechanics' liens, the power of the state was to be wielded to enforce equality of opportunity and to prevent unfair discrimination. While William Leggett expressed the extreme laissez-faire view, George Henry Evans on occasion advocated government monopoly of public utilities like ferries and canals in preference to either private monopoly or unrestricted competition, seeing the state as the instrument of the whole people. The Workingmen generally, as well as the "purified" Democracy of the 'forties, leaned toward Leggett's view, as exemplified by the successful effort to limit the state's economic role in the 1846 constitution. The opposition in New York during this period to state action in the economic field seems to depart from the pattern in the neighboring states of Massachusetts and Pennsylvania, and this can in part be attributed to the influence of the Locofoco tradition.[3]

A similar inconsistency is evident in the Workingmen's attitude toward paper money and banking, combining the hard-money doctrines more suited to a simpler economy with a demand for unrestricted competition in banking under a "general law." Bray

Hammond perhaps overstresses the predominance of antibank sentiment in the movement, and underestimates their desire for easier access to credit, in viewing the Locofocos as "an urban and industrial phase of traditional agrarianism produced by the economic pressure which was exerted on the less fortunate part of the population by industry and enterprise, by steam and credit."[4] While some in the movement subscribed to the agrarian ideal of a simple, non-commercial society, others visualized an expansive economy with no limits to individual enterprise. For the most part, the Workingmen as spokesmen of the unprivileged were struggling—journeyman and master, manufacturer and merchant—against an aristocratic system which would deny to all but a few the opportunity to partake in the future of the new nation.

The Workingmen demonstrated the Jacksonian dilemma: "the Jacksonian struggle," as elucidated by Marvin Meyers, "to reconcile again the simple yeoman values with the free pursuit of economic interest, just as the two were splitting hopelessly apart."[5] Some shared the qualms of Albert Gallatin, the voice of the Jeffersonian conscience. "We have rioted in liberty and revel in luxury," he declared in 1841, and have substituted "the thirst of gold for the honest endeavors to acquire by industry and frugality a modest independence." Five years earlier, in the midst of the speculative mania, he had even more emphatically epitomized the tenor of the Jacksonian revolution: "The energy of this nation is not to be controlled; it is at present exclusively applied to the acquisition of wealth and to improvements of stupendous magnitude. Whatever has that tendency, and of course an immoderate expansion of credit, receives favor. The apparent prosperity and the progress of cultivation, population, commerce, and improvement are beyond expectation." He concluded ruefully: "I would have preferred a gradual, slower, and more secure progress. I am, however, an old man, and the young generation has a right to govern itself."[6] Subordinating their scruples, many Workingmen took advantage of the improved opportunities for the enterprising, but it was the succeeding generation who truly benefited from their fathers' crusade. The new business world of the Civil War era, as Bray Hammond has emphasized, "was not a mere expansion of the old . . . dominated by descendants of the merchants who had dominated the old or by their traditions." Instead, "it was dominated by self-made men" who "exulted in their humble origins and acquisitive achievements."[7] The New York Workingmen may not have recognized, or approved, the face of postwar America, but their efforts had contributed to produce it.

Notes

INTRODUCTION

1. See Thomas C. Cochran, "The Presidential Synthesis in American History," *American Historical Review*, LIII (July 1948), 748–59.

2. Samuel E. Morison and Henry S. Commager, *The Growth of the American Republic* (4th ed., 2 vols., New York, 1950), I, 472. See also John W. Ward, *Andrew Jackson, Symbol for an Age* (New York, 1955).

3. See, e.g., his *United States, 1830–1850* (New York, 1935), pp. 24–25.

4. *The Age of Jackson* (Boston, 1945), p. 283.

5. *Ibid.*, pp. 307–8, 344.

6. "The Jackson Wage-Earner Thesis," *American Historical Review*, LIV (January 1949), 305.

7. Richard Hofstadter, *The American Political Tradition and the Men Who Made It* (New York, 1948), p. 55; Bray Hammond, "Public Policy and National Banks," *Journal of Economic History*, VI (May 1946), 82

8. *History of Labour in the United States* (2 vols., New York, 1918), I, 12; the detailed account of this period by Helen L. Sumner and Edward B. Mittelman covers pp. 169–470.

9. On Philadelphia see William A. Sullivan, "Did Labor Support Andrew Jackson?" *Political Science Quarterly*, LXII (December 1947), 569–80; "Philadelphia Labor during the Jackson Era," *Pennsylvania History*, XV (October 1948), 305–20; and *The Industrial Worker in Pennsylvania 1800–1840* (Harrisburg, 1955). Cf. Louis H. Arky, "The Mechanics' Union of Trade Associations and the Formation of the Philadelphia Working Men's Movement," *Pennsylvania Magazine of History and Biography*, LXXVI (April 1952), 142–76. On Boston see Edward Pessen, "Did Labor Support Jackson?: The Boston Story," *Political Science Quarterly*, LXIV (June 1949), 262–74. On Newark see Milton J. Nadworny, "New Jersey Workingmen and the Jacksonians," *Proceedings of the New Jersey Historical Society*, LXVII (July 1949), 185–98.

10. *History of Labour*, I, 5.

11. John R. Commons and associates, eds., *A Documentary History of American Industrial Society* (11 vols., Cleveland, 1910), V, 141–42.

12. Edward Pessen, "The Workingmen's Movement of the Jacksonian Era," *Mississippi Valley Historical Review*, XLIII (December 1956), 431. See also Dixon Ryan Fox, *Decline of Aristocracy in the Politics of New York* (New York, 1919), 352–408.

13. New York *American*, October 29, November 3, 1829; all newspapers hereinafter cited were published in New York City, unless otherwise indicated.

CHAPTER 1

1. See Claude G. Bowers, *Party Battles of the Jackson Period* (Boston and New York, 1922), chap. 2.

2. Fox, *Decline of Aristocracy,* pp. 347–50; Jackson's statewide majority was about 25,000 less than that of Governor Van Buren. See also *American,* November 10, 13, 1828.

3. For the history of the Philadelphia Workingmen's Party cf. Commons, *History of Labour,* I, 184–216; and Arky, "The Mechanics' Union of Trade Associations," pp. 142–76. It is difficult, if not impossible, to assess the influence of this movement, though it seems inconceivable that New Yorkers could have been ignorant of its existence.

4. Miss Wright delivered a series of lectures in New York before Owen's arrival; *Free Enquirer* (New Harmony, Ind.), February 11, 1829. The first issue of the paper published in New York was that of March 4, 1829; both Owen and Miss Wright were listed as editors.

5. *Morning Herald,* February 26 to March 4, 1829; *American,* March 3, 20, 1829.

6. [George H. Evans], "History of the Origin and Progress of the Working Man's Party in New York," *Radical* (Granville, N.J.), January 1842; Evans does not so state, but it is probable that the building trades were most concerned by this demand. A brief notice of the meeting appeared in *Commercial Advertiser,* April 25, 1829.

7. Brief proceedings of the meeting were published in *Free Enquirer,* April 29, 1829, and *Morning Herald,* May 1, 1829. See also *Farmers', Mechanics', and Working Men's Advocate* (Albany, N.Y.), June 30, 1830.

8. *Radical,* January 1842; this assertion cannot be proved, as no list of the Committee members has been found.

9. *Free Enquirer,* August 19, September 23, 30, 1829. Evans, then a young printer associated with Owen, was chairman of this committee.

10. For the proceedings of the meeting see *Morning Courier and New-York Enquirer,* October 23, 1829, and *Working Man's Advocate,* October 31, 1829. This was the first issue of the latter newspaper, printed, edited, and published by George Henry Evans.

11. Skidmore's occupation was given in *Courier and Enquirer,* October 28, 1829; for his political background see *American,* September 18, October 15, 1828. The *Free Enquirer,* June 17, 1829, carried a notice announcing the impending publication by subscription of his book.

12. *Working Man's Advocate,* October 31, 1829.

13. *Ibid.* For Wood's political background see *American,* September 27, 1828; he also received the National Republican nomination for State Senator in 1829.

14. *Courier and Enquirer,* October 28, 1829. For the 1828 political activities of Potter and Friend see *American,* September 18, 19, October 15, 1828; for Blatchley's background see *ibid.,* March 9, 1829.

15. The different accounts of the meeting are from the October 31,

1829, issues of the *Working Man's Advocate, American,* and *Courier and Enquirer.* For the preceding Association meeting see *Free Enquirer,* November 7, 1829.

16. For the origin of the "Pewter Mug" faction and the election results see *Courier and Enquirer,* October 31, November 2, 12, December 16, 1829.

17. *Ibid.,* November 12, 13, 1829.

18. *Evening Journal,* November 9, 1829. For the prospectus of the *Daily Sentinel* see *Courier and Enquirer,* December 15, 1829; this paper did not appear until February 1830, largely because of financial difficulties.

19. For biographical information on Cook and Crolius see *Longworth's Directory of New York City,* 1828–29; Edwin Williams, *New-York Annual Register for the Year of Our Lord 1830,* p. 129; *Proceedings and Address of the Republican Young Men of the State of New-York, Assembled at Utica, on the 12th day of August, 1828,* p. 4; *Morning Herald,* July 1, December 19, 1829; *American,* September 17, 19, 27, October 9, 15, November 1, 1828.

20. For the debate on party organization see *Working Man's Advocate,* November 21, 28, December 5, 19, 1829; *Evening Journal,* December 4, 14, 1829; Skidmore's views were published by Evans as letters from "Marcus." The proceedings of the December 29 meeting were detailed and discussed in *ibid.,* December 30, 31, 1829, January 2, 1830.

21. *Working Man's Advocate,* January 16, 23, 1830; *Evening Journal,* January 18, 1830. For the background of the Executive Committee officers see *Directory,* 1829–30; *American,* September 27, October 30, 1828; *Courier and Enquirer,* October 28, November 10, 1829; *Evening Journal,* November 28, 1829; *Sentinel and Working Man's Advocate,* June 16, 1830.

22. *Evening Journal,* January 26, 28, February 25, 1830; for the publication of Skidmore's paper (no copies of which have been located) see *Working Man's Advocate,* April 17, 1830, and *Free Enquirer,* May 1, 1830.

23. *Working Man's Advocate,* March 13, April 24, 1830.

24. Jabez D. Hammond, *History of Political Parties in the State of New-York, from the Ratification of the Federal Constitution to December, 1840* (4th ed., 2 vols., Cooperstown, 1846), II, 330–33. For the upstate parties and Evans' comment see *Evening Journal,* March 5, 1830; *Farmers', Mechanics', and Working Men's Advocate,* April 28, 1830; *Working Man's Advocate,* April 24, 1830.

25. *Farmers', Mechanics', and Working Men's Advocate,* May 26, 1830; *Working Man's Advocate,* May 22, 1830.

26. Cook was first listed as co-editor in *Evening Journal,* February 2, 1830. The first issue of the *Sentinel* was February 15, 1830; it was at first conducted by six journeyman printers, but later merged with the *Working Man's Advocate* until discontinued by Evans in 1833; see *Sentinel and Working Man's Advocate,* June 23, 1830, and *Working Man's Advocate,* July 6, 1833.

27. For accounts of the meeting see *Free Enquirer*, June 5, 1830; *Working Man's Advocate*, May 22, 29, 1830; *Sentinel and Working Man's Advocate*, June 16, 1830. No copies of the *Evening Journal* have been found for this crucial period, but for the same viewpoint see *Farmers', Mechanics', and Working Men's Advocate*, May 26, 29, 1830.

28. *Sentinel and Working Man's Advocate*, June 16, 1830; *Farmers', Mechanics', and Working Men's Advocate*, June 19, 1830.

29. *Working Man's Advocate*, May 29, June 5, 1830; *Sentinel and Working Man's Advocate*, June 16, 19, 23, 26, 1830; *Farmers', Mechanics', and Working Men's Advocate*, June 23, July 10, 1830.

30. *Sentinel and Working Man's Advocate*, July 3, 10, 1830; *American*, June 29, July 1, 1830. For the background of Lamb and Leavens see *ibid.*, September 17, October 30, 1828; *Directory*, 1830–31. For the election results and the reaction see *Sentinel and Working Man's Advocate*, July 17, 1830.

31. *Courier and Enquirer*, July 19, 1830; *Sentinel and Working Man's Advocate*, July 21, 1830.

32. *Ibid.*, July 17, 24, 1830; for Evans' statement see *ibid.*, July 21, 1830.

33. On the convention see *Farmers', Mechanics', and Working Men's Advocate*, April 24, July 21, 31, August 7, 28, 1830; *Working Man's Advocate*, September 4, 1830. For the movement toward coalition see *Farmers', Mechanics', and Working Men's Advocate*, October 6, 16, 1830; *Working Man's Advocate*, October 9, 1830; *American*, October 16, 1830.

34. *Sentinel and Working Man's Advocate*, July 10, 1830. For efforts at reconciliation see *Working Man's Advocate*, October 9, 16, 1830; *Farmers', Mechanics', and Working Men's Advocate*, October 9, 1830; *American*, October 16, 1830.

35. *Working Man's Advocate*, September 18, October 9, 16, 23, 1830; Smith had been listed as the Buffalo agent for the *Free Enquirer* since early 1829; see the issue of March 11, 1829. On the Skidmore faction see *Working Man's Advocate*, September 25, 1830; the election results were in *ibid.*, November 13, 1830.

36. *Free Enquirer*, November 13, 1830; *Working Man's Advocate*, November 13, 1830. After the election the Workingmen joined with Tammany in celebrating the recent French Revolution; *ibid.*, November 20, December 4, 1830.

37. Letter published in *ibid.*, November 13, 1830.

CHAPTER 2

1. *Working Man's Advocate*, September 17, 1831.

2. *Ibid.*, February 19, 1831; for establishment of the associations see *ibid.*, January 1, 22, March 5, 12, 26, 1831.

3. *Ibid.*, April 9, 1831; for the election see *American*, April 19, 1831.

4. *Working Man's Advocate*, October 15, 22, 29, 1831.

5. *Ibid.*, October 29, 1831.

6. For the election and its aftermath see *American*, November 16, 1831; *Working Man's Advocate*, November 12, 26, 1831.

7. *Ibid.*, April 3, 17, 1830, January 29, June 11, September 24, 1831; on Johnson see also Schlesinger, *Age of Jackson*, pp. 140–42.

8. *Working Man's Advocate*, March 24, 1832. For the Johnson rally see *Courier and Enquirer*, March 13, 16, 1832; this paper, partisan to Van Buren, charged the Workingmen with responsibility for the call, which Evans denied.

9. *Working Man's Advocate*, March 31, 1832; see *ibid.* for proceedings of the meeting.

10. *Ibid.*, February 4, June 2, 1832; for other statements on Van Buren see *ibid.*, September 3, 1831, June 9, 1832.

11. *Ibid.*, September 22, 1832; *Sentinel*, September 27, 28, 1832.

12. *Ibid.*, September 12, 13, 1832; see also *ibid.*, September 26, October 15, November 5, 1832. Evans criticized some candidates on the Tammany Assembly ticket in *ibid.*, October 20, 1832.

13. *American*, September 21, 1832. On Wells see *Evening Journal*, February 1, 1830; *American*, October 6, 24, 30, November 5, 1832; *Working Man's Advocate*, May 29, 1830, November 10, 1832. Edward J. Webb, a former Clay supporter, urged the Workingmen to vote for Jackson in *Sentinel*, November 5, 1832. For the election results see *ibid.*, November 4, 1832.

14. *Whig*, November 13, 1832; this was an Antimasonic paper.

15. *Evening Star*, November 2, 8, 1833; see *American*, November 11, 1833, for the election results.

16. On the controversy see *Evening Star*, January 25, 1834; *American*, February 25, 1834; *Evening Post*, January 31, February 5, 1834. For Evans' view see *Man*, March 3, 1834; this was a new daily paper, successor to the *Sentinel*.

17. For views of the Park meeting see *American*, February 7, 8, 10, 1834; *Evening Post*, February 10, 1834; *Evening Star*, February 8, 10, 11, 1834. On the dismissals see *Evening Post*, February 10 to 13, 1834; *Courier and Enquirer*, February 10, 1834. The latter had moved into the Clay camp in 1832; see *ibid.*, October 1, 1832.

18. *Evening Star*, January 31, February 13, March 7, 20, 1834. For the meetings see *ibid.*, March 14, 24, 28, 29, 1834; cf. *Niles' Weekly Register* (Baltimore, Md.), April 5, 1834.

19. *Working Man's Advocate*, February 1, March 29, April 5, 1834; *Man*, March 3, April 4, 1834.

20. For accounts of the rioting see *Evening Star*, April 10 to 14, 1834; *Evening Post*, April 11, 1834; *Working Man's Advocate*, April 12, 1834; *Niles' Register*, April 12, 19, 1834. For the election results see *American*, April 18, 1834.

21. *Working Man's Advocate*, April 19, 1834; Webb's statement was made in a letter published in the *Evening Star*, May 27, 1834.

22. *Man*, May 7, 12, 17, 19, 1834.

23. *Ibid.*, May 10, 15, July 8, 1834. Leggett conducted the paper dur-

ing most of the controversy, Bryant traveling in Europe from mid-1834 to early 1836; see Allan Nevins, *The Evening Post: A Century of Journalism* (New York, 1922), chap. 6.

24. *Times,* May 20, 1834; *Man,* May 21, 22, 1834.

25. *Ibid.,* July 8, 1834; see also *Working Man's Advocate,* August 30, 1834.

26. *Man,* October 1 to 4, 7, 10, 1834; *Evening Post,* October 3, 9, 1834.

27. For meetings on the prison-labor question and Moore's appointment see *Evening Star,* January 15, April 5, May 26, July 5, 1834; *Working Man's Advocate,* September 13, 1834. The best summary of the Auburn Plan, as the prison system was called, and the nature of the complaints against it are to be found in the "Report of the Commissioners appointed under the 'act concerning State Prisons' to the legislature of the State of New York, January 29, 1835," *New York Assembly Documents,* 58th Session (1835), No. 135, pp. 1–18.

28. *Working Man's Advocate,* November 8, 1834.

29. On the Democratic nominations see *ibid.,* October 18, November 1, 1834; *Man,* October 30, 1834; *Evening Post,* October 31, 1834. See *Working Man's Advocate,* November 15, 1834, for the election results.

CHAPTER 3

1. *Times,* November 15, 17, 1834.

2. *Working Man's Advocate,* November 22, 1834; see also *ibid.,* November 29, 1834; *Evening Post,* November 14, 15, 20, 29, December 30, 1834, January 3, 1835.

3. *Working Man's Advocate,* January 31, February 14, 1835; see also *Times,* May 12, 1835; *Independent Press,* October 1, 1835.

4. *Working Man's Advocate,* February 21, March 14, 1835; *Times,* May 13, 22, 1835. On the prison-labor question see *Evening Post,* February 10, April 28, 1835; *Man,* February 9, 1835; *Times,* February 10, 1835.

5. For the Johnson dinner and the ward meetings see *Working Man's Advocate,* September 12, October 10, 17, 24, 1835; F. Byrdsall, *History of the Loco-Foco or Equal Rights Party, Its Movements, Conventions and Proceedings, With Short Characteristic Sketches of Its Prominent Men* (New York, 1842), pp. 19–20.

6. On Evans see *Working Man's Advocate,* August 29, October 31, 1835; *Radical,* January 1841. On Leggett see *Working Man's Advocate,* November 7, 21, 1835; Richard Hofstadter, "William Leggett, Spokesman of Jacksonian Democracy," *Political Science Quarterly,* LVIII (December 1943), 584, 592.

7. Byrdsall, *History,* pp. 22–23.

8. *Working Man's Advocate,* October 24, 1835; Byrdsall, *History,* p. 16. For the relationship to the Workingmen's Party see *ibid.,* pp. 13–15.

9. *Ibid.,* p. 21.

10. *Ibid.*, pp. 23–27; *Working Man's Advocate,* November 7, 1835. For Bennett's eye-witness account see *Herald,* October 30, 1835.

11. Byrdsall, *History,* pp. 28–31. For the press reaction, including the views of the *Times,* see *Niles' Register,* November 7, 1835.

12. Byrdsall, *History,* pp. 31–32.

13. For the election results see *Working Man's Advocate,* November 7, 1835; the *Evening Post* was quoted in *ibid.,* November 21, 1835. During Leggett's illness the paper was conducted by some of his friends, particularly Theodore Sedwick, Jr.; see Nevins, *Evening Post,* p. 152.

14. Byrdsall, *History,* pp. 32–37.

15. *Ibid.,* pp. 37–43; for the Declaration of Principles see *ibid.,* pp. 39–40.

16. *Ibid.,* pp. 46–49. Cf. *Democrat,* April 2, 1836; this was the Locofoco party organ, established early in March by John Windt. For Ming's political background see *Working Man's Advocate,* October 4, 1834, October 17, November 7, 1835.

17. On the effect of the inflation and the activities of the Trades' Union see Commons, *Documentary History,* V, 286–322. For the trial of the journeyman tailors see *Union,* June 14, 1836; *New-Yorker,* June 4, 25, 1836. Proceedings of the Park meeting were detailed in Byrdsall, *History,* pp. 52, 56; *Evening Post,* June 14, 1836.

18. Byrdsall, *History,* pp. 54–55; for Evans' views see *Working Man's Advocate,* September 12, 1835.

19. Byrdsall, *History,* pp. 56–61.

20. *Ibid.,* pp. 61–77; cf. *Proceedings of the Convention of Mechanics, Farmers and Working Men of the State of New-York, held at the City of Utica, in the County of Oneida, on the 15th, 16th, and 17th Sept. 1836; with the Address of the Convention to the People of the State of New-York* (n.p., n.d. [1836]), pp. 1–6.

21. Byrdsall, *History,* pp. 79–87; see also *Democrat,* October 8, 26, 29, 1836; *Times,* November 2, 1836.

22. Byrdsall, *History,* pp. 88–92; *Times,* October 19, 1836.

23. *Ibid.,* November 3, 6, 1836; Byrdsall, *History,* pp. 92–93, 181–82.

24. *Ibid.,* p. 94; *Times,* November 14, 1836; *Democrat,* November 26, 1836.

25. Byrdsall, *History,* pp. 97–98; this statement was made in reference to a special election in December, in which the Locofoco candidate polled enough votes to elect the Whig nominee, much to the despair of the Democracy. For an analysis of the legislative role of the Locofocos in the Assembly, see Carl N. Degler, "An Inquiry into the Locofoco Party" (unpublished M.A. thesis, Columbia University, 1947).

26. For accounts of the Park meeting and flour riot see Byrdsall, *History,* pp. 99–105, 108–13; *Niles' Register,* February 18, 25, 1837; *New-Yorker,* February 18, March 11, 18, 1837. For the effects of the Panic see *ibid.,* June 10, 24, October 7, 1837; *New Era,* October 7, 1837.

27. Byrdsall, *History,* pp. 135–39. The Locofocos held another state

convention, but little was accomplished since few counties were represented; *ibid.*, pp. 162–63.

28. On the Conservative schism see *ibid.*, p. 171; Fox, *Decline of Aristocracy*, pp. 398–401; William Trimble, "Diverging Tendencies in the New York Democracy in the Period of the Loco Focos," *American Historical Review*, XXIV (April 1919), 404–12.

29. Byrdsall, *History*, pp. 161–62, 174–76; see also Fox, *Decline of Aristocracy*, p. 399.

30. Byrdsall, *History*, pp. 177–79, 186–87.

31. *Ibid.*, p. 187; *New-Yorker*, November 4, 18, 1837.

32. Byrdsall, *History*, p. 188.

33. On Leggett and the Locofoco contribution see Trimble, "Diverging Tendencies," pp. 416–21; Schlesinger, *Age of Jackson*, pp. 257–60; Hofstadter, "William Leggett," pp. 592–94.

CHAPTER 4

1. *History of Labour*, I, 12–18, 232–33, 459–62; see also *Documentary History*, V, 141–42, 203–7.

2. See, e.g., Vernon L. Parrington, *Main Currents in American Thought* (3 vols. in 1, New York, 1927), II, 145–46, 244; Charles A. and Mary R. Beard, *Rise of American Civilization* (2 vols. in 1, New York, 1934), I. 542, 573, 580; Mary R. Beard, *American Labor Movement, A Short History* (New York, 1938), pp. 33–57; Schlesinger, *Age of Jackson*, pp. 205–9; Philip S. Foner, *History of the Labor Movement in the United States* (New York, 1947), pp. 140–66.

3. Dorfman, "The Jackson Wage-Earner Thesis," p. 296.

4. *Ibid.*, p. 305.

5. *Young Men's Advocate*, January 24, 1833.

6. *Times*, September 15, 1834; *Working Man's Advocate*, September 20, 27, November 8, 1834.

7. *Evening Journal*, January 9, 1830.

8. *Ibid.*, February 25, 1830.

9. *Working Man's Advocate*, March 27, April 3, 1830; *Radical*, January 1842.

10. For excellent summaries of this situation see Commons, *History of Labour*, I, 335–47; George R. Taylor, *Transportation Revolution, 1815–1860* (New York, 1951), pp. 215–20, 250–52.

11. See, e.g., John R. Commons, "American Shoemakers, 1648–1895; A Sketch of Industrial Evolution," *Quarterly Journal of Economics*, XXIV (November 1909), 39–84.

12. *Evening Journal*, February 18, 1830.

13. *Working Man's Advocate*, June 8, 1833.

14. *Evening Journal*, October 17, 1829; for a discussion of the rivalry between merchants and manufacturers see August B. Gold, "A History of Manufacturing in New York City, 1825–1840" (unpublished M.A. thesis, Columbia University, 1932), pp. 3–37, 109–18.

15. *Working Man's Advocate,* April 12, 1834.

16. *Sentinel,* November 6, 1832; *Man,* March 22, 1834; *Working Man's Advocate,* April 5, 12, 26, May 3, 1834.

17. *American Apprenticeship and Industrial Education* (New York, 1921), pp. 55–60.

18. *National Trades' Union,* September 6, 1834. No file of this newspaper has been found, so references are to typewritten extracts by John R. Commons and associates, State Historical Society of Wisconsin, or mircrofilm at Columbia University.

19. *Man,* May 30, 1834.

20. *Working Man's Advocate,* March 13, 1830, June 29, 1833.

21. *Ibid.,* November 20, 27, December 4, 1830.

22. *American,* January 14, 1830; *Working Man's Advocate,* April 2, 1831, September 13, 1834; *Courier and Enquirer,* November 18, 1829. Other organizations were the New York Beneficial Society and the Greenwich Village Mechanics' Library; see *Evening Journal,* January 9, March 5, 1830.

23. *American Apprenticeship,* p. 56.

24. *Constitution and By-Laws of the New-York Typographical Society, With a List of Members* (New York, 1848) ; *Working Man's Advocate,* June 16, 25, 1831. See also George A. Stevens, *Typographical Union No. 6: A Study of a Modern Trade Union and Its Predecessors* (Albany, 1913), pp. 105–13; Ethelbert Stewart, ed., *Documentary History of the Early Organizations of Printers* (Indianapolis, 1907), pp. 42–48.

25. For the 1831 strikes see *Working Man's Advocate,* May 21, 28, 1831; for the carpenters' Society see "Constitution and By Laws of the New York Society of Journeyman House Carpenters, Adopted November 19, 1833" (MS., New York Public Library).

26. *Working Man's Advocate,* May 18, 25, 1833; *Courier and Enquirer,* May 21, 1833; Commons, *Documentary History,* V, 212–13.

27. *Working Man's Advocate,* July 13, 27, August 3, 1833; *Courier and Enquirer,* July 26, 1833. The constitution was published in *National Trades' Union,* August 9, 1834, quoted in Commons, *Documentary History,* V, 215–18; the provisions cited are from Articles XI, XII and XIV. For the growth of the Union and the December celebration see *ibid.,* V, 203–4; *Evening Star,* December 3, 1833.

28. *Man,* May 3, June 13, 1834; *National Trades' Union,* August 2, 16, 23, 1834; the objectives of the convention were described in *ibid.,* August 16, 1834. For the list of delegates and proceedings of the meeting see *Man,* August 26–30, September 2, 6, 1834 (also reprinted in large part in Commons *Documentary History,* VI, 196–224). For Commons' summation see *ibid.,* VI, 192–93.

29. *Working Man's Advocate,* June 8, November 30, 1833; *Man,* May 28, June 14, 1834, March 26, April 3, May 20, 1835; *Union,* May 26, 1836; *Courier and Enquirer,* June 13, 16, 1836; *National Trades' Union,* April 18, May 2, 7, 23, 30, June 6, July 4, October 17, 1835, February 13,

27, March 5, 12, 19, 1836. See also Commons, *Documentary History*, V, 220–97; Evans Woolen, "Labor Troubles between 1834 and 1837," *Yale Review*, I (1892), 87–100.

30. *National Trades' Union*, April 4, 1835, April 16, 1836.

31. *Man*, June 9, 10, 23, 1834; *National Trades' Union*, September 6, 27, October 25, 1834.

32. *Niles' Register*, July 5, 1834; *National Trades' Union*, August 9, 1834.

33. *Journal of Commerce*, June 1, 1833; *Evening Star*, December 3, 1833, June 10, 1834; *Niles' Register*, August 23, 1834, May 9, 1835.

34. *National Trades' Union*, September 27, 1834; see also *ibid.*, August 9, 1834.

35. *Ibid.*, December 13, 20, 27, 1834, January 24, 1835.

36. For masters' combinations see Commons, *Documentary History*, V, 206, 308–13; *National Trades' Union*, June 13, 1835, February 13, 20, 27, 1836. The resolution of the Master Tailors was published in *Courier and Enquirer*, March 9, 1836, quoted in Commons, *Documentary History*, V, 314–15.

37. For a full account of the strike and trial see *Union*, May 26 to June 14, 1836; this was a new penny daily, sponsored by the General Trades' Union, which first appeared in April. For the Park meeting see Byrdsall, *History*, pp. 51–52. Greeley's comment appeared in *New-Yorker*, June 25, 1836.

38. *Ibid.*, June 10, October 7, 1837; cf. *New Era*, March 17, October 7, 1837.

39. For a detailed biographical study of Moore see Walter Hugins, "Ely Moore: The Case History of a Jacksonian Labor Leader," *Political Science Quarterly*, LXV (March 1950), 105–25.

40. James W. Moore, *Rev. John Moore of Newtown, L.I., and Some of His Descendants* (Easton, Pa., 1903), pp. 316–17; obituary in *Kansas National Democrat* (Lecompton, Kan.), February 2, 1860. The date of Moore's marriage could not be discovered, but his first child was born in New York in 1825, according to Ely Moore, Jr., "The Lecompton Party Which Located Denver," Kansas State Historical Society *Collections*, VII (1901–2), 446 n. For Coutant's occupation and political activity see *Directory*, 1827–28; *Minutes of the Common Council of the City of New York, 1784–1831* (21 vols., New York, 1930), *passim* (see the index for specific references); *Morning Courier*, November 3, 1828.

41. Deeds and Conveyances recorded in the Office of the Register of the City and County of New York (filed and indexed in the Hall of Records, New York City), Liber 231, p. 476 and *passim;* see also *Index of Conveyances: Grantors* (New York, 1858), VI; *Daily Whig*, June 7, 1839. Coutant had engaged in land speculation in Manhattan for several years; see *Minutes of the Common Council*, XI, 559, 614; Deeds and Conveyances, Libers 67–466 (1804–44), *passim*.

42. For Coutant's election see *Standard*, November 9, 1830. It cannot be established whether Moore was appointed when Coutant first took

office or subsequently; the *Directory* does not list him as assistant register until 1833, continuing the citation in the 1834–35 edition, when Moore and Coutant were out of office; see also *Evening Star,* November 1, 1838.

43. *Working Man's Advocate,* March 17, 1832; Moore's speech was printed in William Emmons, *Authentic Biography of Col. Richard M. Johnson of Kentucky* (New York, 1833), pp. 61–65. For his return to party orthodoxy see *Evening Post,* October 30, 1832.

44. Ely Moore, *Reply to a Pamphlet Entitled "A Statement of Facts in Relation to the Origin, Progress and Prospects of the New-York & Harlem Rail Road Company"* (New York, 1833) ; *Evening Post,* March 15, 18, 1833.

45. *Working Man's Advocate,* June 30, 1832; Commons, *Documentary History,* V, 214–15; Stevens, *Typographical Union,* pp. 162–65. The charges against Moore appeared in *Daily Whig,* June 7, 1839, and *Evening Star,* October 31, 1838.

46. *Address Delivered Before the General Trades' Union of the City of New-York, December 2, 1833* (New York, 1833), pp. 11–13; this has been reprinted in slightly abridged form in Joseph L. Blau, ed., *Social Theories of Jacksonian Democracy* (New York, 1947), pp. 289–300.

47. *Man,* April 4, May 17, 1834; see also *Evening Star,* February 5, 21, 1834.

48. For the prison-labor question see Commons, *Documentary History,* V, 51; *Evening Star,* November 19, 1833, January 15, April 5, 1834. Moore's role in the movement is detailed in *ibid.,* May 26, 28, 1834, November 2, 1838; *Man,* May 27, 31, 1834. For the report and its opposition see *New York Assembly Documents,* 58th Session (1835), No. 135; *Evening Post,* February 10, April 28, 1835; *Man,* February 9, 22, March 2, 7, 1835; *National Trades' Union,* May 30, August 29, 1835. Moore made an appearance at the 1835 convention of the National Trades' Union but contributed little to the proceedings; Commons, *Documentary History,* VI, 228–29, 237–39.

49. *Evening Post,* October 9, 31, November 11, 1834; *Times,* October 9, 1834; *Man,* October 10, 16, 30, November 1, 1834.

50. For his Congressional speeches see *Congressional Globe,* 24th Congress, 1st Session, Appendix, pp. 444–47; 25th Congress, 1st Session, Appendix, pp. 138–46; his other activities are detailed in *ibid.,* 24th Congress, 1st Session, p. 213; 25th Congress, 3d Session, Appendix, pp. 134–35. For assessments of his Congressional career see "Glances at Congress," *United States Magazine and Democratic Review* (Washington, D.C.), I (October 1837), 74–76; "Historical Register," in *ibid.,* IV (February 1838), 41–69, and (November 1840), 177–210; Charles F. Adams, ed., *Memoirs of John Quincy Adams* (12 vols., Philadelphia, 1877), IX, 405-6; Benjamin Perley Poore, *Perley's Reminiscences of Sixty Years in the National Metropolis* (2 vols., Philadelphia, 1886), I, 150–151; *Democrat,* May 2, 1836; *Union,* May 19, 26, 1836.

51. Byrdsall, *History,* pp. 79, 83, 89–90, 94; *Democrat,* October 5, 29, 1836; *Times,* November 2, 1836.

52. Moore in the House, October 13, 1837, *Congressional Globe,* 25th Congress, 1st Session, Appendix, pp. 138–39.

53. *Daily Whig,* March 21, 1838; *New-Yorker,* December 30, 1837; *Evening Star,* October 16, November 3, 1838; *New Era,* November 2, 1838.

54. *Evening Star,* May 21, 23, 1839; *Evening Post,* October 26, November 5, 9, 1842, October 25, November 7, 8, 1844; *Plebeian,* March 23, 29, 1844; *Register of Officers and Agents in the Service of the United States, 1845,* p. 221; *Warren Journal* (Belvidere, N.J.), June 6, 1850; Ely Moore, Jr., "The Story of Lecompton," Kansas State Historical Society *Collections,* XI (1909–10), 463–64; Albert H. Greene, "United States Land Offices in Kansas," and Franklin G. Adams, "The Capitals of Kansas," in *ibid.,* VIII (1903–4), 1–5, 331–43; *Kansas National Democrat* (Lecompton, Kan.), November 5, 12, 1857, February 2, 1860.

55. "Address Delivered Before the General Trades' Union, September 25, 1834," published in *Man,* November 24 and 25, 1834; see also his *Oration Delivered Before the Mechanics and Working Men of the City of New York, on the Fourth of July, 1843* (New York, 1843), p. 22.

56. *Address on Civil Government: Delivered Before the New York Typographical Society, Feb. 25th, 1847* (New York, 1847), pp. 8–45; *Warren Journal,* June 13, August 1, October 31, 1850; also his speech reported in *Plebeian,* March 29, 1844.

57. *Working Man's Advocate,* December 4, 1830, May 9, October 11, 1834; *Courier and Enquirer,* July 26, 1833; *Man,* April 4, 1834; *National Trades' Union,* August 9, December 6, 1834, January 31, 1835; *Democrat,* April 2, 1836; Byrdsall, *History,* p. 146. For his occupation see *Directory,* 1836–37 to 1838–39; *Doggett's New York City and Co-Partnership Directory,* 1842–43.

58. *Courier and Enquirer,* July 26, 1833; *National Trades' Union,* August 9, November 8, 1834; *Man,* September 2, 1834, February 26, March 2, 17, July 6, 1835. For his political activities see *Working Man's Advocate,* April 5, October 11, November 1, 1834, March 14, 1835; *Times,* October 31, 1834; *Jeffersonian,* December 11, 1834; *Man,* April 4, 1835; *Union,* June 14, 1836; Byrdsall, *History,* p. 93; *New Era,* March 19, 25, 1840. His Tammany career is based on Edwin P. Kilroe, "Tammany Society or Columbian Order, Membership List, 1789–1924," p. 14, typescript in Kilroe Tammaniana, Columbia University. For his occupational history see *Directory,* 1836–37 to 1841–42; *Doggett's Directory,* 1842–43 to 1845–46.

59. For his career in the Union see *National Trades' Union,* May 2, 1835; *Man,* May 13, 1835; *Working Man's Advocate,* August 29, 1835; *Union,* May 16, June 14, 1836; *New Era,* December 8, 1836. For his occupation see *Directory,* 1833–34 to 1837–38; he was listed without occupation in 1838–39 and 1839–40, and as editor from 1840 to 1845. However, Byrdsall, *History,* p. 187, listed him as a locksmith on the 1837 Locofoco ticket.

60. *Democrat,* April 2, October 8, 1836; Byrdsall, *History,* pp. 37,

88, 135, 140, 172–75, 187–88; for his character sketch see *ibid.*, p. 134. For his connection with Tammany and his activities in the 1840's see Kilroe, "Membership List," p. 154; *New Era,* November 3, 1838, February 24, March 25, 1840; *Evening Post,* October 19, 1842; *Plebeian,* November 2, 1842, March 12, 1844; *Aurora,* August 2, 1843. His relations with the Calhoun faction are detailed in Joseph A. Scoville to Hunter, August 29, September 11, November 21, 1842, in C. H. Ambler, ed., "Correspondence of Robert M. T. Hunter, 1826–76," American Historical Association, *Annual Report* (1916), II, 40–42, 51–52; Scoville to Calhoun, October 25, 1842, in J. Franklin Jameson, ed., "Correspondence of John C. Calhoun," American Historical Association, *Annual Report* (1899), II, 856–57; Henry P. Barber to Calhoun, December 29, 1843, in C. S. Boucher and R. P. Brooks, eds., "Correspondence Addressed to John C. Calhoun, 1837–49," American Historical Association, *Annual Report* (1929), II, 196. See also Fernando Wood to ———, February 20, 1843, Van Buren Papers, Library of Congress.

61. *Evening Star,* March 24, 28, 29, 1834; *Mercantile Advertiser and New-York Advocate,* September 20, October 15, 31, 1834. See also *Working Man's Advocate,* November 1, 1834; *National Trades' Union,* October 11, 1834.

62. *Courier and Enquirer,* October 23, 26, 28, 1829; *Evening Journal,* December 26, 1829, March 31, 1830; *Sentinel and Working Man's Advocate,* June 19, August 11, 1830; *Farmers', Mechanics', and Working Men's Advocate,* August 7, 28, 1830; *Working Man's Advocate,* September 4, October 30, 1830; *American,* March 7, April 9, 1834; Byrdsall, *History,* pp. 93, 146; *Evening Star,* October 30, 1838. For his occupation as a carpenter see *Directory,* 1825–26 to 1841–42.

63. Kilroe, "Membership List," p. 169; *Directory,* 1825–26 to 1838–39; *Evening Journal,* December 31, 1829, January 14, 1830; *Working Man's Advocate,* June 5, September 4, 11, 25, 1830; *Farmers', Mechanics', and Working Men's Advocate,* August 28, 1830; *Standard,* October 25, 1830; *Daily Whig,* July 3, 1832; *Evening Star,* September 20, 1834.

64. *Courier and Enquirer,* July 26, 1833; *National Trades' Union,* August 29, 1834. According to the previously cited manuscript "Constitution of the Journeyman House Carpenters," Odell joined the Society on June 18 and Townsend on July 2; the Union preliminary convention was held July 15.

65. For the National Trades' Union convention and the debate on politics see *Man,* September 2, 6, 1834; also published in Commons, *Documentary History,* VI, 196–97, 211–16. For Townsend's and Odell's resignations and Odell's reappointment see *National Trades' Union,* November 8, 1834, January 17, August 22, 1835.

66. Byrdsall, *History,* pp. 67–71, 88, 92–94, 146, 172, 175, 187. Marcy's characterization of Townsend was in a letter to P. M. Wetmore, October 25, 1837, quoted in Schlesinger, *Age of Jackson,* p. 199 n. For his later career see *Directory,* 1839–40 to 1841–42; *Doggett's Directory,* 1842–43 to 1844–45.

67. For Commerford in Brooklyn see *Sentinel and Working Man's Advocate*, August 4, 1830; *Working Man's Advocate*, October 23, 1830; he was first listed as a chairmaker in New York in *Directory*, 1831–32, the citation continuing annually to 1841–42. His 1834 political activities were detailed in *Working Man's Advocate*, April 5, 1834; *Man*, May 9, 17, 1834. For his participation in the labor movement see *ibid.*, August 29, September 2, 17, 1834; *National Trades' Union*, November 29, December 13, 1834. The only references found to the United Working Men are notices of meetings in *ibid.*, September 20, October 11, 1834; the corresponding secretary was William Froment, a turner who had been active in the Workingmen's movement since early 1830, moving to Albany in 1835, where he became agent of the *Working Man's Advocate*.

68. *Man*, February 26, April 15, 1835; *Working Man's Advocate*, January 3, 1835; Byrdsall, *History*, pp. 17, 36, 54, 75, 79, 93; the quotation is from *ibid.*, p. 51.

69. *Man*, March 2, June 15, July 6, 1835; *Working Man's Advocate*, August 29, September 19, 1835; *New Era*, December 8, 1836; *National Trades' Union*, August 1, 15, 29, October 10, 1835, February 13, March 26, 1836. See *ibid.*, January 30, February 27, 1836, for the establishment of the *Union*; the first issue appeared on April 21 and the last on July 6, 1836. Byrdsall, *History*, p. 51, states that Commerford was editor, but his name was carried on the masthead only as president of the G.T.U.; see *Union*, April 21, 1836.

70. *Radical*, December 1841; Byrdsall to Calhoun, November 6, 1842, July 19, 1847, in Jameson, "Correspondence of Calhoun," pp. 862, 1126. See also *Evening Post*, October 17, 1842.

71. *Working Man's Advocate*, April 20, May 11, September 7, 1844; *Subterranean*, March 7, September 26, 1846, January 9, 1847. His Trades' Union address was published in *Working Man's Advocate*, September 19, 1835. For his attitude toward Nativism see *ibid.*, May 4, 1844; *Champion of American Labor*, April 3, 1847.

72. *Tribune*, June 7, 1850; *Doggett's Directory*, 1842–43 to 1848–49. For his political activities see *Tribune*, October 8, 1860. His final years are discussed in Helene S. Zahler, *Eastern Workingmen and National Land Policy* (New York, 1941), pp. 103–4, 172 n; Lewis Masquerier, *Sociology: or the Reconstruction of Society, Government, and Property* (New York, 1877), pp. 102, 125.

73. *Working Man's Advocate*, November 1, 1834; Masquerier, *Sociology*, pp. 106–7. For his association with printers' associations see *Standard*, November 19, 1830; *Working Man's Advocate*, June 18, 25, 1831, June 30, 1832, June 29, 1833; *Evening Post*, February 10, 1834. *Directory*, 1825–26 to 1834–35, listed him as a printer, changing the listing in 1835–36 to Windt and Conrad, "printers and manufacturer of Compo."

74. *Man*, April 4, May 15, 17, 1834; *Jeffersonian*, December 11, 1834; *Working Man's Advocate*, October 11, 18, November 1, 8, 1834, January 3, March 14, September 12, October 17, 31, 1835; Byrdsall, *History*, pp.

17, 37, 48, 88, 100, 146, 178–79; *Democrat,* March 9, 1836; *Evening Post,* October 28, 1837.

75. Thomas N. Carr to Van Buren, September 15, 1843, Van Buren Papers; *Working Man's Advocate,* March 16, April 6, September 28, 1844; Masquerier, *Sociology,* pp. 95, 106–7.

76. For a discussion of Moore, Slamm, and Commerford as typical spokesmen of the labor movement see Edward Pessen, "Social Philosophies of Early American Leaders of Labor" (unpublished dissertation, Columbia University, 1954), pp. 60–70.

77. This information was compiled principally from Commons, *Documentary History,* V and VI, supplemented by *Working Man's Advocate, Man,* and *National Trades' Union;* the members of the Society of Journeyman House Carpenters were listed in the manuscript "Constitution and By Laws," the only such listing found for the period.

78. Note especially the discussion of politics at the first N.T.U. convention; *Man,* September 6, 1834.

79. *National Trades' Union,* September 20, October 11, 1834.

80. *Ibid.,* July 5, September 13, 1834.

81. Byrdsall, *History,* pp. 52, 94; cf. Trimble, "Diverging Tendencies," p. 399 n.

82. *Man,* June 14, 1834, June 5, 19, 1835.

83. *Evening Post,* November 21, December 6, 1834, March 10, 1835; *Plaindealer,* December 10, 1836, February 18, 1837. These editorials can also be found in Theodore Sedgwick, Jr., ed., *A Collection of the Political Writings of William Leggett* (2 vols., New York, 1840), I, 106–10, 162–66, 226–29; II, 125–26, 221–24.

84. See, for example, *Working Man's Advocate,* February 12, 19, March 5, July 9, August 6, 1831; *Man,* May 27, June 19, 1835; *National Trades' Union,* June 6, 27, August 8, 22, 1835.

85. *Man,* May 23, 1835; *National Trades' Union,* October 10, 1835, February 6, March 26, 1836. For the coming of the factory system see Taylor, *Transportation Revolution,* pp. 229–49, 270–300.

86. *National Trades' Union,* February 20, 27, April 9, 1836.

CHAPTER 5

1. Trimble, "Diverging Tendencies," p. 401; see also his "Social Philosophy of the Loco-Foco Democracy," *American Journal of Sociology,* XXVI (May 1921), 710.

2. Parrington, *Main Currents,* II, 244; cf. Schlesinger, *Age of Jackson,* p. 307.

3. Statistical studies using the career-line approach include E. Pendleton Herring, *Federal Commissioners: A Study of Their Careers and Qualifications* (Cambridge, Mass., 1936); Cortez A. M. Ewing, *Judges of the Supreme Court 1789–1937* (Minneapolis, 1938); C. Wright Mills, "The American Business Elite: A Collective Portrait," *Tasks of Economic History* (Supplemental Issue of *Journal of Economic History*),

V (1945), 20–44; William Miller, "American Historians and the Business Elite," *Journal of Economic History,* IX (November 1949), 184–208.

4. *Working Man's Advocate,* August 11, 1832. For a recent assessment of his role in the movement see Edward Pessen, "Thomas Skidmore, Agrarian Reformer in the Early American Labor Movement," *New York History,* XXV (July 1954), 280–96.

5. *Free Enquirer,* March 30, 1834. This memoir was written by Amos Gilbert, a former editor of the paper with whom Skidmore had often disagreed violently, and was apparently based on the testimony of Skidmore's friends.

6. *Ibid.,* April 6, 1834. Skidmore was not listed in the *Directory* until 1830–31, when his occupation was given as printer, but he was referred to as a machinist during the political campaigns of 1829 and 1830; see *Courier and Enquirer,* October 28, 1829, and *Working Man's Advocate,* September 25, 1830.

7. Skidmore to Clinton, August 22, 1822, DeWitt Clinton Papers (X, 53), Columbia University; no reply has been found to this letter.

8. *American,* September 18, October 15, 1828; see also *Courier and Enquirer,* October 28, November 13, 1829.

9. *Free Enquirer,* June 17, 1829; *Courier and Enquirer,* November 12, 1829; *Evening Journal,* December 31, 1829, February 11, 1830; *Working Man's Advocate,* April 17, 1830.

10. *Free Enquirer,* June 25, July 2, December 17, 1831.

11. *Ibid.,* April 13, 1834.

12. *Working Man's Advocate,* August 11, 1832; *Free Enquirer,* April 6, 13, 1834.

13. *Directory,* 1828–29; Williams, *Annual Register* (1830), p. 129; *Morning Herald,* November 19, December 19, 1829.

14. *American,* September 17, 27, 1828; *Proceedings, Convention of 1828,* p. 4.

15. *Evening Journal,* February 2, 1830; *Working Man's Advocate,* August 28, 1830.

16. *American,* April 8, 16, 1834.

17. *Dictionary of American Biography* (21 vols., New York, 1937), XIV, 118–20; *Appleton's Cyclopedia of American Biography* (6 vols., New York, 1888), IV, 615–16. The best biography is Richard W. Leopold, *Robert Dale Owen, A Biography* (Cambridge, Mass., 1940).

18. *Free Enquirer* (New Harmony, Ind.), February 11, 1829; the first issue published with a New York City date line was on March 4. *Free Enquirer,* June 24, August 19, 1829.

19. *Ibid.,* November 7, 14, 1829.

20. *Ibid.,* November 5, 1831; for Owen's marriage see *Working Man's Advocate,* April 28, 1832; *DAB,* XIV, 118–20. On Robinson see *Directory,* 1830–31; *Sentinel and Working Man's Advocate,* August 11, 1830; *Working Man's Advocate,* December 4, 1830, January 1, 22, March 5, 12, 1831.

21. *Free Enquirer,* June 8, 1833; *DAB,* XIV, 118–20.

22. *DAB,* VI, 201–2; this sketch states, without further clarification, that the Evans family was "lower middle-class." See also Frederick W. Evans, *Autobiography of a Shaker* (New York, 1888), pp. 2–6, 11–13. G. H. Evans, in an obituary of his father, who died in Binghamton in 1833, also referred to his military experience; see *Working Man's Advocate,* April 6, 1833. Some of George's Binghamton cousins were printers, according to F. W. Evans, *Autobiography,* p. 12; Edwin T. Evans, probably one of them, advertised his half-interest in the *Broome Republican* (published in Binghamton) for sale; see *Working Man's Advocate,* February 1, 1834.

23. *Directory,* 1828–29; *Free Enquirer,* March 4, 11, July 15, 22, 1829. Frederick Evans sheds no light on this period, since he was visiting in England during most of this time and, upon his return in June 1830, became a Shaker, thus effectively breaking contact with his agnostic brother; *Autobiography,* pp. 13–25.

24. *Working Man's Advocate,* October 31, 1829; Masquerier, *Sociology,* p. 99. For a comparison of Skidmore, Owen, and Evans as spokesmen of the movement see Pessen, "Social Philosophies of Early American Leaders of Labor," pp. 16–35.

25. For Evans' journalistic career see *Courier and Enquirer,* December 15, 1829; *Working Man's Advocate,* February 13, 1830, February 19, August 6, October 22, 1831, July 6, 1833, August 29, September 19, October 31, 1835; *Sentinel and Working Man's Advocate,* June 23, 1830; *Man,* February 18, 22, 1834; *Radical,* January, February 1841, February 1843.

26. Masquerier, *Sociology,* pp. 95–98; *Radical,* March 1841. Of the 40 names listed by Evans as active in the Association, at least 14 (or 35 percent) were former Workingmen; see *Working Man's Advocate,* March 16, July 20, September 7, 28, 1844.

27. For a modern analysis of Evans' program and influence, see Zahler, *Eastern Workingmen,* pp. 21–39. See also *Working Man's Advocate,* May 4, 11, September 28, October 5, November 2, 9, 1844. Evans joined forces briefly with Mike Walsh, the colorful demagogue and Tammany baiter; see *ibid.,* October 12, December 21, 1844; *Subterranean,* February 24, November 2, 1844. For Evans' last years see Masquerier, *Sociology,* pp. 99–102; *DAB,* VI, 202.

28. William C. Bryant, "William Leggett," *Democratic Review,* VI (July 1839), 17–28; *DAB,* XI, 147–48; *Appleton's Cyclopedia,* III, 679. See also Hofstadter, "William Leggett," pp. 581–94.

29. *DAB,* XI, 147–48; Nevins, *Evening Post,* chap. 6; Parke Godwin, *A Biography of William Cullen Bryant* (2 vols., New York, 1883), I, 262. For references to *The Critic,* see *Evening Post,* October 18, 1828; *Courier and Enquirer,* June 22, July 1, 1829; this periodical first appeared in November 1828, and was discontinued in June 1829.

30. *DAB,* XI, 147–48; *Appleton's Cyclopedia,* III, 679; *Evening Star,* May 30, 1839. For Leggett's abolitionist views, see especially *Plaindealer,* December 24, 31, 1836, January 14, 1837. His letter declining

the nomination, dated October 24, 1838, was published in Sedgwick, *Political Writings,* II, 334–36.

31. Gorham's first appearance in the movement was as chairman of a ward meeting in early December 1829, and his last as a Rump Assembly candidate in November 1837; in between, he served on the General Executive Committee of the Workingmen's Party in 1830, 1831, and 1834, was nominated in 1830 for County Register, and attended the Locofoco state convention. See *Evening Journal,* December 5, 1829, February 1, 1830; *Working Man's Advocate,* October 9, 23, 1830, March 26, 1831; *Man,* May 17, 1834; Byrdsall, *History,* pp. 75, 172, 187. His occupation was listed consistently in the *Directory* from 1827–28 to 1842–43. For Byrdsall's characterization see *History,* pp. 106–7.

32. *Sentinel and Working Man's Advocate,* June 12, 1830; *Working Man's Advocate,* September 11, October 30, 1830, January 22, 29, 1831, November 7, 1835; Byrdsall, *History,* pp. 25–26. Curtis' first appearance as a Workingman was in January 1830, as a member (and later chairman) of the General Executive Committee; *Evening Journal,* February 1, 1830; *Sentinel and Working Man's Advocate,* August 14, 1830. For his occupational history, see Gold, "History of Manufacturing," p. 52; *Directory,* 1825–26 to 1841–42.

33. The only Byrdsall found in any Directory is "William F., late merchant," in *Doggett's Directory* for 1844–45; this may have been his father, for the residence listed is in the Eighth Ward, which Byrdsall represented as a Locofoco.

34. Byrdsall, *History,* pp. 34–43, 56–61, 179–84.

35. Joseph A. Scoville to Hunter, September 11, 1842, and J. Francis Hutton to Hunter, September 26, 1843, in Ambler, "Correspondence of Robert M. T. Hunter," pp. 44–48, 64–65; Byrdsall to Calhoun, October 11, 1842, February 22, July 29, November 12, 1847, and Henry P. Barber to Calhoun, December 29, 1843, in Boucher and Brooks, "Correspondence Addressed to John C. Calhoun," pp. 178, 196, 369, 389, 410; Byrdsall to Calhoun, November 6, 1842, August 25, December 2, 1844, February 14, July 19, 1847, in Jameson, "Correspondence of John C. Calhoun," pp. 862, 966, 1004–5, 1105, 1126.

36. See *Register of Officers and Agents* (1847), p. 70; (1849), p. 65; (1851), p. 67; (1853), p. 84; Kilroe, "Membership List," p. 23.

37. For Ming's early publishing activity see Clarence S. Brigham, *History and Bibliography of American Newspapers, 1690–1820* (2 vols., Worcester, Mass., 1947), I, 680–81, 704–5. His activities as a Workingman and a Democrat are detailed in *Courier and Enquirer,* October 28, November 12, 1829; *Working Man's Advocate,* September 25, November 13, 1830, November 1, 1834; *Man,* April 6, 1835. For his occupational history see *Directory,* 1825–26 to 1841–42; *Doggett's Directory,* 1842–43 to 1844–45; *Register of Officers and Agents* (1835), p. 40; (1837), p. 48; (1845), p. 153; (1847), p. 74.

38. For his occupational history see *Directory,* 1825–26 to 1841–42; *Doggett's Directory,* 1842–43 to 1844–45. For his political history see

Evening Post, October 3, 1828; *Standard,* November 2, December 23, 1830; *Sentinel,* October 23, 1832; *American,* April 9, 1834; *Times,* November 5, 1834; *Working Man's Advocate,* October 4, December 27, 1834; October 17, November 7, 1835; *Man,* April 1, 14, 15, 1835; *Niles' Register,* February 18, 1837; see also Byrdsall, *History,* pp. 17, 25, 36, 46, 55, 100, 145, 172, 176. For his career in the Custom House see *ibid.,* pp. 104–8; *Register of Officers and Agents* (1831), p. 55; (1835), p. 40; (1837), p. 48; (1845), p. 153; (1847), p. 74. For his relations with Van Buren during the latter's 1839 visit to New York see Allan Nevins, ed., *Diary of Philip Hone* (2 vols., New York, 1927), I, 404. For his activities in 1842 see *Evening Post,* May 13, 16, 18, 1842; Arthur M. Mowry, *Dorr War* (Providence, 1901), p. 172. His 1855 oration was published in the *Times,* July 6, 1855; see also Edwin P. Kilroe, *St. Tammany and the Origin of the Society of Tammany or Columbian Order in the City of New York* (New York, 1913), p. 224.

39. *Directory,* 1826–27 to 1827–28, lists Hogbin as a grocer, but he is listed as a tinsmith in 1828–29 and a turner in 1830–31; beginning in 1831–32 through 1841–42 (except for 1833–35) the listing is tinware, the same occupation being continued in *Doggett's Directory,* 1842–43 to 1844–45. See also advertisements in *Working Man's Advocate,* February 12, 1831, March 14, 1832; *Sentinel,* September 22, 1832; *Man,* July 2, 1835. For his Tarrytown residence see *Working Man's Advocate,* May 18, 1833, June 20, 1835. His principal political activities were detailed in the following: *Evening Journal,* January 18, 1830; *Sentinel and Working Man's Advocate,* August 14, 1830; *Working Man's Advocate,* October 9, 1830, January 22, March 26, 1831; Byrdsall, *History,* pp. 55, 178, 188; *Evening Post,* October 28, 1837.

40. Much of the biographical information on the Cozzens family comes from the sketches of Frederick's son, Frederick S. Cozzens, an author and wine merchant in New York; see *DAB,* IV, 490; *Appleton's Cyclopedia,* I, 762–63. For their occupations and relations with Tammany see *Directory,* 1825–26 to 1841–42 (Frederick is listed without occupation here, except in 1838–39 where the citation is "cupper and leecher") ; see also Kilroe, "Membership List," pp. 36, 401, 403–4, 469. For his activities in the Workingmen's movement see *Working Man's Advocate,* June 5, September 25, October 16, 23, 1830; *Sentinel and Working Man's Advocate,* July 3, 8, 1830; *Man,* May 17, 1834; Byrdsall, *History,* pp. 48, 55, 138.

41. *Courier and Enquirer,* October 28, November 12, December 3, 1829; *Evening Journal,* November 28, December 4, 1829, January 6, 18, February 27, March 27, 1830; *Working Man's Advocate,* May 29, September 18, October 16, 23, 1830; *Sentinel and Working Man's Advocate,* June 26, August 14, 1830. For his occupation see *Evening Journal,* February 1, 1830; *Sentinel,* September 22, 1832; the *Directory* lists him without occupation during this period. For his activities in 1834, see *Working Man's Advocate,* November 8, 1834.

42. *Courier and Enquirer,* December 16, 1829; *Evening Journal,*

February 1, 25, March 9, 1830; *Morning Herald,* March 8, 1830; *Working Man's Advocate,* May 29, August 21, September 18, October 16, 1830; *Sentinel and Working Man's Advocate,* July 10, 1830. For his occupation see *Directory,* 1828–29 to 1830–31. For his later political career see *Working Man's Advocate,* March 17, November 10, 1832; *American,* March 28, April 4, 5, 16, 1834.

43. *Evening Journal,* February 1, 1830; *Working Man's Advocate,* May 29, October 23, 1830; *Sentinel,* June 23, 1830. For his occupations see *Directory,* 1830–31 to 1836–37; *American,* April 8, 1834. For Darling as a Democrat see *Working Man's Advocate,* April 5, December 27, 1834, January 3, September 12, October 17, 1835; Byrdsall, *History,* p. 31.

44. *Working Man's Advocate,* March 31, 1832, October 11, 1834, January 10, September 12, October 17, 1835; Byrdsall, *History,* pp. 16–17, 31; *Directory,* 1828–29 to 1842–43.

45. *Working Man's Advocate,* October 31, 1829, July 10, 1830, October 11, 18, 1834, October 17, 1835; *Evening Journal,* January 6, 1830; *Man,* May 17, 1834; Byrdsall, *History,* p. 17. For his occupations see *Directory,* 1825–26 to 1840–41; *Register of Officers and Agents* (1845), p. 159.

46. *Morning Herald,* July 3, 1829; *Free Enquirer,* July 15, 1829, July 16, 1831, December 22, 1832, February 9, April 13, 1833; *Working Man's Advocate,* March 17, June 2, 1832. For the Paine birthday dinners see *Free Enquirer,* February 25, 1832, February 9, 1833, February 1, 1835. See *Directory,* 1830–31, and advertisements in *Working Man's Advocate,* November 6, 1830, and November 30, 1833, for his occupation; the quotation is from the 1830 advertisement. The high points in his political career were described in *Evening Journal,* January 11, 1830; *Working Man's Advocate,* May 22, August 21, 1830, January 1, 22, October 1, 22, March 24, September 22, 1832, January 5, 1833; *Radical,* January 1841.

47. *Directory,* 1828–29 to 1841–42; for Pyne's nationality see Masquerier, *Sociology,* p. 126. See also *Sentinel and Working Man's Advocate,* June 26, 1830; *Working Man's Advocate,* September 25, 1830, March 26, 1831, August 29, September 19, 1835; *Man,* May 15, 1834; Byrdsall, *History,* p. 37; *Radical,* January 1841; *Doggett's Directory,* 1842–43 to 1844–45.

48. In a letter published in the *Man,* May 13, 1835, Webb gave his age as sixty-three. An editorial in the *American,* February 8, 1834, referred to him as an Englishman, and the *Free Enquirer,* May 1, 1830, published a notice of a lecture by Webb based on "his recollections of the excitement produced in England by the revolutionary events of France"; in addition, a letter from "An American" in *Working Man's Advocate,* September 22, 1832, charged that Webb had not been a citizen long enough to have knowledge of American politics. His advertisement announcing his official debut as an architect, appearing in *Sentinel and Working Man's Advocate,* June 23, 1830, stated that he had had forty years' experience as a "practical builder and house carpenter." His son

who took over the business was probably George Webb, a carpenter who briefly took part in the Workingmen's Party; see *Directory,* 1830–31; *Evening Journal,* December 31, 1829, January 14, 1830. For the elder Webb's occupation see *Directory,* 1825–26 to 1841–42; *Doggett's Directory,* 1842–43 to 1844–45; he was listed as a carpenter through 1829–30, and as an architect throughout the succeeding years. The notice of his architectural lectures appeared in *Working Man's Advocate,* February 25, 1832.

49. For Webb's lectures see *Evening Journal,* January 8, 1830; *Working Man's Advocate,* January 23, 30, 1830; *Free Enquirer,* May 1, 1830. For accounts of his political speeches see *Evening Journal,* December 11, 12, 1829; *Working Man's Advocate,* December 4, 1830, October 11, 1834, February 28, 1835; *Jeffersonian,* April 17, 1835; *Man,* April 11, 13, 1835. For his letters see *Working Man's Advocate,* November 14, 21, 28, December 19, 1829, September 15, 22, 1832, January 19, 1833; *Evening Journal,* December 12, 1829; *Sentinel,* September 22, 1832; *Man,* May 13, 1835.

50. *Courier and Enquirer,* October 28, December 16, 1829; *Evening Journal,* December 30, 1829, January 6, 1830; *Working Man's Advocate,* October 31, 1829, June 5, October 23, 1830, March 26, 1831, April 5, 1834; *American,* February 8, 1834; Byrdsall, *History,* pp. 55, 88, 138, 140, 146.

51. For Vale as a Workingman see *Man,* May 15, 1834; *Working Man's Advocate,* October 25, November 1, 1834; Byrdsall, *History,* p. 55. Biographical information is in *Appleton's Cyclopedia,* VI, 225; Masquerier, *Sociology,* pp. 105–6; *Directory,* 1830–31 to 1841–42; *Doggett's Directory,* 1842–43 to 1844–45. For his lecturing and writing activities see *Free Enquirer,* January 8, March 19, April 23, May 21, October 1, December 17, 1831, November 17, December 8, 1832, October 19, 1833, January 4, 1835; *Working Man's Advocate,* March 17, April 7, 1832, April 20, November 30, 1833, April 5, 1834; *Man,* April 25, 1835; *Radical,* April 1841. His *Political Economy,* in slightly abridged form, was published in Blau, *Social Theories,* pp. 237–60.

52. *DAB,* II, 46–47; *Appleton's Cyclopedia,* I, 192; *Olive Branch and Christian Inquirer,* May 17, June 14, 1828; *Directory,* 1825–26 to 1830–31. For the Pestalozzi Institute see *Evening Journal,* January 19, February 23, 1830; he is listed as Barnabas Bates A.M. In regard to the *Every Day Mail* see *ibid.,* February 19, March 17, 1830; *Free Enquirer,* April 24, 1830; *Farmers', Mechanics', and Working Men's Advocate,* July 24, 1830.

53. *Working Man's Advocate,* April 2, October 8, 22, November 5, 1831, March 17, 24, 1832, October 11, 25, 1834; *American,* March 28, 1834; *Evening Star,* March 28, April 5, 1834; Byrdsall, *History,* pp. 17, 34.

54. *Ibid.,* p. 37.

55. *Directory,* 1833–34 to 1836–37; *Working Man's Advocate,* April 6, 1833, August 23, 1834; *New Era,* February 25, 1840; *DAB,* II, 46–47.

See also *Register of Officers and Agents* (1835), p. 294; (1837), p. 319; (1843), p. 75; (1845), p. 159; (1847), p. 67; (1849), p. 63.

56. For Blatchley's Workingmen's Party activities see *Courier and Enquirer,* October 28, November 12, 1829; *Sentinel and Working Man's Advocate,* June 26, July 24, 1830; *Working Man's Advocate,* August 21, 1830, November 5, 1831. For his family and professional background see Boyd Crumrine, *History of Washington County, Pennsylvania* (Philadelphia, 1882), p. 848; Stephen Wickes, *History of Medicine in New Jersey* (Newark, 1879), pp. 152–57; letter in files of Morristown National Historical Park, Morristown, New Jersey, dated September 26, 1923, from Dr. Christopher J. Colles (a great-grandnephew of Blatchley) to Henry C. Pitney, Secretary of the Washington Association of New Jersey, documenting a portrait of Blatchley presented to the Association. See also *Directory,* 1828–29 to 1830–31; *Courier and Enquirer,* October 31, November 11, 13, 1829; *Working Man's Advocate,* November 14, 21, 28, December 5, 12, 19, 26, 1829, January 9, May 29, 1830; *Evening Journal,* January 30, February 8, 1830.

57. On Judd see *Evening Journal,* February 1, 25, 1830; *Working Man's Advocate,* October 18, 1834; *Directory,* 1828–29 to 1830–31; [Joseph A. Scoville,] *Old Merchants of New York City* (3 vols., New York, 1872), I, 100–101. For Gedney see *Evening Journal,* December 4, 1829; *Directory,* 1828–29 to 1830–31; *Appleton's Cyclopedia,* II, 622.

58. For the Bruces in the Workingmen's movement see *Working Man's Advocate,* September 25, October 23, November 13, 1830, November 5, 1831. For their occupations and biographies see *Directory,* 1828–29 to 1830–31; *DAB,* III, 181; *Appleton's Cyclopedia,* I, 418–19.

59. *Man,* May 9, 1834, April 1, 1835; *Working Man's Advocate,* April 5, October 11, 25, 1834, October 17, 1835; *Appleton's Cyclopedia,* I, 708; *National Cyclopedia of American Biography* (13 vols., New York, 1892–1906), V, 480; *Directory,* 1836–37; advertisement in *Sentinel and Working Man's Advocate,* June 16, 1830. For his relations with Tammany see Kilroe, "Membership List," p. 33.

60. *Working Man's Advocate,* September 18, October 23, November 13, 1830, October 29, November 5, 1831; for his praise of Evans see letter in *ibid.,* August 27, 1831. His biography is detailed in *DAB,* VII, 1–3; *Appleton's Cyclopedia,* II, 538; *National Cyclopedia,* VIII, 289; Henry B. Caldwell, "John Frazee, American Sculptor" (M.A. thesis, New York University, 1951). For an account of his early life see "Autobiography, John Frazee, First American Sculptor, b. 1790 Rahway, N.J.," MS., New York Public Library (copied in 1944 by H. A. Frazee, from Marsh papers in New Jersey Historical Society). See also *Directory,* 1828–29 to 1830–31; advertisements in *Working Man's Advocate,* November 6, 1830, June 2, 1832; *Man,* May 20, 1834. For his work on the Custom House see Talbot Hamlin, *Greek Revival Architecture in America* (New York, 1944), pp. 154–56; I. N. P. Stokes, *Iconography of Manhattan Island, 1498–1909* (6 vols., New York, 1918–28), V, 1775; *Commercial Advertiser,* July 13, 1842.

61. *DAB*, IV, 409–10; Edward C. Mack, *Peter Cooper, Citizen of New York* (New York, 1949), pp. 19, 57–58, 67–68; *Morning Courier*, November 11, 1828; *Man*, May 17, 1834; *Times*, October 3, 1836.

62. Mack, *Peter Cooper*, pp. 22, 168, 393; *Working Man's Advocate*, January 16, May 29, August 21, 1830, January 22, March 12, 1831; *Evening Journal*, February 1, 1830; *Sentinel*, June 23, 1830; *Sentinel and Working Man's Advocate*, July 14, August 11, 1830.

63. Mack, *Peter Cooper*, pp. 22, 169–72; *Evening Journal*, January 6, 1830; *Sentinel and Working Man's Advocate*, July 14, August 11, 1830; *Working Man's Advocate*, October 9, 23, 1830, October 22, 1831, January 5, 1833; *Man*, May 17, 1834.

64. Mack, *Peter Cooper*, p. 60; *Working Man's Advocate*, January 16, October 16, 1830.

65. On Henry Riell as a Workingman and Democrat, see *Evening Journal*, January 18, 1830; *Sentinel and Working Man's Advocate*, June 19, August 11, 14, 1830; *Working Man's Advocate*, October 23, 1830; January 22, 1831, October 11, 1834, January 3, 10, August 29, 1835; *Jeffersonian*, November 13, 1834; *Man*, April 14, 1835. On the Riell brothers as Locofocos, see Byrdsall, *History*, pp. 17, 31, 37, 54, 93, 151, 173–77, 182–83. For their occupational history, as well as their father's, see *Directory*, 1828–29 to 1841–42; *Doggett's Directory*, 1842–43 to 1844–45.

66. For the Milledoler's occupations see *Directory*, 1826–27 to 1839–40; their father's life is sketched in *DAB*, XII, 618–19. For their political activities see *Working Man's Advocate*, November 5, 1831, October 4, 11, 18, 1834, January 3, 10, March 14, September 12, October 17, 1835; Byrdsall, *History*, pp. 16–17, 31, 79; Kilroe, "Membership List," p. 115.

67. The sketch of George W. Matsell in *Appleton's Cyclopedia*, IV, 260–61, deals mainly with his career after 1843. For the Matsell's occupational history see *Directory*, 1832–33 to 1841–42; *Doggett's Directory*, 1842–43 to 1844–45. It seems logical to assume that their father was George Matsell, listed as a tailor in the *Directory*, 1825–26 to 1838–39, for his address is the same as the brothers from 1832 to 1835. Advertisements for the bookstore, listing books for sale, were in *Working Man's Advocate*, June 1, 1833, September 19, 1835, and *Free Enquirer*, September 7, 1834. For their political activities see *Man*, May 15, 1834; *Working Man's Advocate*, February 7, 1835; Byrdsall, *History*, pp. 61, 88, 172; Kilroe, "Membership List," p. 113. For Matsell and Fernando Wood see *DAB*, XX, 456.

68. Vincent F. Holden, *Early Years of Isaac Thomas Hecker* (Washington, 1939), pp. 1–42, 180–82; *Appleton's Cyclopedia*, III, 156–57; *Directory*, 1828–29 to 1841–42. For John's Locofoco activities see Byrdsall, *History*, pp. v. 140, 146. For Isaac's communitarian experience see Alice F. Tyler, *Freedom's Ferment; Phases of American Social History to 1860* (Minneapolis, 1944), pp. 173, 179, 385.

69. *Directory*, 1825–26 to 1841–42; *Doggett's Directory*, 1842–43 to 1844–45; Daniel T. Ronk, *Hasbrouck family births, marriages and deaths,*

copied from old church and cemetery records (Brooklyn, 1917), pp. 20, 62. For his political career see *American*, March 6, 1834; *Working Man's Advocate*, October 18, 1834, March 14, 1835; *Man*, April 11, 1835; *Democrat*, October 5, 8, 1836; Byrdsall, *History*, pp. 38, 55, 79–80, 138, 173–79. For Fenelon Hasbrouck see Ronk, *Hasbrouck family*, p. 54; *Directory*, 1838–39 to 1841–42; Byrdsall, *History*, p. 146.

70. *New Era*, February 25, 1840; *Aurora*, September 5, 1843.

71. His father, Col. Moses Jaques, served in the First Regiment of the Essex County (N.J.) Militia; see William S. Stryker, comp., *Official Register of the Officers and Men of New Jersey in the Revolutionary War* (Trenton, 1872), pp. 341, 353. See also Kilroe, "Membership List," p. 85; *Directory*, 1825–26 to 1837–38; *Working Man's Advocate*, March 17, 1832, October 17, 1835; Byrdsall, *History*, pp. v, 20, 36, 42, 71–74, 97, 135–37, 145.

72. *Ibid.*, pp. 42–43.

73. Nevins, *Evening Post*, pp. 152–53; Sedgwick's *What Is a Monopoly* (New York, 1835) has been reprinted, somewhat abridged, in Blau, *Social Theories*, pp. 220–36. For biographical information on the Sedgwicks see *DAB*, XVI, 549–52; *Appleton's Cyclopedia*, V, 452; Joseph Dorfman, *Economic Mind in American Civilization* (2 vols., New York, 1946), II, 650–52, 655.

74. For Vethake's article see *Evening Post*, October 21, 1835; it has been reprinted in Blau, *Social Theories*, pp. 211–19. For biographical information on the Vethakes see Dorfman, *Economic Mind*, II, 654–55, 731–43. John was first listed in the *Directory* in 1833–34 as an M.D., the citation continuing through 1841–42; in 1840–41 he was listed as "M.D., U.S. inspector." For his political activities see *Working Man's Advocate*, October 25, December 27, 1834, January 3, September 12, October 31, 1835; *Man*, April 9, 1835; Byrdsall, *History*, pp. 17, 20–21, 36. For his 1845 appointment to the Custom House see *Register of Officers and Agents* (1845), p. 155.

75. *Directory*, 1828–29 to 1841–42; Roosevelt was not listed from 1831 through 1837; see also *Doggett's Directory*, 1842–43 to 1844–45. For his writings see *Working Man's Advocate*, November 30, 1833; Dorfman, *Economic Mind*, II, 652–53, 660–61. For his political activities see *Democrat*, October 5, 8, November 26, 1836 (this paper began publication March 9, 1836); *Man*, March 10, 1835; Byrdsall, *History*, pp. 48, 79, 88, 92–97, 114. For his invention see *Official Catalogue, 38th Annual Fair of the American Institute* (New York, 1869), p. 43. The quotation is from Byrdsall, *History*, pp. 92–93.

76. *Free Enquirer*, October 27, 1832; *Working Man's Advocate*, October 23, 1830; *Directory*, 1826–27 to 1836–37, 1842–43 (with the exception of the period 1826–30, he is listed here without occupation); Kilroe, "Membership List," p. 77. For his political career see *Morning Courier*, November 11, 1828; *Working Man's Advocate*, October 23, November 13, 1830, January 1, April 2, November 5, 1831; September

12, October 31, 1835; *Courier and Enquirer,* November 2, 1829; *American,* November 11, 1833; *Times,* October 31, 1834; Byrdsall, *History,* p. 79; *Democrat,* October 5, 1836; *Whig,* October 26, 1839. For his humanitarian activities see *Standard,* December 25, 1830; *Free Enquirer,* February 2, 1833, February 23, 1834; *Evening Star,* October 3, 1833, February 7, 1834; *Times,* February 20, 1835; *Herald,* November 4, 1835; *Whig,* November 4, 1839. See also Herttell's *The demurrer; or, Proofs of error in the decision of the Supreme court of the State of New York requiring faith in particular religious doctrines as a legal qualification of witnesses* (New York, 1828) ; and *Correspondence on the subject of life and death* (Boston, 1845).

77. *Working Man's Advocate,* October 20, 1832, November 1, 1834, October 10, 1835; *DAB,* III, 432–33. For his railroad activities see *Evening Star,* October 5, 8, December 2, 1833, January 6, 1834; *Farmers', Mechanics',* and *Working Men's Advocate,* August 4, 1830. He was listed as a merchant in the *Directory,* 1825–26, being included without occupation in subsequent years. For his association with Astor see Kenneth W. Porter, *John Jacob Astor, Business Man* (2 vols., Cambridge, Mass., 1931), I, 296–97, 318, 533–39, II, 592–93, 999.

78. *DAB,* III, 432–33; Schlesinger, *Age of Jackson,* pp. 62–63. For examples of opposition to his tariff views see *American,* October 14, 1828; *Evening Journal,* March 23, 1830; *Morning Herald,* April 22, 1830. His relations with the Locofocos are detailed in Byrdsall, *History,* pp. 20, 79, 94.

79. John C. Fitzpatrick, ed., "Autobiography of Martin Van Buren," American Historical Association, *Annual Report (1918),* II, 655; Byrdsall, *History,* p. 96. For the close relationship between Van Buren and Cambreleng see Van Buren Papers, notably the following: Van Buren to Cambreleng, November 6, 1825, October 29, November 3, 7, 9, 1826, April, 1829; Cambreleng to Jackson, April 15, 1829.

80. See, e.g., [Alonzo Potter,] "Trades' Unions," *New-York Review, II* (January 1838), 5–48. For a discussion of the role of immigrants in the Workingmen's and Locofoco Parties see Robert Ernst, *Immigrant Life in New York City 1825–1863* (New York, 1949), pp. 168–69.

CHAPTER 6

1. This analysis of the *Directory* appeared in Williams, *Annual Register for 1834,* quoted in *Man,* May 17, 1834; only 53 occupations were listed, less than half of those utilized in Table I.

2. Williams, *Annual Register for 1837,* p. 345.

CHAPTER 7

1. Proceedings of the meeting of October 19, 1829, in *Courier and Enquirer,* October 23, 1829; and Skidmore, *The Rights of Man to Prop-*

erty! (New York, 1829), especially chap. 4, reprinted in Blau, *Social Theories*, pp. 355–64.

2. *Sentinel and Working Man's Advocate*, June 23, 1830; see also the debate between Skidmore and Owen in *Free Enquirer*, January 9, 23, 1830.

3. *Courier and Enquirer*, November 3, 1829; see also Frances Wright, *A Course of Popular Lectures* (New York, 1829), pp. 150–70, reprinted in part in Blau, *Social Theories*, pp. 282–88.

4. "Address of the Trustees of the Public School Society," quoted in *Free Enquirer*, September 30, 1829; see also *Evening Journal*, March 2, 1830.

5. See Tyler, *Freedom's Ferment*, pp. 240–41; and W. O. Bourne, *History of the Public School Society of the City of New York* (New York, 1873).

6. *Working Man's Advocate*, December 5, 1829, May 1, 1830, December 20, 1834; for the discussion of manual labor schools see *ibid.*, December 5, 1829, December 22, 1832, September 26, 1835; *Man*, May 27, August 28, 1834.

7. *Working Man's Advocate*, December 22, 1832.

8. See especially Miss Wright's lecture quoted in Blau, *Social Theories*, pp. 286–88.

9. *Sentinel and Working Man's Advocate*, June 23, 1830.

10. *Working Man's Advocate*, October 22, 1831; *Man*, May 19, August 2, 1834.

11. Byrdsall, *History*, p. 88; this statement in October 1836 is the only mention of education in this book.

12. *Working Man's Advocate*, June 18, 1831.

13. Sidney L. Jackson, *America's Struggle for Free Schools* (Washington, 1941), pp. 171–73; see also the same author's "Labor, Education, and Politics in the 1830's," *Pennsylvania Magazine of History and Biography*, LXVI (July 1942), 279–93.

14. *Sentinel and Working Man's Advocate*, June 23, 1830.

15. *Courier and Enquirer*, October 23, November 3, 1829.

16. L. W. Meyer, *Life and Times of Colonel Richard M. Johnson of Kentucky* (New York, 1932), pp. 256–63; Schlesinger, *Age of Jackson*, pp. 136–40. Johnson's famous report is reprinted in Blau, *Social Theories*, pp. 274–81. For meetings and discussions in New York see *Courier and Enquirer*, December 7, 15, 22, 29, 1829; *Evening Journal*, December 31, 1829, January 15, 16, March 16, 1830; *Working Man's Advocate*, January 2, 1830.

17. *Free Enquirer*, March 6, 1830; *Working Man's Advocate*, February 27, 1830, January 12, 19, 1833, February 7, 1835; *Man*, February 26, May 14, 1834. See also Fox, *Decline of Aristocracy*, pp. 388–90.

18. *Evening Journal*, January 2, 1830; *Working Man's Advocate*, September 18, November 6, 1830, October 22, 1831; *Man*, May 19, 1834.

19. Byrdsall, *History*, pp. 165–66.

20. *Journal of Commerce,* October 15, 1834; *Daily Whig,* March 26, 1838, January 17, June 18, 1839. For Evans' views see especially *Man,* October 16, November 1, 1834, June 4, 5, 1835. See also Schlesinger, *Age of Jackson,* pp. 142, 350–56.

21. Samuel Rezneck, "The Depression of 1819–1822: A Social History," *American Historical Review,* XXXIX (October 1933), 44–45; Tyler, *Freedom's Ferment,* p. 285; Meyer, *Richard M. Johnson,* pp. 282–88.

22. Edwin T. Randall, "Imprisonment for Debt in America: Fact and Fiction," *Mississippi Valley Historical Review,* XXXIX (June 1952), 89–102. For substantiating evidence see Thomas Herttell, *Remarks on the Law of Imprisonment for Debt* (New York, 1823); *Working Man's Advocate,* December 5, 1829, December 4, 1830, February 7, 1835.

23. *Evening Journal,* December 4, 1829, January 2, February 17, 1830.

24. *Working Man's Advocate,* February 27, April 3, August 21, September 18, November 6, 1830, January 1, 22, 1831; *Farmers', Mechanics', and Working Men's Advocate,* May 26, July 14, September 1, 1830, January 5, 8, February 23, 1831. For the Antimasons see Charles McCarthy, "Antimasonic Party, A Study of Political Antimasonry in the United States, 1827–1840," American Historical Association, *Annual Report* (1902), I, 404–5.

25. *Working Man's Advocate,* April 30, 1831; see also F. T. Carlton, "Abolition of Imprisonment for Debt in the United States," *Yale Review,* XVII, 343–44.

26. *Working Man's Advocate,* January 19, April 20, May 4, 1833; *American,* September 30, 1833.

27. These resolutions were passed at Locofoco meetings, March 6 and June 24, 1837, and at the State convention, September 11, 1837; Byrdsall, *History,* pp. 111, 149, 167.

28. Louis Hartz, *Economic Policy and Democratic Thought: Pennsylvania, 1776–1860* (Cambridge, Mass., 1948), pp. 219, 223; cf. Dorfman, "Jackson Wage-Earner Thesis," p. 305.

29. *Working Man's Advocate,* October 9, 1830; *American,* October 28, November 7, 1831; Commons, *History of Labour,* I, 180.

30. *Evening Journal,* January 2, 1830; *Farmers', Mechanics', and Working Men's Advocate,* May 26, September 1, 1830; *Sentinel and Working Man's Advocate,* June 23, 1830; *Working Man's Advocate,* September 18, November 6, 1830, October 22, 1831. The demand was part of the Workingmen's program as late as 1834; *Man,* May 19, 1834.

31. *American,* October 27, 28, 1831; *Working Man's Advocate,* January 21, March 10, 1832.

32. *American,* November 4, 7, 1831; Fox, *Decline of Aristocracy,* p. 359. For Evans' statement see *Working Man's Advocate,* January 5, 1833.

33. Fox, *Decline of Aristocracy,* p. 359. The *National Trades' Union,* September 6, 1834, also denounced the militia system, but, somewhat surprisingly, the Locofocos failed to include it in their catalogue of evils.

34. W*orking Man's Advocate,* November 21, 1829; *Evening Journal,* January 2, 1830; *Farmers', Mechanics', and Working Men's Advocate,* September 1, 1830. This movement was supported briefly by the Tammany "organ"; see *Courier and Enquirer,* November 11, 12, 17, 1829.

35. *Evening Journal,* January 2, 1830; Byrdsall, *History,* pp. 27, 85.

36. *Evening Journal,* March 31, 1830; *Working Man's Advocate,* April 3, 1830; *Farmers', Mechanics', and Working Men's Advocate,* March 12, 1831.

37. *Working Man's Advocate,* April 19, 1834; see also *ibid.,* April 12, November 29, 1834; *Man,* February 20, 1834. The brunt of the Whig attack was directed against naturalized citizens, most of whom voted for the Democrats. For the 1840 agitation on this question see *Democratic-Republican New Era,* February 29, March 19, 20, 25, 1840.

38. *Sentinel and Working Man's Advocate,* June 23, 1830; *Working Man's Advocate,* August 21, September 18, November 6, 1830. Evans' statement was in *ibid.,* October 29, 1831; see also *ibid.,* March 21, 1835. Congressional districts were first established for the election of 1842; *Plebeian,* November 5, 1842.

39. *Courier and Enquirer,* October 23, 1829; *Farmers', Mechanics', and Working Men's Advocate,* September 1, 1830; *Working Man's Advocate,* June 16, 1832, February 9, 1833; *American,* April 13, 1831.

40. *Working Man's Advocate,* December 31, 1831; see also *Man,* May 16, 1834.

41. *Working Man's Advocate,* June 23, 1832; *Sentinel,* October 8, 1832; *Man,* June 28, 1834. For the letter from "A Working Man" see *Working Man's Advocate,* June 23, 1832; cf. other denunciations of lawyers in *Evening Journal,* March 31, 1830; *Sentinel and Working Man's Advocate,* June 23, 1830; Byrdsall, *History,* pp. 73–74.

42. *Man,* June 28, 1834; Byrdsall, *History,* pp. 73, 165; other statements by the Locofocos on this subject are quoted in *ibid.,* pp. 88, 149. For the demands of the Workingmen's Party see *Working Man's Advocate,* April 3, November 6, 1830. The statement on capital punishment is in Byrdsall, *History,* p. 166; this principle was previously upheld by Evans in the *Man,* May 19, 1834.

43. *Working Man's Advocate,* April 9, 1831.

44. *Courier and Enquirer,* October 23, December 3, 1829; *Free Enquirer,* November 7, 1829. See also *Evening Journal,* November 28, December 4, 1829, January 2, 1830.

45. Henry W. Farnam, *Chapters in the History of Social Legislation in the United States to 1860* (Washington, 1938), pp. 153–54; for the 1823 movement see *Courier and Enquirer,* December 2, 1829. As Farnam indicates, this principle was not found in the English common law, but was probably derived from Roman law; Jefferson, who was instrumental

in securing passage of the Maryland law, was familiar with French jurisprudence, based on Roman law. For the background of the Pennsylvania law of 1803, see Hartz, *Economic Policy*, pp. 191–92.

46. *Courier and Enquirer,* December 9, 1829. For other examples see *ibid.,* December 5, 1829; *Evening Journal,* October 28, 1829; *Sentinel,* September 28, 1832.

47. *Courier and Enquirer,* November 9, December 2, 1829; *Working Man's Advocate,* December 12, 1829.

48. *Laws of the State of New York, 1830,* Chapter 330, quoted in Charles C. Nott, *A Treatise on the Mechanics' Lien Laws of the State of New York* (Albany, 1856), pp. 224–26. See also *State of New York, Report of the Joint Legislative Committee Investigating the Lien Law,* Legislative Document (1930) No. 72 (Albany, 1930), p. 5; Commons, *History of Labour,* I, 329.

49. The last Workingmen's meeting which passed a resolution advocating a lien law was held on March 29, 1830; *Working Man's Advocate,* April 3, 1830. The act was published in *ibid.,* May 1, 1830. For Evans' listing of "Workingmen's Measures" after this time see *ibid.,* November 6, 1830, October 22, 1831. Gustavus Myers, *History of Tammany Hall* (New York, 1901), p. 99, asserts primarily on the basis of comparative election figures that about 4,000 Workingmen rejoined the Democracy because of this act. The Locofocos in 1836 asked that the lien law be amended "as really to afford a lien of security, plain and useful to working men"; Byrdsall, *History,* p. 88.

50. For the law of 1832 and subsequent legislation see Nott, *Mechanics' Lien Laws,* p. 227 (citing Chapter 120, *Laws of 1832*), pp. 217–22; S. F. Kneeland, *A Treatise upon the Principles Governing the Acquisition and Enforcement of Mechanics' Liens* (New York, 1876), pp. 366–73; *Report of the Joint Legislative Committee* (1930), p. 5.

51. *Working Man's Advocate,* September 18, 1830.

52. This point has been made in Hartz, *Economic Policy,* p. 221, with reference to the parallel movement in Pennsylvania; see also *ibid.,* pp. 191–93.

53. *Working Man's Advocate,* December 19, 1829.

54. Farnam, *Social Legislation,* p. 152.

CHAPTER 8

1. Quoted in James D. Richardson, *A Compilation of the Messages and Papers of the Presidents 1789–1897* (10 vols., Washington, 1896), II, 590. For comment on this passage see especially William Leggett's editorial in *Evening Post,* November 21, 1834; also quoted in Blau, *Social Theories,* pp. 74–75.

2. *Working Man's Advocate,* April 9, 1831. Evans specifically excepted the duty "to establish or to encourage Public Education."

3. *Evening Post,* November 21, 1834; see also *ibid.,* January 3, 1835,

for his denunciation of legislation "conferring partial or exclusive monopolies on small fractions of society."

4. *Working Man's Advocate,* January 3, 1835; Theodore Sedgwick, Jr., *What Is a Monopoly? or Some Considerations upon the Subject of Corporations and Currency* (New York, 1835), quoted in Blau, *Social Theories,* p. 222.

5. *Man,* July 17, 1834; see also *ibid.,* May 28, 1835; *Sentinel,* November 1, 1832. In the mid-1840's Evans attempted to revive the Workingmen's movement, making land reform the fundamental issue; Zahler, *Eastern Workingmen,* pp. 21–39.

6. Robert G. Albion, *Rise of New York Port* (New York, 1939), pp. 12–13, 276–79. For the number of auctioneers and their comparative prosperity (based on the duties they collected) see also Williams, *Annual Register* (1830), p. 130; *Courier and Enquirer,* December 12, 1829. The two firms of John Hone and Sons and Haggerty and Austin divided nearly half the business between them.

7. James Auchincloss to Martin Van Buren, January 12, 1829, Van Buren Papers; Albion, *New York Port,* pp. 279, 410; the latter page contains a tabular listing of New York auction sales from 1818 to 1841, based on *New York Assembly Documents* (1843), No. 10, pp. 130–31.

8. *American,* October 11, 13, 16, 21, 23, 1828; for Cambreleng's reply to the charges see *Evening Post,* October 22, 1828. For a detailed account of the movement see Horace Secrist, "The Anti-Auction Movement and the New York Workingman's Party of 1829," *Transactions* of the Wisconsin Academy of Science, Arts and Letters, XVII (1914), 149–66; it is interesting that this group used two devices later adopted by the Workingmen, the pledge and the Committee of Fifty.

9. For the election results see *ibid.,* p. 156; for later meetings of this group see *Morning Herald,* May 8, 1829; *Courier and Enquirer,* December 9, 11, 1829. See also James Auchincloss to Martin Van Buren, January 12, 1829, and Van Buren's undated reply, Van Buren Papers.

10. *Evening Journal,* January 2, 1830. For other resolutions on auctions see *Courier and Enquirer,* October 23, 1829; *Free Enquirer,* November 7, 1829.

11. *Working Man's Advocate,* December 12, 1829.

12. For the political careers of Mathews and Curtis see *Evening Post,* October 21, 1828; *Evening Journal,* January 20, February 1, 1830; *Working Man's Advocate,* September 18, October 23, November 13, 1830. Their occupations are given in *Directory,* 1830–31.

13. *Working Man's Advocate,* September 18, 1830. But the auction system was among the monopolies denounced in the 1834 Constitution of the Workingmen's Association; *Man,* May 19, 1834.

14. *Farmers', Mechanics', and Working Men's Advocate,* May 26, 1830. For the protectionist movement in New York see Williams, *Annual Register* (1830), pp. 206–7; *Report of the 3d Annual Fair of the American Institute of the City of New-York* (New York, 1830); *Life*

and Annual Members of the American Institute . . . Together with the names of its Officers, Directors and Trustees from its organization in the year 1828 to the present time (New York, 1882); *Morning Herald,* July 6, 1829; *American,* October 19, 1831, June 8, 11, 1832; *Working Man's Advocate,* November 5, 1831, July 13, 1833.

15. Albion, *New York Port,* pp. 61–63; Fox, *Decline of Aristocracy,* pp. 331–34; Turner, *United States 1830–1850,* pp. 401, 421.

16. *Working Man's Advocate,* June 16, 1832; Byrdsall, *History,* pp. 85, 142.

17. R. B. Westerfield, "Early History of American Auctions," in *Transactions* of the Connecticut Academy of Arts and Sciences, XXIII (1920), 169–70, 202.

18. See table in Albion, *New York Port,* p. 410.

19. See Chapter 6, Table I. For a description of the price fluctuations see the account in *Niles' Register,* quoted in Albion, *New York Port,* p. 279. The three auctioneers were Thomas Tripler, Abraham LeFoy, and Isaac Underhill; according to Williams, *Annual Register* (1830), p. 130, listing the duties paid by auctioneers in 1829, Tripler and LeFoy were so far down the list that their gross business could not have been large; Underhill was not listed, apparently obtaining his appointment in 1830.

20. Albion, *New York Port,* pp. 279–80.

21. For provisions of the charter see Moore, *Reply to a Pamphlet,* pp. 6–9; *American,* March 31, June 10, 1831. For the attacks see *ibid.,* April 11, October 10, 1831; *Working Man's Advocate,* October 29, 1831.

22. *Evening Post,* February 22, March 1, 1833.

23. *Ibid.,* March 1, 14, 1833; Moore, *Reply to a Pamphlet,* pp. 2–5, 12–21. For the later history of the company see *New-Yorker,* October 5, 1839; J. W. Greene, "The New-York & Harlem Railroad," *New-York Historical Society Quarterly Bulletin,* IX (1926). The railroad became an issue in the struggle for power within the Tammany organization, particularly in the selection of Common Council candidates; Moore became involved in this fight in the Fifteenth Ward. See *Working Man's Advocate,* March 23, April 20, 1833; *Evening Post,* March 15, 20, April 12, 1833; *Standard,* March 18, 22, 1833.

24. *Working Man's Advocate,* November 22, 1834; the *Evening Post* and the *Times* were quoted in *ibid.,* November 15, 22, 29, 1834.

25. *Ibid.,* November 29, 1834, January 3, 10, 1835; for Leggett's discussion of joint-stock partnerships see *Evening Post,* December 30, 1834.

26. *Courier and Enquirer,* December 22, 1829. For a description and evaluation of the Auburn system see Tyler, *Freedom's Ferment,* pp. 274–77.

27. *Mechanics' Gazette,* May 17, 1823, quoted in Commons, *Documentary History,* V, 51.

28. *Farmers', Mechanics', and Working Men's Advocate,* June 26,

July 3, 14, 1830, March 12, 1831; *Sentinel and Working Man's Advocate,* July 3, 1830; *Working Man's Advocate,* March 5, 19, 1831.

29. For the journeymen's protests and the N.T.U. resolution see *Man,* June 7, 23, August 28, 1834; *Working Man's Advocate,* March 29, April 5, 1834. The prospectus appeared in *National Trades' Union,* July 5, 1834; for the letter see *Evening Star,* April 5, 1834.

30. These conclusions are based on testimony by mechanics summarized in "Report of the Commissioners," p. 13. For meetings on prison labor, dominated by employers, see *Evening Star,* November 19, 1833, January 15, July 5, 1834; *Man,* May 24, 31, July 1, 1834.

31. *Times,* October 17, 1834; *Evening Star,* July 5, 1834.

32. *Working Man's Advocate,* September 13, 1834; see also *ibid.,* November 1, 1834, and *Man,* August 1, 1834. For the proceedings of the convention see *Niles' Register,* September 20, 1834; *National Trades' Union,* September 30, 1834. For resolutions of the Workingmen on prison labor see *Working Man's Advocate,* April 5, October 18, 1834.

33. For passage of the act and Moore's appointment see *Evening Post,* May 26, 1834; *Evening Star,* May 26, 28, 1834; *Man,* May 31, 1834. The other commissioners were Elisha Litchfield, a prosperous upstate merchant and former Congressman, and Arphaxad Loomis, a lawyer elected to Congress in 1836; see *Biographical Directory of the American Congress* (Washington, 1928), pp. 1229, 1238. For a detailed account of Moore's lobbying activities see letters from "A Mechanic" in *Evening Star,* October 31 to November 6, 1838.

34. "Report of the Commissioners," pp. 13–14, 16–18, 21–25.

35. *Man,* February 9, 19, 26, 1835; *Evening Post,* February 10, April 28, 1835; *Times,* February 10, 20, 1835; Albany *Argus* quoted in *Transcript,* February 18, 1835; *National Trades' Union,* February 21, 28, 1835.

36. For the proceedings of the G.T.U. see *Man,* March 2, 17, 30, 1835; *National Trades' Union,* May 2, 1835. For the mechanics' meeting see *Man,* February 26, 1835; the resolution of the General Committee was published and discussed in *ibid.,* March 7, 20, 1835; see also *Times,* March 18, 1835.

37. *Man,* May 1, 6, 1835; *Working Man's Advocate,* September 5, 1835. For the state convention see *Mechanic,* August 25, 1835. The Locofoco resolutions are in Byrdsall, *History,* pp. 167, 172. For the 1838 and 1839 campaigns see *Evening Star,* October 31, November 3, 1838; *Whig,* November 1, 1839.

38. *Evening Post,* April 28, 1835. See also *Man,* June 7, 1834; *Working Man's Advocate,* September 13, 1834.

39. For the practice in Pennsylvania and Massachusetts see Hartz, *Economic Policy,* pp. 204–7; Oscar and Mary F. Handlin, *Commonwealth; A Study of the Role of Government in the American Economy: Massachusetts, 1774–1861* (New York, 1947), pp. 67–80.

40. *American,* October 22, 1828; this article gave an itemized list of

6,892 positions. See also Edwin Williams, *New-York As It Is, in 1834* (New York, 1834), pp. 163–73, for a listing of licensed occupations. About 3,000 grocery and tavern licenses were issued in 1833, and nearly $100,000 was realized by the city from license fees, 80 percent of which came from market and tavern fees; *ibid.*, pp. 169, 178–80. See also Thomas F. DeVoe, *The Market Book* (New York, 1862), *passim.*

41. For resolutions on the subject see *Evening Journal*, March 10, 1830; *Working Man's Advocate*, November 6, 1830, March 14, 21, 1835; *Man*, April 13, 1835; Byrdsall, *History*, pp. 103, 135, 166. The memorial was published in *Evening Journal*, March 17, 1830.

42. *Working Man's Advocate*, November 29, 1834.

43. *Democrat*, March 18, 1836.

44. *Man*, March 26, April 13, 1835.

45. *Morning Herald*, April 15, 1829; *Working Man's Advocate*, July 23, 1830, October 11, 1834, February 21, March 14, 1835; *Man*, March 23, 1835.

46. Letter in *Working Man's Advocate*, March 14, 1835; *Man*, March 25, 1835. This compromise proposal was not offered by the Workingmen, but by an Alderman in the Common Council.

47. *Working Man's Advocate*, June 25, 1831, March 21, 1835. See also *Courier and Enquirer*, June 20, 1829.

48. *Man*, June 29, 1835. The Workingmen generally ignored the temperance movement, regarding it as dominated by the "Church and state aristocracy," but Evans in 1830 mentioned the "intemperate use of intoxicating liquors" by laborers and expressed the hope that the Workingmen would choose a candidate for governor who was "temperate in all habits"; *Working Man's Advocate*, August 21, 1830. See also *Free Enquirer*, March 25, 1829.

49. *Working Man's Advocate*, February 14, 1835; *Man*, June 13, July 3, 1835.

50. *Evening Journal*, March 17, 1830.

51. *Working Man's Advocate*, August 23, December 13, 1834, March 14, 1835; *Man*, April 11, 13, 1835; Byrdsall, *History*, p. 135. For the ferry tolls see *Working Man's Advocate*, October 31, 1835.

52. *Ibid.*, December 13, 1834; see also *ibid.*, January 10, March 21, 1835.

53. *Evening Post*, February 18, October 10, 1835. Leggett was actually replying to a proposal advanced by the Whig New York *American.*

54. *Working Man's Advocate*, December 13, 1834. The attack on the ferry and market monopolies was linked with the demand, discussed in the previous chapter, for a salaried Common Council; this reform, it was asserted, would enable antimonopolists to be elected to overthrow the power of "landed interests" who by maintaining a revenue system based on license and franchise fees kept property taxes low and rents high. See *ibid.*, March 21, 1835; *Man*, April 3, 11, 1835; Byrdsall, *History*, pp. 102–3.

55. Henry B. Shafer, *American Medical Profession, 1783 to 1850* (New York, 1936), pp. 205–10; see also speech of Job Haskell reported in *Man,* April 30, 1835. For the Rutgers controversy see *Rutgers Medical College, Announcement, 1826* (New York, 1826); *Statesman,* November 8, 10, 1827.

56. The law of 1828 was cited in the "Report of the Attorney-General, on a resolution from the Assembly," *New York Assembly Documents,* 53d Session, vol. 2, No. 199 (Albany, 1830); see also *Courier and Enquirer,* October 19, 1829. For the debate on this law see memorials published in *American,* September 24, 1828; *Evening Post,* October 2, 1828.

57. *Courier and Enquirer,* October 19, 21, 23, 27, November 9, 1829; the quotation is from a letter by "One Who Knows" in *ibid.,* October 23, 1829. The court ruling was cited in "Report of the Attorney-General."

58. For the 1830 legislation see *Man,* April 30, 1835. Advertisements of botanic physicians and others are in *Working Man's Advocate,* May 22, October 30, 1830. The medical electrician was Jonas Humbert, Jr., formerly a baker like his father; the latter was the Skidmore candidate for lieutenant governor in 1830, but was later denounced by the Workingmen for his agitation against the bakers' strike. See *ibid.,* September 25, 1830; *Man,* June 24, 26, 1834; *Directory,* 1828–29 to 1830–31.

59. "Memorial of the Medical Society of the city and county of New-York," *New York Assembly Documents,* 55th Session, vol. 3, No. 249 (Albany, 1832), pp. 1–3. This memorial was presented January 31, 1832, and the bill based on its demands was introduced early in March; see "Remonstrance of Joseph M. Smith et al., of the city of New-York, against any alteration of the law regulating the practice of physic in this State," in *ibid.,* vol. 3, No. 262. This movement began in October 1831, when a committee of the County Medical Society prepared a circular letter calling for "a uniformity of usage in examinations"; it was published in *Working Man's Advocate,* November 26, 1831.

60. "Remonstrance of the State Medical Society," *New York Assembly Documents,* 55th Session, vol. 3, No. 185, pp. 4–5.

61. "Memorial of J. A. Smith and others, of the Medical Profession in the city of New-York," *ibid.,* vol. 3, No. 250, pp. 1–2; the signers were the seven members of the faculty of the College of Physicians and Surgeons.

62. "Memorial of the Medical Society of the city and county of New-York," *ibid.,* vol. 3, No. 244, pp. 1, 4–5.

63. "Remonstrance of physicians and surgeons in the city of New-York," *ibid.,* vol. 3, No. 261, p. 2; virtually the same charge was made in *ibid.,* vol. 3, No. 244, p. 3. For the reply to this charge see "Remonstrance of Doctors T. R. Beck and James McNaughton," *ibid.,* vol. 3, No. 272; these men were professors at the College of Physicians and Surgeons, Western District.

64. "Remonstrance of seventy-six practitioners of medicine in the city of New-York," *ibid.,* vol. 3, No. 246; this was about one-fourth of

the membership. See also "Report of Mr. Winfield, from the committee on medical societies and colleges," *ibid.*, vol. 3, No. 251, pp. 3–4.

65. *Working Man's Advocate,* April 19, November 8, 1834.

66. For Evans' views see *ibid.*, November 26, 1831. For the physicians' participation see *American,* September 24, 1828; *Courier and Enquirer,* October 19, 22, November 9, 1829; *Man,* May 15, 1834; *New York Assembly Documents* (1832), No. 261, pp. 4–5, and No. 246, pp. 2–3.

67. *Working Man's Advocate,* May 3, December 20, 1834; see also *ibid.*, April 19, November 8, 1834.

68. *Man,* April 27, 1835. For the medical bill and the praise of Haskell see *ibid.*, April 27, 30, May 7, 1835.

69. *Ibid.*, April 27, 1835; Byrdsall, *History,* p. 166.

70. Shafer, *Medical Profession,* pp. 210, 233–36. An example of the popular attack on physicians was the charge that many had deserted the city during the cholera epidemic; *Sentinel,* September 26, 1832. There was a parallel movement to repeal medical laws in Massachusetts; see Handlin, *Commonwealth,* pp. 223–24.

71. Resolution of Workingmen's meeting published in *Working Man's Advocate,* October 11, 1834.

CHAPTER 9

1. Report and resolutions of October 19, 1829, meeting in *Courier and Enquirer,* October 23, 1829; see also *Working Man's Advocate,* October 31, 1829.

2. Bray Hammond, "Free Banks and Corporations: The New York Free Banking Act of 1838," *Journal of Political Economy,* XLIV (February 1936), 185; Charles A. Conant, *A History of Modern Banks of Issue* (4th ed., New York, 1909), p. 370.

3. Margaret G. Myers, *New York Money Market: Origins and Development* (New York, 1931), pp. 5–6.

4. Hammond, "Free Banks and Corporations," pp. 186–88; Robert E. Chaddock, *Safety Fund Banking System in New York, 1829–66* (Washington, 1910), p. 235.

5. *Ibid.*, pp. 242–47; Myers, *Money Market,* p. 156. For the Bank of America scandal see Fox, *Decline of Aristocracy,* pp. 166, 226–28.

6. Chaddock, *Safety Fund,* pp. 243, 247; for the contemporary evaluation see Hammond, *History of Political Parties,* I, 337.

7. Chaddock, *Safety Fund,* pp. 252–55; Myers; *Money Market,* p. 82.

8. Chaddock, *Safety Fund,* pp. 259–63; Conant, *History,* pp. 370–71.

9. Chaddock, *Safety Fund,* pp. 236–40, 263–71; Harry E. Miller, *Banking Theories in the United States Before 1860* (Cambridge, Mass., 1927), pp. 150–51. For the quotation see *American,* April 3, 1829; other criticisms can be found in *ibid.*, November 26, 1829; *Evening Journal,* March 13, 1830. The same arguments were used by the "Pewter Mug" faction in the 1829 election.

10. Ralph C. H. Catterall, *Second Bank of the United States* (Chicago, 1903), pp. 24–26, 164–68; Conant, *History*, pp. 343–48; Bray Hammond, "Jackson, Biddle, and the Bank of the United States," *Journal of Economic History*, VII (May 1947), 2–4; Myers, *Money Market*, pp. 160–62; Sister M. Grace Madeleine, *Monetary and Banking Theories of Jacksonian Democracy* (Philadelphia, 1943), pp. 42, 67–68; Fritz Redlich, *Molding of American Banking: Men and Ideas* (New York, 1947), Part I, pp. 96–181. See also the account in Bray Hammond, *Banks and Politics in America from the Revolution to the Civil War* (Princeton, 1957), chap. 12.

11. Myers, *Money Market*, pp. 61, 69; Catterall, *Second Bank*, p. 165; Chaddock, *Safety Fund*, p. 270; Bray Hammond, "The Banks, the States, and the Federal Government," *American Economic Review*, XXIII (December 1933), 626.

12. Myers, *Money Market*, pp. 162–64. Slightly more than one million dollars was actually withdrawn by drafts on the Bank, the remaining ten million dollars of government deposits being drawn out gradually in the normal course of federal expenditures; however, the order resulted in all federal revenues being deposited in the designated state banks.

13. *Evening Journal,* January 2, 1830.

14. *Working Man's Advocate,* August 21, 1830; the quotation was in *ibid.,* February 12, 1831.

15. *Ibid.,* April 2, 1831. Two years later Evans maintained that the Bank of the United States was the greater evil because of its "dangerous power"; *ibid.,* January 26, 1833.

16. Chaddock, *Safety Fund,* pp. 275–76, 279, 284. See also Fritz Redlich, "Free Banking: The History of an Idea and Its Exponents," in *Essays in American Economic History* (New York, 1944), p. 133; and Hammond, "Free Banks and Corporations," p. 193.

17. William Gouge, *A Short History of Paper Money and Banking in the United States* (Philadelphia, 1833), Part I, p. 74. Evans praised this book highly, reporting that he had sold nearly 150 copies in slightly more than a year; *Working Man's Advocate,* March 23, 1833, September 13, 1834. For another example of oversubscription of stock see *Man,* June 17, 1834.

18. Sedgwick, *What Is a Monopoly?* quoted in Blau, *Social Theories,* p. 232; *Evening Post,* March 25, 1835, quoted in Dorfman, *Economic Mind,* II, 653.

19. *Man,* June 4, 1834; see also *Working Man's Advocate,* February 8, 1834.

20. *Evening Post,* January 3, 1835. For a similar statement written two years before see Gouge, *Short History,* Part I, pp. 135–40.

21. Miller, *Banking Theories,* pp. 142–45. For a discussion of the English experience see Norman J. Silberling, "Financial and Monetary Policy of Great Britain During the Napoleonic Wars: II. Ricardo and

the Bullion Report," *Quarterly Journal of Economics,* XXXVIII (May 1924), 397–439.

22. *Man,* March 5, 1834. This statement was made to a delegation of merchants from Philadelphia.

23. Chaddock, *Safety Fund,* p. 278; Redlich, "Free Banking," p. 137. For the Locofoco demands see *Man,* May 19, 1834; Byrdsall, *History,* pp. 88, 102. The legislature restored small bills in 1838 because of a scarcity of specie during the Panic; Fox, *Decline of Aristocracy,* pp. 402–3.

24. Neil Carothers, *Fractional Money: A History of the Small Coins and Fractional Paper Currency of the United States* (New York, 1930), p. 80.

25. *Ibid.,* pp. 62, 66–67, 72-81.

26. *Working Man's Advocate,* April 5, 1834. For the specie importation see quotations from *Journal of Commerce* in *Man,* February 20, May 23, June 27, 1834.

27. Carothers, *Fractional Money,* pp. 89–93; see also *Man,* May 31, June 24, July 1, 1834. White, a Democratic Congressman since 1828, was a merchant and later a bank director; *Directory,* 1833–34; *Democrat,* October 8, 1836.

28. *Man,* June 26, 1834; Leggett's editorial is quoted in *ibid.,* July 8, 1834. For the reaction of banking theorists see Dorfman, *Economic Mind,* II, 609–10.

29. Carothers, *Fractional Money,* pp. 79, 97–101.

30. Editorial in *Evening Post* quoted in *Man,* July 8, 1834.

31. Miller, *Banking Theories,* pp. 40–44, 70–71, 82. The statement on overissue was made by Albert Gallatin; see also Henry Adams, *Life of Albert Gallatin* (Philadelphia, 1879), pp. 652–53, 662–64.

32. *Working Man's Advocate,* December 31, 1831.

33. Memorial of citizens published in *ibid.,* April 3, 1830; letter from "A.B." in *ibid.,* October 10, 1835; *Man,* March 22, 1834. See also *ibid.,* August 8, 1834; *Working Man's Advocate,* March 14, 1835; *Evening Post,* August 6, 1834, March 10, 11, 1835.

34. *Man,* May 10, 1834.

35. *Working Man's Advocate,* December 31, October 8, December 24, September 3, November 12, 1831. Some banking theorists condemned banks for lending notes which they freely manufactured, while others insisted that overissue could only be avoided if banks loaned their credit instead of their capital; Miller, *Banking Theories,* pp. 82, 147. See also Abraham H. Venit, "Isaac Bronson: His Banking Theory and the Financial Controversies of the Jacksonian Period," *Journal of Economic History,* V (November 1945), 202, 204.

36. *Working Man's Advocate,* January 28, 1832. See also *ibid.,* February 11, 1832, April 13, 20, 1833; Miller, *Banking Theories,* p. 82.

37. *Working Man's Advocate,* April 27, 1833.

38. *Ibid.,* June 29, 1833. William Gouge was quoted on "the constant tendency of banks." In *ibid.,* August 30, 1834, Eleazar Lord was cited

on convertibility and overissue, although characterized as a "Knight of the Rag Mill."

39. *Ibid.*, April 6, 1833.

40. *Ibid.*, December 5, 1829; *Man*, May 22, 1834.

41. Isaac Bronson, John McVickar, and Eleazar Lord were the chief proponents of this plan. See Miller, *Banking Theories*, pp. 147, 152; Venit, "Isaac Bronson," pp. 204–6; James A. Hamilton, *Reminiscences, or Men and Events at Home and Abroad During Three-Quarters of a Century* (New York, 1869), pp 82–84; Redlich, "Mercantilist Thought and Early American Banking," in *Essays*, pp. 121–23.

42. *Working Man's Advocate,* December 12, 1829, August 23, 1834. A writer in the *Evening Post,* quoted in *ibid.,* September 19, 1835, proposed "a circulating medium, based upon mortgages of real property" in order to aid "the agricultural portion of the community." The Free Banking Act of 1838 provided for notes based upon the security of both bonds and mortgages.

43. Byrdsall, *History*, pp. 101, 111–12.

44. *Working Man's Advocate,* October 29, 1831. According to *ibid.,* September 19, 1835, "when business is good and things are going on smoothly they get out too much money, which causes a rise in the price of all sorts of produce, encourages speculation and overtrading, and by these means the markets are overstocked." See also *Man,* May 22, 1834.

45. Letter in *Working Man's Advocate,* April 27, 1833; editorial in *ibid.,* July 9, 1831.

46. *Ibid.*, January 17, 1835; Evans made essentially the same statement earlier in *ibid.*, January 21, 1832.

47. *Ibid.*, December 17, 1831, January 7, 1832, April 20, 1833. For nearly two years this writer carried on an extensive debate with "A Journeyman Printer," "A Working Man," and editor Evans.

48. *Ibid.*, June 22, 1833.

49. *Ibid.*, February 18, 1832.

50. See *ibid.*, February 8, 1834; *Man*, May 7, 1834. Cf. *Free Enquirer,* May 22, 1830.

51. *Working Man's Advocate,* October 1, 1831.

52. For favorable remarks on savings banks see *Sentinel,* September 26, 1832; *Working Man's Advocate,* June 22, 1833. For denunciations see *Man,* March 3, May 10, 1834.

53. *Working Man's Advocate,* November 19, 1831; see also *ibid.,* January 22, 1831, December 21, 1833. For Leggett's criticism see *Evening Post,* August 6, 1834.

54. *Evening Journal,* March 15, 1830; *Free Enquirer,* May 22, 1830.

55. *Working Man's Advocate,* December 17, 1831; see also letter from "A Mechanic" in *ibid.,* January 17, 1832.

56. *Ibid.,* April 6, 13, 1833; Herttell's speech was given in the New York Assembly on March 19, 1833. See also *ibid.,* November 19, 1831, for Evans' earlier reaction to a similar proposal.

57. *Evening Post,* August 26, November 21, 22, 1834, January 3,

1835. "A Mechanic" quoted Thomas Cooper in support of free banking; *Working Man's Advocate*, June 22, 1833. For other statements by Leggett, as well as letters from "Hard Money" written in support of his stand, see *ibid.*, April 19, September 27, 1834; *Man*, May 15, 21, 1834.

58. Quoted in Redlich, "Free Banking," p. 134.

59. *Ibid.*, pp. 139–40; Dorfman, *Economic Mind*, II, 522. McVickar derived the idea of bond-backed notes from Isaac Bronson; see Venit, "Isaac Bronson," pp. 203–4. Eleazar Lord repeated this proposal in 1829; see *Working Man's Advocate*, August 23, 30, 1834; Redlich, "Free Banking," p. 147.

60. Quoted in *Working Man's Advocate*, January 3, 1835; see also *Evening Post*, December 30, 1834, January 23, 26, 1835.

61. Sedgwick, *What Is a Monopoly?* in Blau, *Social Theories*, p. 223; this was a collection of a series of articles by "Veto" which appeared in the *Evening Post* during the fall and winter of 1834–35. For the identity of "Veto" see Schlesinger, *Age of Jackson*, p. 188.

62. *Working Man's Advocate*, January 3, 10, 1835. For Leggett's views see *Evening Post*, January 20, 1835.

63. *Working Man's Advocate*, October 24, 1835.

64. Letter from "A New Yorker" in the *Evening Post*, quoted in *Working Man's Advocate*, September 19, 1835, with Evans' comment.

65. *Evening Post*, October 21, 1835; also published in Blau, *Social Theories*, p. 218.

66. Byrdsall, *History*, pp. 39, 73; see also *ibid.*, pp. 88, 112–13, 172.

67. Hammond, "Free Banks and Corporations," pp. 192–94; see also Redlich, "Free Banking," pp. 148–50.

68. Cf. Samuel Rezneck, "Social History of an American Depression, 1837–1843," *American Historical Review*, XL (July 1935), 675; and Redlich, "Free Banking," pp. 153–57.

69. Conant, *History*, pp. 374–75; Hammond, "Free Banks and Corporations," pp. 197–207. For the widespread influence of the Free Banking Act see Leonard C. Helderman, *National and State Banks, A Study of Their Origins* (Cambridge, Mass., 1931), pp. 143, 156, and *passim*; cf. Hammond, *Banks and Politics*, chap. 18.

70. For a discussion of this relationship between the demand for free banking and the desire for credit, and the Mercantilist background of the controversy, see Bray Hammond, "Long and Short Term Credit in Early American Banking," *Quarterly Journal of Economics*, XLIX (November 1934), 79–90, 95–103; and "Free Banks and Corporations," p. 191; Redlich, *Essays*, pp. 107–10, 113–15, 132, 137.

71. Chaddock, *Safety Fund*, pp. 275–76; Myers, *Money Market*, pp. 45–55. The statement on the "legitimate function of banks" was by Isaac Bronson; see Venit, "Isaac Bronson," pp. 203–4.

72. Gouge, *Short History*, Part I, pp. 35–37. See also Miller, *Banking Theories*, pp. 92–96.

73. *Working Man's Advocate*, December 5, 1829; *Evening Journal*, January 15, 1831. The latter article hailed the recent establishment of

the Mechanics' Bank, under the auspices of the General Society of Mechanics and Tradesmen, as a step toward improving the situation.

74. *Working Man's Advocate*, October 29, 1831; for criticisms of savings banks see *ibid.*, September 22, 1832; *Sentinel*, September 26, 1832.

75. *Working Man's Advocate*, September 3, October 8, 1831.

76. *Ibid.*, January 21, 1832.

77. *Ibid.*, February 18, 1832.

78. "Gracchus" in *ibid.*, January 28, 1832; "A Working Man" in *ibid.*, April 13, 1833; "Plebeian" in New Bedford *Working Man's Press*, quoted approvingly by Evans in *ibid.*, April 20, 1833; "A Journeyman Mechanic" in *ibid.*, April 26, 1834.

79. *Man*, May 17, 1834.

80. Leggett in *Evening Post*, quoted in *Working Man's Advocate*, October 25, 1834; *Plaindealer*, June 3, 1837.

81. Sedgwick, *What Is a Monopoly?* in Blau, *Social Theories*, pp. 230–31.

82. *Evening Post*, October 21, 1835.

83. Byrdsall, *History*, pp. 140, 149.

84. Hammond, "Long and Short Term Credit," p. 95.

85. *Ibid.*, pp. 93–94, 102; Gallatin's statement was quoted in *ibid.*, p. 96 n. See also Redlich, *Essays*, p. 132.

86. Helderman, *National and State Banks*, pp. 25–29. Cf. Bray Hammond, "Banking in the Early West: Monopoly, Prohibition, and Laissez Faire," *Journal of Economic History*, VIII (May 1948), 1–25.

87. Myers, *Money Market*, pp. 172–73; Conant, *History*, p. 356. For further details on the suspension see Hammond, "Jackson, Biddle, and the Bank of the United States," pp. 12–23.

88. Byrdsall, *History*, p. 151; Gouge, *Short History*, Part I, p. 138. See also Dorfman, *Economic Mind*, II, 610–13.

89. *Working Man's Advocate*, May 7, December 24, 1831; for the resolution see *ibid.*, February 8, 1834. See also letters from "Gracchus" and "A. B." in *ibid.*, January 28, 1832, December 21, 1833.

90. Myers, *Money Market*, pp. 174–84; Dorfman, *Economic Mind*, II, 613–18. For Gallatin's views and his position in New York see Adams, *Gallatin*, pp. 657–61; Bray Hammond, "The Chestnut Street Raid on Wall Street, 1839," *Quarterly Journal of Economics*, LXI (August 1947), 605–18; Hammond, "Jackson, Biddle, and the Bank of the United States," pp. 12–23.

91. See *Working Man's Advocate*, December 24, 1831, April 13, 1833, April 19, 1834.

92. Miller, *Banking Theories*, pp. 12–14, 112–19; Myers, *Money Market*, pp. 87–93. Bronson was one of the few who, as early as 1827, realized the role of deposits; Venit, "Isaac Bronson," pp. 203–4.

93. Helderman, *National and State Banks*, pp. 9–10, 39–46, and *passim;* Hammond, "Banking in the Early West," pp. 1–5, 23–24, main-

tains that prohibition, rather than laissez faire and free banking, was most characteristic of the Western agrarians.

94. On this point see Miller, *Banking Theories,* p. 95.

95. "Public Policy and National Banks," pp. 84, 82.

CHAPTER 10

1. See Wilfred E. Binkley, *American Political Parties, Their Natural History* (New York, 1945), pp. 141–45.

2. Albion, *New York Port,* pp. 1–15, 418–19, and *passim.*

3. Fox, *Decline of Aristocracy,* pp. 22–25, 431–36.

4. Article I, Section 3, of the constitution of 1846 in *Manual for the Use of the Legislature of the State of New York, 1866* (Albany 1866), p. 40. The school fund was established by Art. IX, Sec. 1, in *ibid.,* p. 69.

5. Art. V, Secs. 1–4, and Art. VI, Secs. 2, 12, and 14, in *ibid.,* pp. 54, 56, 58–59.

6. Art. VI, Sec. 24, and Art. I, Sec. 17, in *ibid.,* pp. 61, 43.

7. Art. V, Sec. 8, in *ibid.,* p. 55.

8. *Ibid.,* pp. 68–69. The constitution also prohibited state assistance by gift or loan to any corporation or association; see Art. VII, Sec. 9, in *ibid.,* p. 66.

9. *Report of the Proceedings and Debates of the Convention of 1821* (Albany 1821), pp. 219–22, quoted in Fox, *Decline of Aristocracy,* pp. 254–55.

CONCLUSION

1. *Decline of Aristocracy,* p. 300. The 1821 constitution, as amended in 1825, provided for universal white male suffrage with a minor residence requirement; Negro voting was restricted by the requirement of a $250 freehold and three years' residence; *ibid.,* pp. 251, 273–74.

2. *Banks and Politics,* p. 329.

3. Cf. Handlin, *Commonwealth,* and Hartz, *Economic Policy.* These writers stress "the myth of laissez faire" in their accounts of the history of Massachusetts and Pennsylvania during this period, concluding that state action in the economic field was the generally accepted pattern until after the Civil War.

4. *Banks and Politics,* p. 574. Hammond also oversimplifies in ascribing these doctrines to farm-bred men now working in factories and shops; he emphasizes further that their entrepreneurial employers, also of rural origin, typified the laissez-faire attitude toward banks.

5. *The Jacksonian Persuasion: Politics and Belief* (Stanford, Calif., 1957), p. 10; see also pp. 92–107.

6. Gallatin to Jonathan Roberts, June 3, 1841, and Gallatin to Badollet, September 3, 1836, in Adams, *Gallatin,* pp. 663–64, 153.

7. *Banks and Politics,* p. 740. According to Mills, "American Business Elite," pp. 20–44, the highest percentage of the business elite in American history with lower- and lower–middle-class origins is to be found in the generation born between 1820 and 1850.

tain than prohibition. Rather than higher fines and free bonking, was
moral characteristic of the Western spectrum.

91. On this point see Weber, *Banking Theory*, p. 95.

92. Fuller, *Public Land System*, *Annual Report*, pp. 43, 82.

CHAPTER 10

1. See W. Floyd E. Bisbley, *Historical Political Papers: Their Natural History* (New York, 1945), pp. 191–95.

2. Cobbin, *New York Post*, pp. 1–15, 418–19 and *passim*.

3. Fox, *Decline of Aristocracy*, pp. 22–23, 411–53.

4. Article I, Section 4 of the Constitution of 1846 in *Manual for the Use of the Legislature of the State of New York* (New York, Albany, 1889), sec. iii. The school fund was established by Art. IX, Sec. 4, in ibid., p. 31.

5. Art. V, Secs. 1–4 and Art. V Laws, X. Id., and 14, in ibid., pp. 41, 54, 91–92.

6. Art. VI, Sec. 24, and Art. 4, sec. 12, in ibid., pp. 91, 93.

7. Art. V, Sec. 8, in ibid., p. 53.

8. Ibid., pp. 98–99. The constitution also prohibited state assistance by gift or loan to any corporation or association; see Art. VII, Sec. 9, in ibid., p. 66.

9. *Report of the Franchise and Colonies* of the Convention of 1847 (Albany, 1847), pp. 210–22, quoted in Fox, *Decline of Aristocracy*, pp. 184–22.

CONCLUSION

1. *Decline of Aristocracy*, p. 300. The 1821 constitution, as amended in 1825, provided for universal white male suffrage and a minor residence requirement; the Negro voting was restricted by the requirement of a $250 freehold and three years' residency; ibid., pp. 270, 272–74.

2. *Banking and Politics*, p. 359.

3. A traditional, *Communists*, "sustain are Economic *Policy*." These writers stress "the growth of laissez-faire" in their accounts of the history of investment and franchise acts during this period, concluding that experimentation in the economic field was the generally accepted answer until after the Civil War.

4. Hartz and Salisbury, p. 304. Hartz did not over-emphasize his state-making these doctrines, he interpreted state non-meddling in *Economic* and almost monopolize further that state entrepreneurial employment should be emphasized. *Greatest* the *Interpretation* of the *content* field.

5. Pax Jacksonus, *Social Policy, Public content*, *Labor Monetary Policy*, 1857, pp. 10; see also pp. 92–103, etc. *Passim*.

6. Gallatin to Jonathan Robert's, June 2, 9, and Gallatin to Thad., ibid., ibid., b. h.v., in *Addr.*, *Gallatin*, pp. 251, 251, 154.

7. Dorset and Pollard, *J. Distribution*, p. 21, The *Constitution Mechanism*, pp. 20–41 are, *rigorous sustentation of the business* allow. American interest with lower class and low *exchangeable* discrepancy case in the bond in the *generation* born between 1821 and 1843.

Bibliography

MANUSCRIPTS

"Autobiography, John Frazee, First American Sculptor, b. 1790 Rahway, N.J." New York Public Library (copied in 1944 by H. A. Frazee from Marsh Papers, New Jersey Historical Society).

DeWitt Clinton Papers. Columbia University.

"Constitution and By Laws of the New York Society of Journeyman House Carpenters, Adopted November 19, 1833." New York Public Library.

Deeds and Conveyances recorded in the Office of the Register of the City and County of New York. Hall of Records, New York City.

Kilroe, Edwin P., "Tammany Society or Columbian Order, Membership List, 1789–1924." Kilroe Tammaniana, Columbia University.

Martin Van Buren Papers. Library of Congress (microfilm at Columbia University).

Washington Association of New Jersey Papers. Morristown National Historical Park, Morristown, New Jersey.

NEWSPAPERS AND PERIODICALS

NEW YORK CITY

American, 1828–34. New-York Historical Society.

Aurora and Union, 1843. New-York Historical Society.

Champion of American Labor, 1847. New-York Historical Society.

Commercial Advertiser, 1829–30. New-York Historical Society.

Democrat, 1836. New York Public Library.

Democratic-Republican New Era, 1840. New-York Historical Society.

Evening Journal, 1829–31. New-York Historical Society.

Evening Post, 1828–44. New York Public Library.

Evening Star, 1833–40. New-York Historical Society.

Free Enquirer, 1829–35. Columbia University.

Herald, 1835–37. New-York Historical Society.

Independent Press, 1835. New-York Historical Society.

Jeffersonian, 1834–35. New-York Historical Society.

Journal of Commerce, 1828–37. New York Public Library.

Man, 1834–35. New-York Historical Society.

Mechanic, 1834–35. New-York Historical Society.

Mercantile Advertiser and New-York Advocate, 1833–38. New-York Historical Society.

Morning Courier, 1827–29. New-York Historical Society.
Morning Courier and New-York Enquirer, 1829–36. New-York Historical Society.
Morning Herald, 1829–30. New-York Historical Society.
National Trades' Union, 1834–36. Typewritten extracts by John R. Commons and others, State Historical Society of Wisconsin (also microfilm, Columbia University).
New Era, 1836. New-York Historical Society.
New-Yorker, 1836–39. Columbia University.
Olive Branch and Christian Inquirer, 1828. New-York Historical Society.
Plaindealer, 1836–37. Columbia University.
Plebeian, 1842–45. New York Society Library.
Sentinel, 1830–32. State Historical Society of Wisconsin (also microfilm, Columbia University).
Sentinel and Working Man's Advocate, 1830. New-York Historical Society.
Standard, 1830. New-York Historical Society.
Statesman, 1827–28. New-York Historical Society.
Subterranean, 1844–47. New-York Historical Society, 1844; New York Public Library, 1845–47.
Times, 1834–37. New-York Historical Society.
Transcript, 1835. Columbia University.
Tribune, 1842–60. Columbia University.
Union, 1836. New York Public Library.
Whig, 1831–33, 1839–40. New-York Historical Society.
Working Man's Advocate, 1829–36, 1844–45. Ohio State Archeological and Historical Society, 1829–32 (microfilm, Columbia University); New-York Historical Society, 1830–33, 1844–45; New York Public Library, 1834–36; State Historical Society of Wisconsin, 1833–36 (microfilm, Columbia University).
Young Men's Advocate, 1832–33. New-York Historical Society.

OTHER

Farmers', Mechanics', and Working Men's Advocate (Albany, N.Y.), 1830–31. New-York Historical Society.
Free Enquirer (New Harmony, Ind.), 1828–29. Columbia University.
Kansas National Democrat (Lecompton, Kan.), 1857–61. Library of Congress.
Niles' Weekly Register (Baltimore, Md.), 1833–37. Columbia University.
Radical, in Continuation of the Working Man's Advocate (Granville, N.J.), 1841–43. Columbia University.
United States Magazine and Democratic Review (Washington, D.C.), 1837–39. Columbia University.
Warren Journal (Belvidere, N.J.), 1850. New Jersey Historical Society.

BOOKS AND ARTICLES

Adams, Charles F., ed. *Memoirs of John Quincy Adams, 1795–1848.* 12 vols. Philadelphia, 1876.

Adams, Franklin G. "The Capitals of Kansas," Kansas State Historical Society *Collections,* VIII (1903–4), 331–43.

Adams, Henry. *Life of Albert Gallatin (1761–1849).* Philadelphia, 1879.

Address of the Republican General Committee of Young Men of the City and County of New-York, Friendly to the Election of Gen: Andrew Jackson to the Presidency, to the Republican Electors of the State of New-York. New York, 1828.

Albion, Robert G. *The Rise of New York Port.* New York, 1939.

Ambler, C. H., ed. "Correspondence of Robert M. T. Hunter 1826–76," American Historical Association, *Annual Report* (1916), II.

Appleton's Cyclopedia of American Biography. 6 vols. New York, 1888.

Arkin, Herbert, and Raymond R. Colton. *An Outline of Statistical Methods.* New York, 1949.

Arky, Louis H. "The Mechanics' Union of Trade Associations and the Formation of the Philadelphia Workingmen's Movement," *Pennsylvania Magazine of History and Biography,* LXXVI (April 1952), 142–76.

Beard, Charles A. and Mary R. *Rise of American Civilization.* 2 vols. in 1. New York, 1934.

Beard, Mary R. *The American Labor Movement, A Short History.* New York, 1938.

Binkley, Wilfred E. *American Political Parties, Their Natural History.* New York, 1945.

Biographical Directory of the American Congress. Washington, 1928.

Blau, Joseph L., ed. *Social Theories of Jacksonian Democracy.* New York, 1947.

Boucher, C. S., and R. P. Brooks, eds. "Correspondence Addressed to John C. Calhoun 1837–1849," American Historical Association, *Annual Report* (1929), II.

Bourne, W. O. *History of the Public School Society of the City of New York.* New York, 1873.

Bower, Robert T. "Note on 'Did Labor Support Jackson?: The Boston Story,'" *Political Science Quarterly,* LXV (September 1950), 441–44.

Bowers, Claude G. *The Party Battles of the Jackson Period.* Boston, 1922.

Brigham, Clarence S. *History and Bibliography of American Newspapers, 1690–1820.* 2 vols. Worcester, Mass., 1947.

Brooks, Richard A. E., ed. *Diary of Michael Floy Jr., Bowery Village, 1833–1837.* New Haven, 1941.

Bryant, William C. "William Leggett," *United States Magazine and Democratic Review,* VI (July 1839), 17–28.

Byrdsall, F. *History of the Loco-Foco or Equal Rights Party, Its*

Movements, Conventions and Proceedings, With Short Characteristic Sketches of Its Prominent Men. New York, 1842.

Caldwell, Henry B. "John Frazee, American Sculptor." Unpublished M.A. thesis, New York University, 1951.

Carlton, Frank T. "Abolition of Imprisonment for Debt in the United States," *Yale Review,* XVII (1908/09), 339–44.

Carothers, Neil. *Fractional Money: A History of the Small Coins and Fractional Paper Currency of the United States.* New York, 1930.

Catterall, Ralph C. H. *The Second Bank of the United States.* Chicago, 1903.

Chaddock, Robert E. *The Safety Fund Banking System in New York, 1829–66.* Washington, 1910.

Cochran, Thomas C. "The Presidential Synthesis in American History," *American Historical Review,* LIII (July 1948), 748–59.

Commons, John R. "American Shoemakers, 1648–1895: A Sketch of Industrial Evolution," *Quarterly Journal of Economics,* XXIV (November 1909), 39–84.

Commons, John R., and associates. *History of Labour in the United States.* 2 vols. New York, 1918.

Commons, John R., and associates, eds. *A Documentary History of American Industrial Society.* 11 vols. Cleveland, 1910–11.

Conant, Charles A. *A History of Modern Banks of Issue.* 4th ed. New York, 1909.

Congressional Globe.

Constitution and By-Laws of the New-York Typographical Society, With a List of Members. New York, 1848.

Croxton, Frederick E., and Dudley J. Cowden. *Applied General Statistics.* New York, 1939.

Crumrine, Boyd, ed. *History of Washington County, Pennsylvania, with Biographical Sketches of Many of Its Pioneers and Prominent Men.* Philadelphia, 1882.

Degler, Carl N. "An Inquiry into the Locofoco Party." Unpublished M.A. thesis, Columbia University, 1947.

DeVoe, Thomas F. *The Market Book.* New York, 1862.

Dewey, Davis R. *State Banking Before the Civil War.* Washington, 1910.

Dictionary of American Biography. 21 vols. New York, 1937.

Doggett's New York City and Co-Partnership Directory.

Dorfman, Joseph. *Economic Mind in American Civilization.* 2 vols. New York, 1946.

———. "The Jackson Wage-Earner Thesis," *American Historical Review,* LIV (January 1949), 293–306.

Douglas, Paul. *American Apprenticeship and Industrial Education.* New York, 1921.

Emmons, William. *Authentic Biography of Col. Richard M. Johnson of Kentucky.* New York, 1833.

Ernst, Robert. *Immigrant Life in New York City 1825–1863*. New York, 1949.

Evans, Frederick W. *Autobiography of a Shaker*. Glasgow and New York, 1888.

[Evans, George H.] "History of the Origin and Progress of the Working Man's Party in New York," *Radical, in Continuation of the Working Man's Advocate* (Granville, N.J.), January 1842 to April 1843.

Ewing, Cortez A. M. *The Judges of the Supreme Court 1789–1937*. Minneapolis, 1938.

Farnam, Henry W. *Chapters in the History of Social Legislation in the United States to 1860*. Washington, 1938.

Fish, Carl R. *The Rise of the Common Man, 1830–1850*. New York, 1927.

Fitzpatrick, John C., ed. "Autobiography of Martin Van Buren," American Historical Association, *Annual Report* (1918), II.

Foner, Philip S. *History of the Labor Movement in the United States*. New York, 1947.

Fox, Dixon R. *The Decline of Aristocracy in the Politics of New York*. New York, 1919.

Godwin, Parke. *A Biography of William Cullen Bryant*. 2 vols. New York, 1883.

Gold, August B. "A History of Manufacturing in New York City, 1825–1840." Unpublished M.A. thesis, Columbia University, 1932.

Gouge, William. *A Short History of Paper Money and Banking in the United States, including an account of provincial and continental paper money, to which is prefixed an inquiry into the principles of the system, with considerations of its effects on Morals and Happiness. The whole intended as a plain exposition of the way in which paper money and money corporations affect the interests of different portions of the community*. Philadelphia, 1833.

Greeley, Horace. *Recollections of a Busy Life*. New York, 1872.

Greene, Albert H. "United States Land Offices in Kansas," Kansas State Historical Society *Collections*, VIII (1903–4), 1–10.

Greene, J. W. "The New-York & Harlem Railroad," *New-York Historical Society Quarterly Bulletin*, IX (1926).

Hamilton, James A. *Reminiscences, or Men and Events at Home and Abroad During Three-Quarters of a Century*. New York, 1869.

Hamlin, Talbot. *Greek Revival Architecture in America*. New York, 1944.

Hammond, Bray. "Banking in the Early West: Monopoly, Prohibition, and Laissez Faire," *Journal of Economic History*, VIII (May 1948), 1–25.

———. *Banks and Politics in America from the Revolution to the Civil War*. Princeton, 1957.

———. "The Banks, the States, and the Federal Government," *American Economic Review*, XXIII (December 1933), 622–36.

———. "The Chestnut Street Raid on Wall Street, 1839," *Quarterly Journal of Economics,* LXI (August 1947), 605–18.

———. "Free Banks and Corporations: The New York Free Banking Act of 1838," *Journal of Political Economy,* XLIV (February 1936), 184–209.

———. "Jackson, Biddle, and the Bank of the United States," *Journal of Economic History,* VII (May 1947), 1–23.

———. "Long and Short Term Credit in Early American Banking," *Quarterly Journal of Economics,* XLIX (November 1934), 79–102.

———. "Public Policy and National Banks," *Journal of Economic History,* VI (May 1946), 79–84.

Hammond, Jabez D. *History of Political Parties in the State of New-York, from the Ratification of the Federal Constitution to December, 1840.* 4th ed. 2 vols. Cooperstown, N.Y., 1846.

Handlin, Oscar, and Mary F. Handlin. *Commonwealth; A Study of the Role of Government in the American Economy: Massachusetts, 1774–1861.* New York, 1947.

Hartz, Louis. *Economic Policy and Democratic Thought: Pennsylvania, 1776–1860.* Cambridge, Mass., 1948.

———. "Seth Luther: Working Class Rebel," *New England Quarterly,* XIII (September 1940), 401–18.

Helderman, Leonard C. *National and State Banks, A Study of Their Origins.* Boston, 1931.

Herring, E. Pendleton. *Federal Commissioners: A Study of Their Careers and Qualifications.* Cambridge, Mass., 1936.

Herttell, Thomas. *Correspondence on the subject of life and death.* Boston, 1845.

———. *The demurrer; or, Proofs of error in the decision of the Supreme court of the State of New York requiring faith in particular religious doctrines as a legal qualification of witnesses.* New York, 1828.

———. *Remarks on the Law of Imprisonment for Debt.* New York, 1823.

Hofstadter, Richard. *The American Political Tradition and the Men Who Made It.* New York, 1948.

———. "William Leggett, Spokesman of Jacksonian Democracy," *Political Science Quarterly,* LVIII (December 1943), 581–94.

Holden, Vincent F. *The Early Years of Isaac Thomas Hecker (1819–1844).* Washington, 1939.

Hugins, Walter E. "Ely Moore: The Case History of a Jacksonian Labor Leader," *Political Science Quarterly,* LXV (March 1950), 105–25.

Index of Conveyances: Grantors. 6 vols. New York, 1858.

Jackson, Sidney L. *America's Struggle for Free Schools; Social Ten-*

sion and Education in New England and New York, 1827–42. Washington, 1941.

———. "Labor, Education, and Politics in the 1830's," *Pennsylvania Magazine of History and Biography*, LXVI (July 1942), 279–93.

Jameson, J. Franklin, ed. "Correspondence of John C. Calhoun," American Historical Association, *Annual Report* (1899), II.

Kilroe, Edwin P. *St. Tammany and the Origin of the Society of Tammany or Columbian Order in the City of New York.* New York, 1913.

Kneeland, S. F. *A Treatise upon the Principles Governing the Acquisition and Enforcement of Mechanics' Liens.* New York, 1876.

Krout, John A., and Dixon R. Fox. *The Completion of Independence, 1790–1830.* New York, 1944.

Leopold, Richard W. *Robert Dale Owen, A Biography.* Cambridge, Mass., 1940.

Life and Annual Members of the American Institute of the City of New-York Together with the names of its Officers, Directors and Trustees from its organization in the year 1828 to the present time. New York, 1882.

Longworth's Directory of New York City.

McCarthy, Charles. "Antimasonic Party, A Study of Political Antimasonry in the United States, 1827–1840," American Historical Association, *Annual Report* (1902), I.

Mack, Edward C. *Peter Cooper, Citizen of New York.* New York, 1949.

Madeleine, Sister M. Grace. *Monetary and Banking Theories of Jacksonian Democracy.* Philadelphia, 1943.

Manual for the Use of the Legislature of the State of New York, 1866. Albany, 1866.

Masquerier, Lewis. *Sociology: or the Reconstruction of Society, Government, and Property.* New York, 1877.

"Memorial of J. A. Smith and others, of the Medical Profession in the City of New-York," *New York Assembly Documents,* 55th Session, vol. 3, No. 250. Albany, 1832.

"Memorial of the Medical Society of the city and county of New-York," *New York Assembly Documents,* 55th Session, vol. 3, No. 244. Albany, 1832.

"Memorial of the Medical Society of the city and county of New-York," *New York Assembly Documents,* 55th Session, vol. 3, No. 249 Albany, 1832.

Meyer, Leland W. *The Life and Times of Colonel Richard M. Johnson of Kentucky.* New York, 1932.

Meyers, Marvin. *The Jacksonian Persuasion: Politics and Belief.* Stanford, Calif., 1957.

Miller, Harry E. *Banking Theories in the United States Before 1860.* Cambridge, Mass., 1927.

Miller, William. "American Historians and the Business Elite," *The Journal of Economic History,* IX (November 1949), 184–208.

Mills, C. Wright. "The American Business Elite: A Collective Portrait," *Tasks of Economic History* (Supplement of *The Journal of Economic History*), V (1945), 20–44.

Minutes of the Common Council of the City of New York, 1784–1831. 21 vols. New York, 1930.

Moore, Ely. *Address on Civil Government: Delivered Before the New York Typographical Society, Feb. 25th, 1847.* New York, 1847.

———. *Address Delivered Before the General Trades' Union of the City of New-York, December 2, 1833.* New York, 1833.

———. "Address Delivered Before the General Trades' Union, September 25, 1834," *Man*, November 24–25, 1834.

———. *Oration Delivered Before the Mechanics and Working Men of the City of New York, on the Fourth of July, 1843.* New York, 1843.

———. *Reply to a Pamphlet Entitled "A Statement of Facts in Relation to the Origin, Progress and Prospects of the New-York & Harlem Rail Road Company."* New York, 1833.

Moore, Ely, Jr. "The Lecompton Party Which Located Denver," Kansas State Historical Society *Collections*, VII (1901–2), 446–50.

———. "The Story of Lecompton," Kansas State Historical Society *Collections*, XI (1909–10), 463–80.

Moore, James W. *Rev. John Moore of Newtown, L. I., and Some of His Descendants.* Easton, Pa., 1903.

Morison, Samuel E., and Henry S. Commager. *Growth of the American Republic.* 4th ed. 2 vols. New York, 1950.

Mowry, Arthur M. *The Dorr War.* Providence, 1901.

Myers, Gustavus. *History of Tammany Hall.* New York, 1901.

Myers, Margaret G. *The New York Money Market: Origins and Development.* New York, 1931.

Nadworny, Milton J. "New Jersey Workingmen and the Jacksonians," *Proceedings of the New Jersey Historical Society*, LXVII (July 1949), 185–98.

National Cyclopedia of American Biography. 13 vols. New York, 1892–1906.

Nevins, Allan, ed. *The Diary of Philip Hone, 1828–1851.* 2 vols. New York, 1927.

———. *The Evening Post: A Century of Journalism.* New York, 1922.

Nott, Charles C. *A Treatise on the Mechanics' Lien Laws of the State of New York.* Albany, 1856.

Official Catalogue, 38th Annual Fair of the American Institute. New York, 1869.

Parrington, Vernon L. *Main Currents in American Thought.* 3 vols. in 1. New York, 1927.

Pessen, Edward. "Did Labor Support Jackson?: The Boston Story," *Political Science Quarterly*, LXIV (June 1949), 262–74.

———. "The Social Philosophies of Early American Leaders of Labor." Unpublished Ph.D. dissertation, Columbia University, 1954.

———. "Thomas Skidmore, Agrarian Reformer in the Early American Labor Movement," *New York History*, XXV (July 1954), 280–96.

———. "The Workingmen's Movement of the Jacksonian Era," *Mississippi Valley Historical Review*, XLIII (December 1956), 428–43.

Poore, Benjamin Perley. *Perley's Reminiscences of Sixty Years in the National Metropolis*. 2 vols. Philadelphia, 1886.

Porter, Kenneth W. *John Jacob Astor, Business Man*. 2 vols. Cambridge, Mass., 1931.

[Potter, Alonzo.] "Trades' Unions," *New-York Review*, II (January 1838), 5–48.

Proceedings and Address of the Republican Young Men of the State of New-York, Assembled at Utica, on the 12th day of August, 1828. Utica, 1828.

Proceedings of the Convention of Mechanics, Farmers and Working Men of the State of New-York, held at the City of Utica, in the County of Oneida, on the 15th, 16th, and 17th Sept. 1836; with the Address of the Convention to the People of the State of New-York. N.p., n.d. [1836.]

Proceedings of a Meeting in Favor of Municipal Reform, Held at Tammany Hall, on Friday Evening, March 22d, 1844. New York, 1844.

Randall, Edwin T. "Imprisonment for Debt in America: Fact and Fiction," *Mississippi Valley Historical Review*, XXXIX (June 1952), 89–102.

Redlich, Fritz. *Essays in American Economic History*. New York, 1944.

———. *The Molding of American Banking: Men and Ideas*. Vol. II, Part 1, of *History of American Business Leaders*. New York, 1947.

Register of Debates in Congress.

Register of Officers and Agents, Civil, Military, and Naval, in the Service of the United States, 1830–1855. (*Biennial Register of all Officers and Agents in the Service of the United States, 1837 to 1855*.)

"Remonstrance of Doctors T. R. Beck and James McNaughton," *New York Assembly Documents*, 55th Session, vol. 3, No. 272. Albany, 1832.

"Remonstrance of Joseph M. Smith et al., of the city of New-York, against any alteration of the law regulating the practice of physic in this State," *New York Assembly Documents*, 55th session, vol. 3, No. 262. Albany, 1832.

"Remonstrance of physicians and surgeons in the city of New-York," *New York Assembly Documents*, 55th Session, vol. 3, No. 261. Albany, 1832.

"Remonstrance of seventy-six practitioners of medicine in the city of New-York," *New York Assembly Documents*, 55th Session, vol. 3, No. 246. Albany, 1832.

"Remonstrance of the State Medical Society," *New York Assembly Documents*, 55th Session, vol. 3, No. 185. Albany, 1832.

"Report of the Attorney-General, on a resolution from the Assembly," *New York Assembly Documents,* 53d Session, vol. 2, No. 199. Albany, 1830.

"Report of the Commissioners appointed under the 'act concerning State Prisons' to the legislature of the State of New York, January 29, 1835," *New York Assembly Documents,* 58th Session, No. 135. Albany, 1835.

Report of the Joint Legislative Committee Investigating the Lien Law. New York Legislative Document No. 72. Albany, 1930.

"Report of Mr. Winfield, from the committee on medical societies and colleges," *New York Assembly Documents,* 55th Session, vol. 3, No. 251. Albany, 1832.

Report of the 3d Annual Fair of the American Institute of the City of New-York. New York, 1830.

Rezneck, Samuel. "The Depression of 1819–1822: A Social History," *American Historical Review,* XXXIX (October 1933), 28–47.

———. "Social History of an American Depression, 1837–1843," *American Historical Review,* XL (July 1935), 662–87.

Richardson, James D., ed. *A Compilation of the Messages and Papers of the Presidents 1789–1897.* 10 vols. Washington, 1896.

Ronk, Daniel T. *Hasbrouck family births, marriages and deaths, copied from old church and cemetery records.* Brooklyn, 1917.

Rutgers Medical College. Announcement, 1826. New York, 1826.

Schlesinger, Arthur M., Jr. *The Age of Jackson.* Boston, 1945.

[Scoville, Joseph A.] *The Old Merchants of New York City.* 3 vols. New York, 1872.

Secrist, Horace. "The Anti-Auction Movement and the New York Workingman's Party of 1829," *Transactions* of the Wisconsin Academy of Science, Arts and Letters, XVII (1914), 149–66.

Sedgwick, Theodore, Jr., ed. *A Collection of the Political Writings of William Leggett.* 2 vols. New York, 1840.

———. *What Is a Monopoly? or some Considerations upon the Subject of Corporations and Currency.* New York, 1835.

Shafer, Henry B. *The American Medical Profession 1783 to 1850.* New York, 1936.

Silberling, Norman J. "Financial and Monetary Policy of Great Britain During the Napoleonic Wars: II. Ricardo and the Bullion Report," *Quarterly Journal of Economics,* XXXVIII (May 1924), 397–439.

Skidmore, Thomas. *The Rights of Man to Property!* New York, 1829.

Stevens, George A. *Typographical Union No. 6: A Study of a Modern Trade Union and Its Predecessors.* Albany, 1913.

Stewart, Ethelbert, ed. *Documentary History of the Early Organizations of Printers.* Indianapolis, 1907.

Stokes, I. N. Phelps. *Iconography of Manhattan Island, 1498–1909.* 6 vols. New York, 1918–28.

Stryker, William S., comp. *Official Register of the Officers and Men of New Jersey in the Revolutionary War*. Trenton, 1872.

Sullivan, William A. "Did Labor Support Andrew Jackson?" *Political Science Quarterly*, LXII (December 1947), 569–80.

———. *The Industrial Worker in Pennsylvania 1800–1840*. Harrisburg, 1955.

———. "Philadelphia Labor During the Jackson Era," *Pennsylvania History*, XV (October 1948), 305–20.

Taylor, George R. *The Transportation Revolution 1815–1860*. New York, 1951.

Trimble, William. "Diverging Tendencies in the New York Democracy in the Period of the Loco Focos," *American Historical Review*, XXIV (April 1919), 396–421.

———. "The Social Philosophy of the Loco-Foco Democracy," *American Journal of Sociology*, XXVI (May 1921), 705–15.

Turner, Frederick J. *The United States 1830–1850*. New York, 1935.

Tyler, Alice F. *Freedom's Ferment; Phases of American Social History to 1860*. Minneapolis, 1944.

Valentine, David T. *Manual of the Corporation of the City of New-York*. New York, 1841.

Van Deusen, Glyndon G. *Thurlow Weed, Wizard of the Lobby*. Boston, 1947.

Venit, Abraham H. "Isaac Bronson: His Banking Theory and the Financial Controversies of the Jacksonian Period," *Journal of Economic History*, V (November 1945), 201–14.

Ward, John W. *Andrew Jackson, Symbol for an Age*. New York, 1955.

Weed, Harriet A., ed. *Autobiography of Thurlow Weed*. Boston, 1883.

Westerfield, R. B. "Early History of American Auctions," *Transactions* of the Connecticut Academy of Arts and Sciences, XXIII (1920), 159–210.

Wickes, Stephen. *History of Medicine in New Jersey*. Newark, 1879.

Williams, Edwin. *New-York Annual Register*, 1830–40.

———. *New-York As It Is, in 1834; and Citizens' Advertising Directory*. New York, 1834.

Woolen, Evans. "Labor Troubles between 1834 and 1837," *Yale Review*, I (1892), 87–100.

Zahler, Helene S. *Eastern Workingmen and National Land Policy, 1829–1862*. New York, 1941.

Index